WITHDRAWN

Ima

D1382369

Women's History

General Editor
June Purvis
Professor of Sociology, University of Portsmouth

Published
Lynn Abrams and Elizabeth Harvey (editors)
Gender relations in German history:
power, agency and experience from the sixteenth to the twentieth century

Jay Dixon
The romantic fiction of Mills & Boon, 1909–95

Carol Dyhouse
No distinction of sex? Women in British universities, 1870–1939

Bridget Hill
Women, work and sexual politics in eighteenth-century England

Linda Mahood
Policing gender, class and family: Britain, 1850–1940

June Purvis (editor)
Women's history: Britain, 1850–1945

Wendy Webster
Imagining home: gender, 'race' and national identity, 1945–64

Barbara Winslow
Sylvia Pankhurst: sexual politics and political activism

Forthcoming titles include:
Shani D'Cruze
Crimes of outrage: sex, violence and working women in Victorian England

Jane McDermid & Anna Hillyar
Midwives of the revolution: female Bolsheviks and women workers in 1917

Imagining home

Gender, 'race' and national identity, 1945–64

Wendy Webster
University of Central Lancashire

UCL logo

First published in 1998 by UCL Press

UCL Press Limited
1 Gunpowder Square
London EC4A 3DE
UK

and

1900 Frost Road, Suite 101
Bristol
Pennsylvania 19007–1598
USA

The name of University College London (UCL) is a registered
trade mark used by UCL Press with the consent of the owner.

British Library Cataloguing-in-Publication Data
A CIP catalogue record for this book is available from the British Library.

Library of Congress Cataloging-in-Publication Data are available

ISBNs: 1-85728-350-3 HB
      1-85728-351-1 PB

Typeset in Classical Garamond.
Printed and bound by T. J. International Ltd, Padstow, UK.

Contents

Acknowledgements

I owe a great debt to Zoe Oxaal, who worked in 1994–5 as a Research Assistant on a project on the oral history of black women in Britain, and to all the women interviewed. Without them this book would not exist. Grateful acknowledgement is also due to the University of Central Lancashire which funded the project.

I would also like to thank all the staff and students with whom I have worked at the University of Central Lancashire over the past five years, and from whom I have learnt so much. For their help on this book I am particularly grateful to Chris Boydell, Liz Brierley, Barbara Jones, Angela Karach, Mary Murthwaite and Ewa Petrus.

I am very indebted to all those who took time from busy schedules to read and comment on drafts of chapters: Judy Giles, Catherine Hall, Joe Pope, Dave Russell, Louise Ryan, Sarah Lawson Welsh and Fiona Williams. Finally, I have to thank Jane Rendall for all her support and encouragement over many years.

Wendy Webster

Introduction

Imagining home is about ideas and images of home in Britain in the period 1945–64, and their significance in constructions of gender, "race" and nation. Drawing on work in a variety of genres, the book reviews different and competing accounts of home produced by politicians, journalists, churchmen, sociologists, health professionals, novelists and film-makers. It draws on oral narratives and life-writing to look at the different meanings of home to women, and the ways in which they negotiated, appropriated or opposed the different roles and identities assigned to them within discourses of race, class, health and nation.

The term "home" is rich in associations. Feminist literature has been particularly concerned with its meaning as a private sphere of intimacy, personal emotion and relationship, domestic and familial life, associated with the lives of women. Feminist historians have traced the development of an ideology of separate spheres from the late eighteenth century, through which the middle classes, in differentiating themselves from other social groups, excluded women from a range of public roles and places.[1] Feminist literature more generally has contested the meaning of home as a place of safety and nurture and in developing themes of domestic violence and abuse, and of women's subordination within the private patriarchy of the family, has seen the home as a main site of oppression for women.[2] Cultural theorists, in developing a literature concerned with notions of location and dislocation, belonging and displacement, migration and exile, have been interested in the associations of home with origins, identity, attachment and settlement, and with its common use as a metaphor for nation.[3] Black feminist literature, intersecting these perspectives, has explored the multiple meanings of home to black women in the contexts of slavery, colonialism and migrations, and argued that the distinction between public and private is raced, and central to the construction of middle-class femininity as white.[4]

The idea of home as an oppressive place for women is apparent in much of the literature on women in Britain in the 1950s – a period which is often seen as a particular nadir when maternity ruled and homes were stultifyingly conformist and dull. Martin Pugh argues that this was a time which saw "the reassertion of domesticity as never before" and Lynn Segal writes of a "monolithic concern with domesticity". "The fixing and freezing of women as mothers and nothing other than mothers," Segal argues, "was central to the vision of the 50s." She sees the decade as one in which "a seemingly endless and all-embracing conservative consensus held sway throughout almost every Western nation, in both northern and southern hemispheres", the conservatism of the period "strongly symbolised through women, marriage and family". In contrast, the 1960s is the period of the "upsurge of youthful protest movements and counter-culture" which "spawned its own fierce rejection of the stifling, inward-looking, acquisitive, post-war suburban family".[5]

Black feminist literature has contested this story, pointing to the importance of colonialism and racism in shaping the meanings of home for black women:

> For Black women there is an inherent contradiction in the very word "home". We can ask ourselves many questions to which there are no easy answers. Where is home for starters? Can you call a country which has systematically colonized your countries of origin, one which refuses through a thorough racism in its institutions, media and culture to even recognize your existence and your rights to that existence – can you call this country "home" without having your tongue inside your cheek? . . . Until we can be both visible and belong, the word "home" will remain for us ambiguous, ironic, and even sarcastic. We will still be "Strangers at Home".[6]

A focus on white women produces a story of the period which emphasizes the way in which maternity ruled, involving immurement with family and submergence in domesticity. A focus on black women produces a very different story – of poorly paid, low-status, full-time employment, separation from family through the process of migration, a search for accommodation in which the sign "no coloureds" was repeatedly encountered. The first view emphasizes patriarchy and sees the family as a main site of women's oppression. The second emphasizes colonialism and racism and sees the family as a main source of support in resistance to it.[7] One aim of this book is to look at the connections between these two stories in exploring the significance of colonialism and racism in shaping the identities of white women, particularly as mothers.[8]

White women were, however, by no means a homogenous group, and a third story sketched here suggests a number of commonalities between black and white migrants. It was the former who were seen as threatening a degeneration of the British race and who were characterized as incapable of domestic or familial life. But white female migrants were also recruited as workers, were often separated from family, worked in low-paid and low-status jobs, and encountered signs on accommodation which announced "no Irish", and in some areas "no Poles or East Europeans".[9] One argument of *Imagining home* is that the role of indigenous women as primarily wives and mothers, centred on domestic and familial life, was facilitated by this recruitment of migrant women to Britain as workers.

In tracing the shifting meanings of home in the period, the opening chapters set these in the context of a central project on which a range of literatures converged during and immediately after the war: post-war reconstruction. One aspect of this identified a range of tasks including the rebuilding of a bankrupt economy, the maintenance of British power and influence in the world, the resolve of "no return" to pre-war mass unemployment, and the building of new estates and new towns. The questions it produced focused on a notion of "our people" – how are "our people" to be housed, how are the Britishness of Australia, Canada and New Zealand to be maintained, how can the needs of our children best be met? Another aspect identified the need for recruitment of migrant labour to rebuild Britain. The questions this produced also focused on a notion of "our people" through their orchestration around a central question – who belongs in Britain?

One main theme traced in the book is the construction of home as white in the raced answers given to the second set of questions. Through a preference for the recruitment of white migrants to the labour market, especially in the government-sponsored scheme for European Volunteer Workers (EVWs), those who were formally aliens were seen as "suitable immigrants" while black migrants, most of whom were formally British subjects, were seen as aliens.[10] Black women were seen as workers, not as wives and mothers, and when their motherhood was made visible in race discourse in the early 1960s it was represented as a threat to the nation. Theories about patriarchy and capitalism do not adequately explain the way in which such strongly contrasting roles were assigned to women on the basis of race. Hazel Carby, emphasizing the recruitment of black women from the Caribbean into the lowest-paid, most menial jobs, argues, "Rather than a concern to protect or preserve the black family in Britain, the state reproduced common-sense notions of its inherent pathology: black women were seen to fail as mothers precisely becuse of their position as workers."[11] At the same time many white female migrants, although constructed as "suitable immigrants" in opposition to black, shared a position as workers.

In Chapter 3 the ways in which colonialism shaped the meanings of home are explored through an analysis of the impact in the metropolis of the decline of British colonial empire, and especially on the ways in which the "immigrant" was constructed.[12] In colonial discourse the colonized were often represented in a pattern of familial imagery where they shared with colonizers membership of one imperial family. Those who migrated to Britain after the war made a passage to the identity of "dark strangers", were seen as importing an alien "colour problem" into the metropolis and became a symbol of national decline.[13] Differences between white and black were constructed through an opposition between an Englishness, characterized by the privacy of domestic and familial life, and "immigrants", who were characterized in terms of an incapacity for domestic and familial life, or domestic barbarism. Within this opposition both the "immigrant" and Englishness were gendered as well as raced – the former seen as a black man, and the latter often embodied in the figure of a white woman. In the context of varied anti-colonial resistances in the period, representations of the colonized in empire and "immigrants" in the metropolis increasingly converged on a common theme – their threat to home.[14]

Obscured within the opposition between British/white and "immigrant"/black, white migrants were more visible on signs advertising accommodation which announced "no coloureds, no Irish". The four-word sign suggests some of the complexities of the influence of colonialism on questions about who belonged in

Britain. Government policies made distinctions between all white migrants – including Irish – as "suitable immigrants" and black migrants as "the colour problem". The sign made no distinction as far as Irish migrants were concerned. Its "coloured" merged people of diverse continents and cultures, most of whom in other contexts were constructed as British subjects. Its "Irish" merged people of the Republic with those of Northern Ireland, who were also constructed as British in other contexts, and might strongly identify with or strongly contest that construction. "No coloureds, no Irish" draws attention to multiple racisms and the presence of some white migrants as well as black who came from countries colonized, or formerly colonized, by Britain.

The opposition between British/white and "immigrant"/black drew particularly on domesticated versions of national identity, constructed between the wars.[15] In the post-war period these were developed into an increasingly classless idea of home as imagery of two nations – rich and poor, employed and unemployed, North and South – was reworked into a distinction between a common Englishness of well-kept homes and families in opposition to "blacks next door". Chapter 4 is concerned with a crop of mid-1950s literature about a "new England", and a dominant account of home, particularly favoured by Conservative politicians by the late 1950s, which emphasized consumption, and was celebrated in the Conservative Party's 1959 General Election slogan "You've never had it so good". After the austerity of the immediate post-war period, and its preoccupations with rationing and shortages, particularly housing shortages, home was increasingly identified as the site of a new affluence. What George Orwell had identified in 1941 as "the germs of the future England", located mainly in the South where "the same kind of life . . . is being lived at different levels, in labour-saving flats or council houses", was seen as spreading across the nation in the development of a "new estate" which signified the notion of a newly classless way of life on newly built estates.[16] The erosion or demise of class and regional differences and of England as two nations was confidently proclaimed. A submerged group was identified mainly in health discourse, not in the language of rich and poor but in a copious post-war literature on the "problem family" whose failings were attributed to "neglectful mothers".[17]

Those who wrote of a new England did not always invoke the

classlessness of "subtopia" as a progressive development. There was anxiety about the Americanization of culture, and its tastelessness and superficiality. The decline of working-class communities was mourned, especially in representations of the North of England, which sometimes invoked an older England through the figure of "our mam", who provided a female counterpart to the solidity of Northern masculinity. In contrast the woman on the new estate was represented as individualistic and acquisitve.

A common thread running through discourses of race and class was anxiety about white masculinity. In race discourse this took various forms. One focus of anxiety was black male sexuality, seen as a threat to white femininity: "our women" were white men's property. Another was the decline of the British colonial empire and the demise of narratives of white male adventure and power in vast territory. The symbols of Englishness in race discourse became the quiet street and privet hedge.

In class discourse where a main emblem of the new England became the television aerial, there was a focus on white masculinity in accounts of a new home-centredness. Representing home as a site of leisure and consumption, erasing domestic work, these accounts proclaimed the advent of a new man who, when he was not passively engrossed in television, did DIY and pushed a pram at weekends. At the same time they wrote the obituary of traditional working-class masculinity associated particularly with heavy industry in Northern England. Anxieties about these developments were often expressed in terms of class in concerns about a decline in Northern working-class community and in men's engagement in politics, trade unionism, and public as opposed to private houses. But in the narratives which reinstated Northern working-class masculinity at the centre of their stories, and which flooded cinema screens and novels in the late 1950s, a major theme was fear of men's emasculation at the hands of women.

The child-centredness of the post-war welfare state – apparent in the wide range of support for mothers and their children – meant that the home became a site of increasing public support and intervention. Despite unprecedented public provision, the home was seen as the place where children's needs could and should best be met. Chapter 5 explores the idea of the "good home", which was elaborated particularly in health discourse. While social progress was associated with the extensive home-building programmes of the 1950s, with the modern housing and facilities that these made available, and with the affluence represented by the new estate and its array of television aerials, the figure at the centre of the good home was the good mother. Reworked in the post-war period around an emphasis on intimacy, emotion and instinct, the concept of the good mother and her intimate relationship with her baby was seen as a basis of national health and public welfare. As the cult of child psychology developed, there was a shift of attention away from hygiene, regularity and discipline to the emotional development of babies and children, and their need for mother-love. The good mother was one who responded to her children's needs rather than constraining their demands through discipline.

The construction of black and Asian people as primitive acquired new meanings when the colonial encounter was reversed through migration to the metropolis, and was no longer represented in terms of colonizers bringing civilization to the primitive, but of "immigrants" bringing physical and moral decline to the civilized. Since they were seen as primitive, black people were not attributed a complicated psychology or the capacity for emotional development. In the 1950s black women were rarely associated with motherhood, and the representation of black people as incapable of personal relationships and family life was particularly associated with black men, who were seen as rootless, transient and untamed. By the mid-1960s, however, this incapacity for relationships became part of the construction of black motherhood when black women's reproduction became an important theme of race discourse and was seen as over-fecund. A main symbol of intimacy, emotional well-being and psychological health – mother-love – was not attributed to black women.

The emphasis on the good mother as the central figure of the good home meant that in the 1950s the hybrid identity of "working wife" attracted considerable attention, anxiety and censure. Chapter 6 is concerned with the ways in which the relationship between home and work was reworked in the period as married women's participation in the labour market increased. There was a range of places from which they received calls to employment – from professional women, including many feminists who advocated dual roles, from employers who needed cheap female labour in occupations that had been feminized before the war, from the government which recruited many married women to work in the expanded post-war welfare state. All these calls were characterized by an emphasis on the priority of women's family responsibilities. Part-time work was often seen as the key to women subordinating their employment to family needs, and it was on these terms that the "working wife" became an increasingly acceptable figure by the early 1960s. But another key was the recruitment of migrant women, whose employment met part of the need for female labour in low-status, low-paid jobs while facilitating the process by which indigenous women's role as primarily wives and mothers could be maintained.

By the early 1960s young educated women living in the suburbs were beginning to produce a version of home which rewrote the story of new England, and particularly its emphasis on "subtopia". The idea that home was not a good place to be pre-dated the Women's Movement of the late 1960s. Already apparent at the end of the 1950s, in letters in the women's page of the *Manchester Guardian* which led to the formation of the National Housewives Register, it was elaborated in the early 1960s in the writings of Hannah Gavron in Britain, and Betty Friedan in America. Friedan was widely read in Britain, and her book discussed at meetings of the National Housewives Register.[18] In developing a critique of home as over-private, isolated and oppressive, these women emphasized the problems of maternity for women as "housebound mothers".

This account, which has informed the view that the 1950s was a nadir for women, does not encompass the very complex range of meanings and values that women assigned to home – the concern of Chapter 7. In 1945 home might have very different meanings for the woman who had worked in domestic service before the war and for the mistress who found herself servantless. It had a particular meaning for Nella Last, who had experienced voluntary war-work as a growth in self-confidence and independence which enabled her to challenge her husband's authority, and who recorded in her diary that:

> I had a pang as I wondered what I would do when all my little war activities stopped . . . if my weak streak would crop up as strong as ever, and I'd give in for peace and to that unspoken, but *very* plain Victorian-Edwardian accusation, "I feed and clothe you, don't I? I've a right to say what you do."[19]

In the 1950s home as a site of affluence had one meaning for the working-class woman who caught a glimpse of "that other life" at gates and between gaps in hedges, as Maureen Lawrence records her mother doing on her trips into the suburbs, and another for the woman in the home behind the gate who might, by the late 1950s, be beginning to write to the *Manchester Guardian* about the alienation of suburbia.[20] Home had quite a different meaning to a Polish woman who, deported to Siberia by the Soviet Union during the war, had made her way to Britain via Africa, India or Palestine, was housed in a Polish resettlement camp after the war, and faced the possibility of permanent exile as the political map of Europe was redrawn.[21] As black women imagined home in the 1950s, it had one dominant meaning for those who found that there were no places for them to live in Britain – back home.

There are many difficulties about the use of language to trace this complex history and I am aware of many problems with my own. I have used "black" mainly to refer to people of the Caribbean and African diasporas in Britain. As such it refers to people who identified as black in various struggles to resist racism. The extent to which this use of the term excludes South Asians in Britain, and the extent to which South Asians should be included under the term "black", has been the subject of considerable debate.[22] Black is also used here to refer to a category constructed in race discourse – for which the term "coloured" was used interchangeably with black – in which South Asians were routinely included. This category comprised those still living under British colonial rule in Africa and the Caribbean throughout much of the period, those who were no longer under British colonial rule in South Asia, and those who migrated to Britain from these areas. The identification of South Asians in Britain as black is particularly apparent to the term "Afro-Asian", which was in common use by the early 1960s to denote "immigration". "Afro-Asian" was also used to denote political unity against racism between African, Caribbean and South Asian people in Britain – for example, in the work of the Afro-Asian Caribbean Conference and its opposition to the Immigration Act of 1962.[23]

Black was constructed in the period not only in opposition to white but also to British. I have generally used white to refer to people who identified as white, some of whom lived in Britain without either being seen as British or identifying as such. I also use white to refer to a category constructed in race discourse. Since this category was seen as superior and was assigned a range of privileges, very few of those who were seen as white refused such an identification. There are, however, problems with this use of the term. Cypriots might be regarded as a group of white migrants who came from a country colonized by Britain and engaged in anti-colonial resistance during the period, but they were not always seen as uncontestably white. For example, while a 1966 survey of racial discrimination by Political and Economic Planning treated Cypriots as a "white Commonwealth immigrant control group against whom the experience of the coloured immigrants can be measured", a study by Clifford Hill in the previous year included Cypriots within the category "coloured Commonwealth citizens".[24] Moreover, the opposition black/white does not adequately convey the range of ways in which people's own identifications in resisting racisms might fall somewhere outside both groups. Groups who were shifted into a black category on arrival in Britain with which they did not generally identify included not only many South Asians, but also many people whose identifications drew on a particularly complex experience of what Winston James calls "pigmentocracy", including Indo-Caribbeans, Anglo-Indians and Anglo-Pakistanis.[25]

One concern of this book is to trace the different constructions of black and white femininities in the period, and the different relationships of black and white women to home and domesticity, but I am also concerned with another main line of division – between what I have called here "migrant women" and "indigenous women". However, I am conscious that both these terms are also problematic. Migrant women excludes those who arrived as refugees, a problem which is compounded when looking at those who were recruited to work in Britain from displaced persons camps in Europe, but were renamed EVWS and so denied refugee status. Indigenous women when used in contrast to migrant women does not acknowledge the diversity of people in Britain before 1945 and all those targetted by multiple racisms who were not post-war migrants.[26]

There are very few terms within the language of race discourse – perhaps none – which can be regarded as unproblematic. A study which used quotation marks around all such terms to signal their problems would have a rash of quotes on every page. I have therefore generally put quotation marks around such terms only on their first use. Since a main theme of the book is the raced and gendered constructions of "immigrant" and "immigration" in a discourse of the "colour problem" which focused on "miscegenation", I have made an exception in the case of these terms, which always appear in quotation marks.[27]

The language of national identity poses further problems, and it is not always clear whether "British" or "English" is appropriate, with writers – especially English writers – often using these terms interchangeably, signalling a history of English dominance in relation to other national identities within Britishness. Since the opposition between British/white and "immigrant"/black drew extensively on domesticated versions of nation apparent in the inter-war period, and developed to signal a particular exclusive, intimate and core identity identified as English, I have generally used "Englishness" for this construction.[28]

Personal narratives

In order to look at the ways in which women negotiated, appropriated or opposed a range of roles and identities assigned to them within ideas of home in the period, I draw extensively on oral narratives and life-writing. These are patchy sources for this period, reflecting the scant attention paid to the 1950s in women's history until recently, with comparatively little work in oral history in comparison with the inter-war period and the war.[29] In contrast in black history the 1950s has received considerable attention, particularly in accounts of the Caribbean diaspora in Britain. There is a substantial literature of oral history collections from black people who migrated to Britain after the war, or who stayed on in Britain after war service, again particularly from the Caribbean.[30] Although there are many autobiographical accounts of the war by white women, there is a dearth of literature which focuses on the 1950s. While there is little autobiography by black women who were adult in the period, one major text – Beryl Gilroy's *Black teacher* – has a main focus on the 1950s and early 1960s.

There is one body of autobiographical literature which does

highlight this period, telling its story from the perspective of girls who grew up in the 1950s. Generally published under a feminist imprint, this genre has enjoyed considerable popularity. *Truth, dare or promise*, a collection of 12 stories of 1950s childhoods, was first published in 1985 and has been in print ever since. Carolyn Steedman's expansion of her own contribution to this collection – in *Landscape for a good woman* – has also been reprinted since its first publication in 1986 and has become a classic.[31]

As Steedman's sub-title – "A story of two lives" – suggests, there is a particular interest in this genre in mother–daughter relationships, with Margaret Forster as well as Steedman situating her own story in relation to her mother's life. Terry Lovell has commented that "the tone of [this] generation towards its mother was distinctly hostile".[32] This is not always the case. Maureen Lawrence, for example, tells of a father who was a stern and constraining patriarch and of her own alliance with her mother against him. However, while not all stories are hostile towards mothers, most chart a progress away from home and from their mothers' lives in a common route from grammar school to university. This is the case even in *Truth, dare or promise*, where, as Laura Marcus comments, despite the focus on accounts of childhood, most end with a coda charting subsequent "success", often in London in the media or as a published writer.[33]

In their interest in their own relationship to their mother's lives, stories of girls' childhoods of the 1950s often tell of a desire to avoid the fate of their mothers. In Carolyn Heilbrun's terms, they represent their mother's lives imprisoned within a romantic and domestic plot, while assigning a quest plot to themselves.[34] Passivity, while a strong theme in some accounts of daughters' sense of self in 1950s childhoods, is commonly attributed to mothers.[35] Ros Coward has argued that "feminism could be called 'the daughters' revolt', so central has been the issue of women defining themselves against a previous generation and distancing themselves from their mothers".[36] This distancing is a major theme in Forster's *Hidden lives*, which charts the common story – in her case from a working-class childhood through grammar school to Oxford to career. In one of the last conversations that she records with her mother before her death, the daughter responds to her mother's statement – "I wish I'd had your life" – by stressing commonalities between them:

A lot of my life, I said, is the same as yours was at my age. She gave a little snort of disbelief but her mouth was full of apple pie and cream. No, really, I said, my day-to-day life is looking after the children, just as you did, and being a housewife, cleaning and tidying and cooking and shopping. It's all easy for me. It isn't the hard slog it was for you, and money makes it all even easier. But the feeling is the same, I get just as tired as you did.[37]

However, this statement is undercut by the way Forster charts her own progress away from her mother's life as part of a story of more general social progress:

It gives me such satisfaction to prove, to myself at least, that what I hoped was true *is* true – my chances, my lot, my expectations, born as I was into a working-class family in which women had always served rather than led, were always hundreds of times better than my grandmother's or mother's. . . Everything, for a woman, is better now, even if it is still not as good as it could be.[38]

The effect of this is often to portray the 1950s as a period in waiting for something else – often identified in some way with the late 1960s, a kind of ante-natal ward before the birth of better times, although not necessarily pregnant with them. The inter-war childhoods of the mother's generation are often erased altogether, survive as the origin of injunctions to daughters not to waste food, or when detailed, as in Steedman and Forster, are told from the perspective of the daughter. The war similarly becomes the daughters' memories of bomb sites or decaying air-raid shelters. The desire to avoid the fate of mothers is seen as the concern of the daughters' generation, and rarely investigated as a theme in the life of their mothers. The waiting is the daughters' perspective and what is awaited is their moment. The youth protest movements, the flight from suburbia or the route to university is their moving on and forward into the late 1960s.

This book attempts to shift attention away from the perspectives of daughters to focus on women for whom the period 1945–64 represented adulthood, not childhood. In drawing on oral narratives and life-writing there are many ethical problems which have been the subject of a substantial feminist literature focusing on imbalances of power.[39] They point to the interviewer's power in a number of areas, especially through her own privileged position as an academic, which often means that she is white and relatively well-paid. Her methods too create a power imbalance. In the interview she sets the agenda through the selection of topics for discussion. In the written account, through processes of editing, selection, interpretation and contextualization, she adapts or appropriates narrators' stories to fit her own needs and concerns. Daphne Patai argues:

> In addition to the characteristic privileges of race and class, the existential or psychological dilemmas of the split between subject and object on which all research depends (even that of the most intense "participant observer") imply that objectification, the utilization of others for one's own purposes (which may or may not coincide with their own ends), and the possibility of exploitation, are built into almost all research projects with living human beings.[40]

This is a powerful critique, acknowledging the complex web of power relationships between women which has been a central concern of different feminisms in the past decade. Oral history could also be seen as a potentially ageist project. Although the realization that a generation is already diminished is one impulse towards the collection of narratives, this involves viewing the lives of narrators as of interest mainly in relation to their pasts. Their presents – one of the main topics they may raise in interviews – are usually excluded from the written account.

However, the central task of oral historians is to listen, a task which is generally undervalued and often feminized across a range of areas including academic work. Their ears have received a good deal of attention in accounts of their role as mediators, and may well be selective and particularly attuned to what they want to hear. But what they hear is also significantly dictated by narrators who may substantially deflect their attention away from their original formulation of their projects, and contribute to some shift in the direction in which knowledge flows. In writing this book, although I have control over the final shaping of the account and its interpretation, voices from oral narrators and life-writing have a major shaping influence, for without their knowledge, understanding and theorizings it would scarcely exist.

This raises problems about claims to single authorship. Anne McClintock argues:

In many oral histories, the multiple authorship of the narrative is submerged in the executive, choreographing authority of the "historian". The oral narrator becomes a Svengali's Trilby, at the beck and call of the master of ceremonies, bestowing prestige and glamour on the historian's professional name without herself benefiting one whit.[41]

This seems to me a problem which is not confined to histories which draw on oral narratives. All work is arguably multiply authored, drawing on a range of oral as well as written sources. The apparatus for acknowledging written sources, while well developed, does not always indicate the extent of an author's debt. There is a similar apparatus for acknowledging oral sources which are formally collected, although in many cases narrators cannot be named because of their wish for confidentiality. It seems likely that much work, such as this book, draws on other less formal oral sources and unpublished written material which can never be properly acknowledged. In my case this includes conversations with friends, students, family and colleagues, oral contributions and papers delivered by students and colleagues in seminars, and unpublished written work in student essays and dissertations. At the same time the convention of single authorship does acknowledge the writer's responsibility for the final written account.

Daphne Patai concludes, "Ultimately we have to make up our minds whether our research is worth doing or not, and then determine how to go about it in ways that let it best serve our stated goals."[42] My goals have led me to make up my mind that I cannot leave out the voices of women from whom my differences include those of race, generation, sexuality, class and income and where the power relationships involved include my position as a white woman of the daughter's generation in an academic post. Audre Lorde, writing of a different context, gave her view of white women who say "I can't possibly teach black women's writing – their experience is so different from mine." "How many years," she asks, "have you spent teaching Plato and Shakespeare and Proust?"[43] Hazel Carby, writing of the same context, makes a similar point about white women who say, "I am reluctant and unable to construct theories about experiences I haven't had," but who theorize about the Brontës despite the fact that they never lived in nineteenth-century Yorkshire.[44] These views are about teaching and theorizing women's writing, and not oral history where the ethical problems are more difficult, but they do suggest that while including voices that speak of "experiences I never had" can involve exploitation and appropriation, excluding them is not an answer.

I am aware, however, of many stories and voices that I have left out in offering a particular and partial version of the story of home in this period. In tracing commonalities and differences in the way that black and white migrants were constructed through a focus on the late 1940s, I exclude the story of many 1950s migrants including Cypriot women. The story of Anglo-Indian and Anglo-Pakistani migration, although it belongs to the late 1940s, is barely mentioned. Through a focus on female migration I generally pay little attention to South Asians in Britain, who were predominantly male in the period under discussion. I also pay scant attention to those who arrived in Britain as refugees rather than migrants – again excluding particularly the 1950s history, including the story of Hungarian refugees – as well as to those living in Britain before 1945 who were the targets of pre-war as well as post-war racisms. It may be that these exclusions serve as an example of the "blind eyes . . . turned to the past" described by Catherine Hall, both knowing and not knowing what it is they do not see.[45] It may be that they allow the kind of account which Friedman describes when she says that: "feminist discourses about race and ethnicity are too often caught up in repetitive cultural narratives structured around the white/other binary".[46]

I have been preoccupied with other "blind eyes" while writing this. Catherine Hall writes:

> In Britain our imperial history is a disturbing one that has involved expropriation and exploitation, relations of domin-ation and subordination, multiple racisms. . . We need to stop "turning a blind eye", knowing and not knowing, acknowledg-ing the presence of empire but at the same time not confronting its meanings, especially its unsavoury ones.[47]

One theme of the book is this "blind eye". In a period which saw the dissolution of much of the British colonial empire it is increas-ingly apparent. Perhaps it began in 1947 when King George VI in his Christmas broadcast to the empire forgot to mention Indian inde-pendence, although this forgetting may have been more about shoring up what remained of imperial power than repressing what was lost.[48] This loss of imperial power, the sharp sense of national decline which it involved, haunts the story told here.[49]

Chapter One

Chapter One

❧

Homecomings

Humphrey Jennings's film *Diary for Timothy* was made in 1944–5 and released in 1946. In marking a moment when the war was coming to an end, the film situates its story in a transitional place between war and post-war. At its centre is the figure of a baby boy born on the fifth anniversary of war – 3 September 1944. The film addresses him, both telling him the story of what has been happening in Britain in the first six months of his life, and entrusting him with the task of making a different world when the war is over. Timothy, representing the future generation, is both what the war has been fought for – "though we didn't exactly know it" – and the symbol of rebirth and renewal.

The film offers an image of nation which is very different from the fervent patriotism invoked during the First World War. What is heroic in *Diary for Timothy* is the quiet courage and endurance of the everyday round, as people keep going despite the weariness of a long war. Britishness is still "the unconquerable spirit and courage of the people" as in Jennings's 1940 *London can take it*, but the meaning of home is beginning to shift from the danger and heroism of the blitz to a place of safety and security. In choosing to place at its centre the figure of a baby boy, and in the intimate diary form in which it addresses him, the film foregrounds gentle domestic images – Timothy with his mother, in his cot, warm and comfortable at home. At the same time, Timothy is constantly reminded of the dangers which surround him. He is shown home as a place of safety for himself, but of danger for others as people shelter from doodlebugs under their kitchen table, and a team go out to rescue those buried in the rubble which had been their home. "It's only chance," he is reminded, "that you're safe and sound."

The transitional place between war and post-war is also evident in the possibility of making the world a different place after the war, although, like Timothy himself, the hopes expressed within the film are still fragile. There is continuing conflict, but the war is coming slowly to an end. Men are shown clearing the beaches of mines and mending the roofs of bomb-damaged houses, signalling a final end to the threat of invasion and the beginnings of reconstruction. Timothy is told that after the war he will be able to run safely on the beach. Renewal is also embodied in images of healing as the film traces the recovery of Goronwy the miner, injured in a pit accident, and Peter the fighter pilot, injured when his plane came down over France. Initially "lying broken and still" in hospital, Peter is shown recovering his confidence and his health – rehabilitated through physiotherapy, and finally going back to flying, limbs restored. Timothy's birth and first months of life also offer an image of new life and renewal as the miserable weather of October 1944 with continuous rain becomes infused with hope in its association with the water of Timothy's baptism.

"We've been doing most of the talking up to now," Timothy is told at the end of the film, before the task of making the world a different place is entrusted to him. This "we" is represented as a community of people in images of social unity – the people's war. Although Timothy is told sternly that he wouldn't be so comfortable if he'd been born in Poland or a Glasgow slum, there are few signs of social conflict or class division, and a common decency is embodied in every figure shown. Division is expressed only through looking back. Through the figure of Goronwy, the Welsh miner, the film establishes its narrative concern not only with war and post-war but also pre-war, evoking the 1930s as unemployment and poverty. Goronwy's message suggests both the fragility and possibility of hope: "I was sitting thinking about the past, the last war, the unemployed, broken homes, scattered families. And then I thought, has all this really got to happen again?"

In tracing the diary of his first six months, Timothy is shown the story of Britain in this period mainly as men's activities as they hew coal, drive trains and fly fighter planes while he lies asleep in his cot. Women are shown as healers who nurture and encourage the progress of Peter's and Goronwy's convalescence and mending, preparing them to venture out into the world again. The gentle domestic images which the film foregrounds are female, associated particularly with Timothy's mother, who is shown indoors – in the nursing home where her son is born, at church for his baptism, but mainly beside Timothy in her domestic world as she baths, feeds and tends to him. In the transitional place between war and post-war, Timothy is also transitional between female and male worlds. His present is female as he lies warm and comfortable in his mother's arms, but his future is in the world of men who speak to him, and the story he is told is one where he will grow into manhood, away from mother and nursery.

No return to the past – the main message that Timothy is offered through Goronwy – imagines the new social order that can be born out of the war and the healing of the social divisions of the 1930s. Class and Englishness linger over the representation of this possibility in a way which suggests considerable limitations to the extent to which the new world envisaged will disrupt an existing social order. The baby at the centre of the film who may make the world a different place is born in a nursing home near Oxford, comes home to a rectory in Henley-on-Thames, and has a choral baptism. The task assigned to him is to listen carefully, and the voices he hears include some from Wales and from the working class. They are all male as not only Peter and Goronwy, but also Bill the engine driver and Alan the farmer speak to him, and are joined by the voice of his father who is serving overseas but sends a letter at Christmas. In a film with a script by E. M. Forster, read by Michael Redgrave, women say almost nothing. Timothy's mother is a passive figure and has no message for him, apart from love. She is waiting for the war to end and for her husband to return.

Images of the war did not always place women on the margins of representations, nor portray them as passive. As war-workers they were used as symbols of heroism, although the emphasis was usually on their taking on work temporarily as a matter of patriotism and citizenship. Jennings's own images of women's war-work were rather unheroic, and in his *The heart of Britain* (1941) they do everyday, routine, tedious things and are content to do so. As the commentary and images tell us:

> Behind this grim work lie an infinite number of patient everyday tasks for the women. Dull jobs, like typing lists of addresses, unending ones like sorting clothes for the homeless. Routines which women fill with love and devotion.

Women as housewives could also serve as symbols of courage and heroism. In *Mrs Miniver* (1942), the Hollywood film based – very loosely – on Jan Struther's creation in *The Times*, it is a middle-class housewife who represents the spirit of Britain. There are many aspects to Caroline Miniver's home front as she encounters a wounded German in her home who threatens her with a gun, is shot at by German planes – which kill her daughter-in-law – while driving her car, and shelters with her family in air-raids which damage her home. Calm in the face of adversity, strong in the face of bereavement, steely during air-raids, Caroline is very far from passive. The film, ending with images of the destruction of the village where she lives – many of its homes in ruins, its church roofless and windowless – shows the "unconquerable spirit and courage of the people" through the continuation of family and village life. As the community attend the ruined church for Sunday worship, it is families, not decent working men, who are shown displaying the determination to carry on, and the central image of such determination is Caroline herself, surrounded by her family, singing "Onward, Christian soldiers".

As the war ended images of women's heroism, whether as warworkers or as housewives, faded. In representing mass unemployment before the war through the figure of Goronwy, *Diary for Timothy* reverted to the pre-war image of unemployment as a male problem and employment as a male preserve – one in which the unemployed man had often been represented in juxtaposition to the young, brightly dressed, made-up and pleasure-seeking factory girl who was seen as barring the door against his chances of employment.[1] Sir Herbert Austin, who employed thousands of women in his car factories, had nevertheless argued that "If we were to take women out of industry I believe we could absorb all the unemployment."[2] One of the major surveys of unemployment – the Pilgrim Trust Report – had called its findings *Men without work*, and identified the "real problem" of female unemployment as the problem of increasing the income brought in by her husband's wage sufficiently for it to be possible for a wife to reject definitely the alternative of going back to work, so settling down instead to make a home. The Report welcomed the existence of a group of women in Blackburn who, despite their tradition of continuous work in the mills, with unemployment "feel the claim of the family to their whole attention".[3]

The shift away from images of women as war-workers is

particularly apparent in the way demobilization was represented as a male return to home and family. Like Timothy's mother, women were increasingly seen as passive figures, who had spent the war waiting for their men's return. Their own return – from the services, from billets where they had been housed during mobilization for war-work, from the Women's Land Army, from evacuation – was obscured. In 1943, a report on *Psychological problems of troops overseas* had recommended that radio and film:

> . . . illustrate essential femininity (as a reassurance against the soldiers' fears about this) and should give forth affection and the suggestion that they are waiting for the return of armies abroad. This need not be done by direct speech, of course; an unconscious glance at a photograph of a soldier on the mantelpiece, or a term of speech – "If our Harry could see me now" – are the sort of thing that can be both natural and implicit ways of conveying this attitude.[4]

As the war ended, the idea that women had spent their time looking at photographs of soldiers on the mantelpiece was common in many representations of demobilization, as magazines, newspapers and cinema screens were flooded with images of heterosexual reunions and their promise of fertility. The housewife, cast in a less heroic role than Mrs Miniver, returned decisively to being "ordinary" and home became the place of peace in opposition to war. In 1945, *Picture Post*'s article on "How to welcome a soldier home" represented the housewife, "Mrs Jim Ford", welcoming Sergeant Jim Ford with slippers by the fire.[5]

Diary for Timothy can thus be read as marking a particular moment when the meaning of home began to be constructed in opposition to war in the notion of a return to the normality and security of family life. The return is not shown in the film, but its hope is expressed through the voice of Timothy's father promising that "we will all be together again", and in the final image where Timothy, lying in his cot and sucking his thumb, is portrayed looking up at a photograph of his father on the wall. This moment also marks a resolve about the shaping of the post-war world which is about the opposite of a return. The final message of the film that Timothy is given is Goronwy's: "Unemployment after the war . . . will it be like that again? Are you going to have greed for money or power ousting decency from the world as they have in the past? Or are you going to make the world a different place – you and the other babies?"

Mending Britain

"Never again" was generally the answer to Goronwy's question – "will it be like that again?" – in visions of reconstruction. These began to emerge during the war with the hope of a new order, expressed as early as 1940 by J. B. Priestley in a broadcast in July and by the Archbishop of Canterbury in a series of broadcasts made in September and October of the same year.[6] In 1941 *Picture Post* published a special edition called "A plan for Britain"; a Cabinet committee was set up on "reconstruction problems"; and discussions about demobilization began. The Beveridge Report was published in December 1942 and in 1943 a Minister of Reconstruction was appointed by the government. J. B. Priestley had already argued in a 1940 broadcast that there was no return, no going back, because "there's nothing that really worked that we can go back to".[7] The resolve – "never again" – as Peter Hennessy writes:

... captures the motivating impulse of the first half-dozen years after the war – never again would there be war; never again would the British people be housed in slums, living off a meagre diet thanks to low wages, or no wages at all; never again would mass unemployment blight the lives of millions; never again would natural abilities remain dormant in the absence of educational stimulus.[8]

This resolve was matched by a contrasting resolve in relation to family life as the return of men promised a restoration of the proper order of the patriarchal family. In 1945 Lord Horder, in his introduction to *Rebuilding family life in post-war Britain*, stated: "To help the people of this land to reconstitute their family life is the purpose of this book. . . . In many cases [family life has been] shattered, broken or disorganised by the social upheaval of a second world war."[9] The book discussed many proposals for "helping", outlining the need for increasing state provision – part of the resolve of "no return" to poverty. But this "helping" was also about the need to return to a pre-war order disrupted by the war, expressed particularly in concerns to stem the rising rates of illegitimacy and divorce.

As these contrasting resolves were addressed, women and men were assigned different roles, as captured in the titles of forces education programmes on the BBC where servicewomen were asked "what ought we to know about food and health in the home", and told about "the weekly wash".[10] Although plans for reconstruction also envisaged a continuation of the need for women to work outside the home, their work in rebuilding family life was prioritized. In so far as men were assigned a role in this, it was mainly through the way in which their return signalled a restoration of the proper order of the patriarchal family. Priority was also given in demobilization arrangements to the task of rebuilding the physical fabric of homes. The creation of a Class B category was designed mainly to release men in the building and ancillary trades to build houses – a task which had become urgent through the impact of bombing and the virtual cessation of house-building during the war.[11] Demobilization arrangements also recognized the need to rebuild family life, giving priority to married women, with priority for married men also discussed, although not implemented.[12]

Mending lives and homes broken by war was a major task assigned to women. As in *Diary for Timothy*, they were given healing tasks, restoring the lives of husbands and children. The way in which such tasks were assigned to women ignored the extent to which they had also suffered in the war as they were given the main responsibility for coping with its psychological and emotional aftermath.

Women, men and children were often haunted by their traumatic experiences during the war. Many had come close to death in a range of settings, including drowning, being buried alive under rubble, being starved and tortured as prisoners-of-war. More had experienced bereavement, evacuation or the violence of killings and maimings both witnessed and delivered. Children as well as adults had experienced bombing raids. Betty Summers records:

> I had a cousin living on the Thames estuary, and when I was stationed in the South and got a 48 hour leave I couldn't really get home, so I used to go and stay with her because her husband was away. She had a little boy of seven. And he had a brainstorm. They'd had so much bombing, and I was staying this particular weekend when it happened. And the sirens went and there was a dugout in the garden, and there was shrapnel raining down, and the guns were all going crackers, and this

child just sat up in bed and screamed and screamed and screamed. It was a brainstorm. We had to get the gear, and get him into the shelter. I remember carrying this screaming child. It had an awful effect on me. What an awful thing for a seven-year old. And after that, they evacuated him, they actually took him to live in the country, in Lincolnshire. He recovered, but it took him a long time. That made a big effect on me. . . . I never want to see another child in that state. Ever.[13]

Those who had been involved in the liberation of concentration camps had witnessed something of the Holocaust. Maureen Lawrence records her father's Sunday morning grief and desolation in the kitchen after his return:

I hear a groaning noise, and only then do I realise that my father is sobbing aloud and that his crying is not like the moist whimpering of a child, but is a dry-voiced sound, a roaring and a gasping, because he is struggling to hold back the flood. Men do not cry. . . Then my mother is in the kitchen. And she is holding him tight, kneeling by his chair to put her face against his head and shushing: There now, it's better now. . . Nothing is ever said. . . Nothing is ever put into words to me, but I pick up clues: his nerves are bad. It is the war and the things he has witnessed in the field and in the camps. . . In the last months of the war he has been with the forces that guard certain camps. What camps? Hush, in front of the child, says my grandmother. The things that he has seen have crept into his soul and he is not the same man. There is a grim bewilderment in my father that manifests itself to me as rage, the obverse side of his Sunday morning grief, that comes out of nowhere, that strikes where it will, that is entirely authorised because it is his rage, his grief, and that gives him terrible power. . . I think my fear of him took its first definite shape that morning. . . His desolation was a dreadful pit opening in front of my eyes. . . Soon it would close over and he would move on to some new place in his experience, ostensibly forgetting or accepting the death chambers except perhaps in the dark night of the soul.[14]

Manuals addressed to women covered trauma, desolation, pain and rage with a coating of sugar as they were advised that the problems they might face from husbands, fathers, brothers or sons would range from snappiness and impatience, fits of moodiness, outbursts of tears, sleepwalking and nightmares to disfigurement, long periods of depression, fits of rage, and violence.[15] "It is a hard task for those who love these men to get through the self-made barriers," counselled *Living together again*, a manual published in 1946 by a doctor and his wife, "but infinite patience, gentleness and an exquisite tact, will gradually wear thin the resistance and enable a truly loving wife or sweetheart to get emotionally near enough to the man to deal quietly with his resistance."[16] There was concern too about the return of children which centred on evacuees, some of whom had spent the entire war away from home. Mothers were counselled that "being uprooted and planted down again too suddenly" might lead to "sleepwalking, night-terrors, a recurrence of bed-wetting, pilfering, playing truant from school and home . . . as well as the more obvious signs of misery, discontent and loss of appetite". They were advised to be understanding and sympathetic, but were told that if this was not enough, "help should be sought from the nearest Child Guidance Clinic".[17]

The return of the father to his children was mainly portrayed as a longed-for event, with little discussion of the problems children might experience on being reunited with a father whom they had rarely or never seen, and the disruptions his return might cause, including the need to adjust to the birth of a new sibling. Advice usually centred on his non-return. *Living together again* suggested ways of coping with questions about a dead parent, or a parent who was absent, because they had gone to live with someone else. In both cases the parent was identified as "daddy": "Daddy prefers to live with Alice. He loves her and is happier with her."[18] There was less advice for war-widows or deserted wives about how to cope with the emotional and financial impact of their husband's absence or death. Phyllis Dewsbury married in 1940, and went to Blackpool to work as a "clippie" on the "balloons" – the double-deckers. Three years later, her husband was killed:

> We lost our youth. I had a brother who volunteered the week that war broke out, and I never saw him until after the war, for five years. And from the time of him going in, I'd been married, had a baby, and was a widow when he came home.
>
> When my husband was first called up, he was away seven months before he got a leave, and then I saw him in between,

and then of course he was killed. When they delivered his clothes it was just like the sides of a dart board. I had to come off the transport when my son was born, and he was a year old the same week that my husband was killed. When he was eighteen months old, I had to go out to work. I got a pension for my husband, a very small pension. In between, my mother went blind, so I had to look after her for a while. My father, he used to come home early from work, and we had to work it between us, and then I had to give up work for a while to look after my son. You didn't get help then – you had to rely more on your family. You got your pension and that was it. It was a bit difficult, but we got through.[19]

Although the return was generally represented as a male concern, particular kinds of reunion were experienced by women as shortages of housing faced some who returned with the prospect of living with parents or parents-in-law indefinitely. Betty Summers records that this was a difficult period. She had served in the Women's Auxiliary Air Force (WAAF) during the war, had married in spring 1945, and came out of the WAAF before the birth of her first child in 1946:

When I went in [to the WAAF] I'd only had two years after school, I was like a kid. And when I came out I was married and couldn't boil an egg. And then I had the baby. I had a good set of parents who took us in, and then J [husband] came out the following year. My parents were very good to me, but I couldn't seem to settle at all. I was restless. I wanted to go off in spite of the baby. I got to used to it, I wouldn't change it now, but I'd had three years of doing as I wanted, more or less.

It was four years after her marriage before Betty Summers and her husband managed to get somewhere to live away from her parents, and by that time she had two children. In retrospect, she looks at the way in which this affected her parents' generation as well as her own:

My parents must have been sick of us. Two babies. When I think of their side of it now. At the time it never entered my mind, but now when I look back, they must have been totally sick, because my father was due to retire, and he got cancer and died. When I think I spoilt their last few years, I often wonder if my mother resented it, but she never showed it if she did.[20]

A 1947 study found that 8 per cent of households still contained one or more married children, some with their spouses, and 7 per cent of households contained boarders.[21]

However, for some women the end of war meant an easing rather than a worsening of overcrowding in the home. Eva Holt worked in munitions in Leeds during the war, and lived with her family in a scullery house, with two bedrooms and a double attic. During the war they had soldiers billeted on them, and also took a family of war-workers from London. This meant they had to make new sleeping arrangements:

> My sister went to sleep with the lady next door. Me and my younger sister slept in the small room, and the soldiers slept in the attic, and the family that were staying with us slept in the big room – we had these pull-out camp beds as we used to call them. And dad went to sleep in another lady's house lower down the street. And mum slept in the same room as me and my sister.[22]

These kind of family separations could also be ended once billettees left, although this was not the kind of reunion that images of demobilization usually portrayed.

The return of men was generally represented as a proper restoration of the order of the patriarchal family, but there were also concerns about the ways in which rising rates of illegitimacy and divorce disrupted this. Divorce rates peaked in 1947, and official concerns were expressed through the government Committee of Inquiry into Matrimonial Breakdown, set up in the same year, which recommended a government grant for the work of marriage guidance dedicated to "the safeguarding of the family unit as the basis of our community life."[23]

As *Living together again* hinted, domestic violence was one experience which disrupted the joy of reunions, although it was surrounded by a general silence. Alice Woodward, who had married in 1944, divorced in 1951:

> He was gentle, he was rather delicate in build, he had straight dark hair and dark brown eyes, he was a nice lad, and I really did fall in love with him. And then of course the inevitable happened, and I got pregnant. And so instead of getting married the next year, we got married in a bit of a hurry, and he left me at home with my gran and he went back to sea. He came

home when my baby was three weeks old. . . . Then he treated me – "I want my dinner here and my pudding there and my cup of tea there." I was only there for his convenience to carry the coal and do the washing and look after the children. I suppose we had nothing in common except bed really.[24]

Alice Woodward's husband also used violence against her, and it was after a particular violent episode that she decided to leave him. The divorce, however, was granted on the grounds of her adultery rather than his violence, and this meant that she was unlikely to get custody of the children, especially since her husband told her that he "would fight me in the court for them right to the bitter end". He did, however, consent to their adoption, and so she decided on this as the best course for the children, and never saw them again. While domestic violence was one reason for post-war divorce, some women stayed in violent marriages because of this threat of separation from their children.

Illegitimacy rates peaked in 1945. Official adoption rates also peaked in 1946 at 21,000, and there were numbers of illegal adoptions which were not covered by official statistics. While it was estimated that one-third of these figures represented the adoption of children by their own mothers, they also represented a range of mothers – both unmarried and married – who were parted from their children in the immediate aftermath of war.[25]

Unmarried women often had little alternative to offering their babies for adoption. Accommodation was a major problem for all those who were rejected by their families, and even for some who were not. Pregnant women in the services were immediately discharged, women living in war-workers' hostels had to give up their room when they stopped working, and those living in private billets were often asked to leave. After childbirth, unmarried mothers had little hope of finding any kind of billet. It was also difficult to find foster mothers or nurseries to care for their children so that they could return to work. Of unmarried mothers who had been servicewomen, 16 per cent went into residential domestic employment as the only alternative to offering their babies for adoption.[26]

There could perhaps be few images more disruptive of a return to the naturalness of the patriarchal family than the man returning to find a baby in a cot who cannot be his. "Bigamy," Lord Elton had declared in 1943, "is almost a national institution."[27] A number of married women also had illegitimate children during the war. While figures on such a subject are unlikely to be accurate, it was estimated that in some towns in 1945, almost half of all illegitimate children were born to married women.[28] Vera married a merchant seaman in 1940, three days before he sailed, and in September of that year gave birth to a daughter. In April 1941 a telegram arrived telling her that her husband was "missing, presumed drowned", and in September 1942 she had a brief affair with another man who was home on leave:

My husband was "missing, presumed drowned". Only someone who has been in this position can really know just what a no man's land that is. . . I was so angry I even thought of suicide, but then I thought it would be wrong for my daughter to be left without any parents, and also that she would have to live with the disgrace of a mother who had taken her own life . . .

It was a very short affair. It felt the right thing to do at the time. It was a way of coming to terms with my husband gone, of stopping grieving and feeling I was really alive again. But soon enough I had a big worry. I knew I was pregnant. . . I longed for the war to end so that I could rent a place for my daughter, my baby son and myself, where we could be a family. It was November 1945 when I got a letter from my husband via the Red Cross. He said his ship had been sunk, but he had been picked up by a Norwegian fishing boat. He had spent some time with a family in a small fishing port there, but when the Germans came he had to go into hiding, moving from place to place. Eventually he was picked up and held prisoner.

He arrived home in January. The months in between had been agony. He was shocked into silence initially – then his anger burst out. I pleaded my side of the case, but he didn't want to know. Eventually he stormed out of the house and I didn't see him for about a week. I learned later that he had spent the time drinking and sleeping in the park. When he did come back, he was calmer. He said he had been thinking things over and that he would try to make a go of it, and we both did try, but he never really accepted that my son was there. We had weeks of calm and then when something went wrong and we quarrelled my affair was brought up. One day he got really angry over something, and became violent. He grabbed my son and shook him and wouldn't let me pick him up. I was terrified. Some time later it happened again, but when things quietened down, he gave me the ultimatum. Him or the boy.

I was devastated. How could I make such a choice? I didn't want to believe what he was saying, but I was also frightened for my son. He was in physical danger as long as the situation continued. By this time I couldn't keep what was happening a secret any longer, so I told mam and she suggested that I contact the local welfare people. The woman . . . suggested my son be taken into a place of safety. It would be in my son's best interest to be out of the violent atmosphere. She reassured me that she had seen other cases like mine and often the husband realised, just by the fact that the wives were prepared to make such sacrifices, that they really had nothing to fear about their wife's fidelity. About seven o'clock that evening, a black car drew up outside the prefab. The woman I had seen earlier and a man got out and came to the door. They said they had come to take my son into care as they were concerned for his safety. . . The whole thing seemed to be over in no time at all, but its consequences have lasted a lifetime.[29]

Initially the authorities would not tell Vera where her son was. Later, they moved him to a children's home which was eight hours' journey away. "All the time I was trying to beg and plead with the local welfare to have my son returned, but they always said that until they could be sure that the home situation had altered, my son was in need of care and protection."[30] It was not until three years later, when her husband left her, that she was told her son had been made a ward of court, and that she had been deemed an unfit mother. It was not until her son was adult that they were reunited.

As Vera's story suggests, married women who had illegitimate children were particularly stigmatized in this period. Illegitimacy of this sort was generally viewed as "the domestic troubles of [male] soldiers", and probation officers were often enlisted by the Army Welfare Service to investigate these troubles. Married women who were suspected of adultery thus came under scrutiny in their homes at the request not only of husbands serving overseas, but also of their commanding officers and padres.[31] Adoption of the wife's illegitimate child was often considered the best way of keeping marriages together, and husbands who were prepared to accept the child were seen as exceptionally understanding. Sheila Ferguson and Hilde Fitzgerald argued that a woman in this situation "could not keep her husband in ignorance because she needed his consent if she offered her baby for adoption. She could ask him to forgive her, but he would rarely be prepared to do so unless she gave up her child."[32] While women like Alice Woodward were parted from their children through divorce, for other women having children adopted was seen as essential in order to keep their marriages together.

Women must bear children

When "Mrs Jim Ford" was portrayed by *Picture Post* welcoming her husband home with fireside slippers, she was also asked about her plans for having children after the war.[33] Reunions were expected to be fruitful, and maternity featured strongly in a prolific literature on pronatalism produced by government, doctors, sociologists, churchmen, demographers and feminists which included the development of work on infertility and medical treatment for it, which was already apparent in 1945.[34] Although concern about declining population in Britain dated from at least the 1880s, and had been exacerbated by low birth rates in the inter-war period, the war and its aftermath sharpened the pens of many pronatalists. At least eight works on the dangers of British depopulation were published or republished in 1945.[35] This was also the year in which the Royal Commission on Population was set up.

The family planning that *Picture Post* suggested for Mrs Ford – "a boy and a girl" – was over-modest by pronatalist standards. Although they did not offer exact prescriptions of family size, many pronatalists would have agreed with Margaret Hadley Jackson, who defined the "sizeable family" as "from four to eight children", the "too small family" as "from nil to three children", and "the solitary ewe lamb" as "a thing to deplore".[36] After the marriage of Princess Elizabeth in 1947, Eva Hubback wrote to Lady Cynthia Colville expressing her opinion that for "Princess Elizabeth to have a rather larger than average family eg. about four children would be the best thing to encourage larger families throughout the country".[37]

A multitude of schemes were proposed to encourage women to have more children. As Denise Riley comments:

15

There is a huge literature, concentrated in 1945 and 1946, which argues for nurseries, after-school play centres, rest homes for tired housewives, family tickets on trains, official neighbourhood baby-sitters, holidays on the social services for poorer families, proper access for all to good gynaecological and obstetric help, a revolution in domestic architecture towards streamlined rational kitchens and a good number of bedrooms, more communal restaurants and laundries.[38]

Few of these schemes were implemented. Family allowances had been at the heart of a long inter-war feminist campaign for family endowment, and it was the intervention of Eleanor Rathbone in Parliament that ensured that they were paid directly to mothers, but the Beveridge Report envisaged them as a measure which would boost the birth rate. This is also how they were popularly understood, illustrating the extent to which the pronatalist message had entered the popular consciousness by the end of the war. A number of feminists associated with the movement for family endowment – notably Eva Hubback, who took over the Family Endowment Society on Eleanor Rathbone's death – had anyway argued their case in these terms. Moya Woodside's investigation of marriage relationships in the urban working classes during the war coincided with the introduction of family allowances. She found that:

Almost all thought of them as an effort to boost the birthrate, rather than as an amelioration of hardship for the more prolific. They were taken as an inducement, a bribe, a payment – and a very inadequate one: "the wife said *she* wasn't going to have a baby for five bob a week". "I'd like to see *them* keep a baby on five shillings." No one thought that the allowances would have any effect in encouraging fertility generally, or that they would influence their own decision.[39]

The impression that family allowances were designed to boost the birth rate may have been reinforced by the fact that they were not paid for "solitary ewe lambs", but only for the second and subsequent children.

The needs of children were another main focus of reconstruction literature and of plans for the wartime and post-war welfare state. State policy was predicated on the assumption that the home was central to children's welfare. "We wish to emphasise . . . the extreme seriousness of taking a child away from even an indifferent home" reported the Care of Children Committee, under the "chairmanship" of Myra Curtis in 1946. "Every effort should be made to keep the child in its home . . . provided that the home can be made reasonably satisfactory."[40] In line with its recommendations, schemes were developed to raise the standards of homes judged inadequate in preference to removing children, and where children could not be kept at home a substitute home – through adoption or fostering – was recommended. Residential care was increasingly seen as a last resort, but where there were no alternatives there was a recognition of the need for small "family" groups. The Curtis Report recommended 8 as ideal and 12 as the maximum, and expressed the hope that institutional care could gradually be eliminated.[41]

A considerable literature developed around evacuation and the psychological and educational problems that this had involved, and produced two very different emphases.[42] In 1943 the importance of cleanliness was still the major theme of the Hygiene Committee of the Women's Group on Public Welfare, which set out to investigate accusations levelled against evacuees, and was addressed to "readers with stout stomachs". Their study compiled the most extraordinary catalogue of bodily dirtiness in British towns, recording in meticulous detail the evidence they collected of the prevalence of lice, skin diseases, insanitary habits, dirty and inadequate clothing, bad sleeping habits and want of discipline. Hygiene, as the committee's name suggested, was the theme which drew together a wide range of topics, including the falling birth rate, diseases of dirt, and incompetent mothering. Their recommendations for child care emphasized the importance of regulation and discipline, including the need to get children to bed at regular times, to ensure their bodily hygiene and good habits over food and drink, and to give sanitary training by checking bad habits which led to enuresis and soiling.[43] John Bowlby's work, also influenced by studies of evacuees' experience of separation from mothers, produced a very different emphasis on the importance of mother-love for children's mental health, emphasizing the importance of a mother's relationship with her children rather than hygiene and discipline.[44]

The view that Bowlby's ideas were taken up as part of a late-1940s campaign to return women to the home and to increase the population is common in many interpretations.[45] While this suggests a patriarchal interest in women as an unpaid workforce in the home, available to care for children and to service men, the extent to which racism was implicated in the construction of women's primary task as motherhood is apparent in most pronatalist literature, where the need to promote a white birth rate was a constant theme, and was usually made explicit. As Mass Observation argued in justification of its 1945 study, *Britain and her birth-rate*, "only those who want the white part of the human race to decrease and eventually to disappear, can legitimately claim that the survey is partisan."[46]

This promotion was sometimes a concern about what was constructed as "the West", with analyses of population decline identifying the United States, western and northern Europe, Canada, Australia and New Zealand as "the zone of low fertility".[47] Statistics which were used to support this view singled out net white reproduction rates in these countries, reflecting fears expressed between the wars that in a country such as New Zealand there was a falling white birth rate while the Maori birth rate was rising.[48] As the Royal Commission on Population saw it in its 1949 Report, since declining population was common to western civilization, and virtually confined to it, this would have serious implications for western prestige, influence, military strength and security, and for the maintenance and extension of western values, ideas and culture.[49] Concerns were equally about the birth rate in Britain and its implications for British influence and power in the world, with the black birth rate in empire presented as a problem of over-population. The Royal Commission on the West Indies in 1945 recommended a reduction in the number of births as an indispensable condition for maintaining the standard of life.[50]

These aspects of pronatalism are apparent in concerns about children born to white British women during the war by black American GIs, who became a focus of race discourse in the late 1940s. Despite the recommendations of the Curtis Committee, embodied in the 1949 Children Act, children of mixed parentage were seen as "unadoptable" – a view which was developed through the 1950s. A Ministry of Health official noted in discussions of these children that "a black child is almost impossible to get adopted, nearly as difficult to board out and therefore is pretty sure to be brought up in some type of Children's Home in this country, if separated from the mother".[51] The League of Coloured Peoples tried to find a home in England where the children could be cared for and decided on a property in Leeds, but nothing came of this initiative.[52] Instead, many of the children were sent to America, sometimes for adoption by their fathers' families, their cases organized by the Family Welfare Association in Britain in conjunction with the International Social Services.[53] The *Daily Mail* explained in 1947, in an article entitled "Britain exports five thousand dusky problem babies", that they were to be "shipped to America in a specially chartered liner . . . [to] save them from growing up social misfits and from possible stigma".[54]

Women must work

Pronatalist prescriptions, with their emphasis on the need for large families, were ostensibly in conflict with a rather different prescription produced by concerns about the labour shortage: *Women must work*. This was the title of a Central Office of Information film released as part of a recruitment campaign in 1947. Aimed at married as well as single women, the campaign also told mothers of young children that there were places in nurseries or creches if they wanted to volunteer.[55] This conflict was resolved in part through stressing the temporary nature of the need for their employment, which was portrayed as a continuation of the war-time emergency. Recruitment posters exhorted, "Women, please lend your support a little longer", and the government encouraged employers to develop a range of schemes for part-time work and shift-work so that employment could be fitted in around the needs of the family. A further way in which conflict was resolved was through the recruitment of migrant women, producing a division of labour where indigenous women were assigned roles which were mainly centred on the home and migrant women were assigned roles as full-time workers.

There were acute shortages of womanpower in a number of areas, including a range of occupations in hospitals. Controls on the engagement and direction of labour, relaxed after the war except in mining and agriculture, were reintroduced for a limited period in 1947, affecting single women as well as men. The recruitment campaign was at its most energetic in the Lancashire textile area, with 61 weaving mills in Nelson alone participating in 1948.[56]

Exports were seen as crucial to economic recovery, and the government looked to the textile industry in particular to spearhead the export drive, interrupting briefly a long history of decline. "Britain's bread hangs by Lancashire's thread" was the slogan. During the war production has been "concentrated" in nucleus mills, with many female textile workers transferring into munitions.[57] When mills were "deconcentrated" and reopened after the war, employers were often desperate for female labour, and even attempted to poach former female skilled workers from other employers.

Bridget Poulton had left school at 14 to work as a weaver in a mill in Preston. During the war, under "concentration", this mill was closed, and she went into munitions. After the war she went back to weaving, at a different mill in Lostock Hall, but when her original mill reopened, they wanted her back:

> I came home one night, and my mother said, "Mr Smith" – that was my old tackler – "he's been round, and Horrockses are opening again. Are you willing to go?" And I thought yes. So I got in contact with him, and he said, "Well, come on the following Monday", so I said, "Well I'll have to serve my notice at Mostons." So when I went to work on the Monday at Mostons, I said, "I want to give my notice in, Horrockses is opening again." "Well you can't go", I was told. I said, "Why, it's my old firm." They said, "It doesn't matter you can't go." So I was really upset. Anyway Mr Smith came round again, so I told him what had happened, and he said, "Oh, I'm not having that, I'll get in touch with Mr Earnshaw." He was the personnel manager from Horrockses, and he came round to see me, and he said, "what's this about?" And I said, "Oh they just said I can't go." So he wrote a letter. So I served my notice.[58]

Poulton was a single woman at this time. But the textile industry was also energetic in trying to recruit married women and mothers, and employers were encouraged by the government to extend day-nursery provision.[59]

Did women want to continue in paid employment once the war was over? This is a question that has attracted particular attention in feminist history.[60] In the light of the responsibility women were given for smoothing the emotional and psychological traumas of war, both short- and long-term, as well as continuing to make do and mend, the opposition by the British Housewives League to married women's employment and its emphasis on returning to a family where men were breadwinners and women were "the respected wife and mother" may have had some appeal.[61] The moment of the League draws attention to the very considerable difficulties women still faced on the home front in the late 1940s.

Housing shortages were the most pressing of these difficulties for many women. The squatters' movement, beginning in the summer of 1946 with the occupation of a disused army camp in Scunthorpe, had led by the autumn to the occupation of over 1,000 camps by more than 40,000 families.[62] Those who had a home frequently lived in very poor accommodation. A 1947 survey found that fewer than half of British households had their own bathroom, while 44 per cent had no water heating appliances of any kind.[63] The very cold winter of 1946–7, coinciding with a fuel crisis, meant that coal shortages and power cuts joined shortages of furniture, carpets, material for clothing and curtains, and prams. In the summer of 1946 women were exhorted in a magazine "Ladies, knit your own knickers". Mrs Price, who had been a corporal in the WAAF serving in Cairo, was demobilized in 1946. She married in 1947 and lived at first in two rented rooms. When she and her husband acquired their own home bought on a mortgage in 1948, she records, "I made my very first stair carpet from three inch wide furniture webbing sewn together on a second hand sewing machine."[64] As rationing continued, the introduction of bread rationing for the first time in the summer of 1946 became the moment of the British Housewives League.

The League called on women to organize in defence of home and of "a free and happy home life". Although officially non-political, many of its core membership were Conservative women who campaigned against Labour government legislation – nationalization, compulsory national insurance and what they saw as the enforcement of the National Health Service on doctors and their patients. Their own discontents with the post-war housewife's lot may well have been reinforced by the difficulties of getting domestic servants, which were not ended by the ending of the war. But other aspects of the League's programme, including an end to rationing and the provision of reasonably priced food, clothing and housing, appealed to a wider constituency, with the League at one time claiming a membership of 100,000.[65]

Despite the evidence of considerable response to their call in the summer of 1946, the extent to which the League represented a particular middle-class ethos and protest is apparent in their neglect of questions of housing shortages – also at their height in 1946. By 1951 the sort of protest which became the core of the League – the view that the policies of the welfare state threatened women's independence and autonomy in running their own homes – was mainly confined to the pages of the *Spectator*, where it was taken up by those who canvassed the need for a "new feminism". Madeleine Henry argued that post-war policies hampered women in their proper task of managing homes and family life, encouraging them instead to work outside the home. She envisaged this as a process of intervention into women's proper ordering of their own affairs, arguing rather fancifully that women were being urged:

> that we cannot keep our children at home when there are such excellent state schools to send them to (from the age of two or three), that we must go without linen, the dream of every woman, to help the dollar drive . . . that we are no longer allowed to buy or cook a normal meal, and that it would be patriotic to close up the flat during the day-time and go out to work in an office or factory for rather less money than our husbands earn from the same effort.[66]

Another writer argued that "shortages of housing, foodstuffs and materials which bear hardly on everyone bear, perhaps, most hardly on women of the middle classes to whom they are the raw material for creating a certain standard of gracious and elegant living".[67]

Women who opposed continued employment in the labour market in the League and the *Spectator* were defeated in the 1950s when married women's participation increased substantially, and a bi-modal pattern began to emerge where they left the labour market on the birth of a first child but returned to it when children were older, frequently part-time. The traditional basis of women's participation was thus decisively shifted; marriage bars were generally dismantled and never reimposed.

This is one answer to the question of whether women wanted to continue in paid employment once the war was over, although there may have been more reluctance in the late 1940s. Whatever the range of answers offered for that period, the evidence suggests that they were reluctant to return to pre-war occupations in traditional areas of employment, particularly domestic service and textile mills. The

post-war period saw the virtual demise of residential private domestic service, which had in any case relied extensively on the
recruitment of migrant women between the wars, including Irish
women and, from the mid-1930s, Jewish women who escaped from
Nazi Germany, as domestics through a Ministry of Labour
scheme.[68] Labour shortages meant that women who had been in
service before the war, and who intensely disliked their work in
private households, had no need to return. Most private domestic
service after the war was on a daily basis, as represented by the
stereotyped figure of Mrs Morgan, the "daily" in *Mrs Dale's Diary*,
the radio soap opera first broadcast in 1948. Middle-class women
who wanted residential servants after the war frequently had to
recruit migrant women, although only so-called "hardship" households were entitled to apply for migrants recruited through official
schemes.[69] As Mrs Smith reported in 1946 on a radio programme,
"I've only got Nanny after about a three months' wait . . . from
Ireland. She wants to leave but doesn't want to leave me stranded.
She gets two pounds a week, but I suppose if she asked for three
pounds, out of pure desperation we'd have to pay it."[70]

Recruitment of women into textile mills in Lancashire was also
well below the targets that were set. Various explanations were given
for this. Historically there had been a high rate of female participation in the labour market in the north-west, with other regions
beginning to match it only in the post-war period.[71] Despite this, it
was argued that the practical difficulties of combining child care,
domestic work and employment were deterring women.[72] These
were difficulties in which women in the north-west were much
better versed than women in most other regions, and some nurseries
were opened by Lancashire textile employers after the war specifically to enable women to combine employment with child care.
Another explanation offered for low recruitment – a reluctance to
return to low-paid work by women who had transferred from
textiles into higher-paid munitions work under "concentration"
during the war – seems more plausible. This was the view of G. D.
H. Cole in 1947:

> Experience of these factories [munitions] made many people
> reluctant to return, or to send their children, to the textile mills.
> This attitude was reinforced by the bad repute into which
> employment in the cotton industry had fallen because of the

23

high rate of unemployment that had prevailed in it year after year. In these circumstances, it was evident that the industry would not get or hold the labour it needed without a substantial improvement in wages even though its output were to fall a long way short of what it had been in the bad times before 1939.[73]

This view of textile employment was particularly relevant to jobs that were unskilled and dirty, within a hierarchy of prestige where women who worked as weavers were at the top and those who worked in the cardroom near the bottom. In 1946 Miss Ayris, a domestic worker, reported that when she went on holiday she never admitted that she was in service. In 1952 Ferdynand Zweig found that some women who worked in textile mills did the same.[74]

The government's attitude to indigenous women was in many ways Janus-faced. Different government departments produced contradictory messages over the closure of war-time nurseries, while in the context of recruitment drives in 1947 the government encouraged employers in textile areas to open nurseries.[75] However, the emphasis on women's recruitment to the labour market as temporary and the encouragement of part-time and shift-work both suggest a reluctance to recruit indigenous women as full-time workers. There was no such reluctance in the case of migrant women. Their employment might also be seen as temporary, especially in the contract basis on which the EVW scheme and bulk recruitment schemes from Italy were organized, but they generally worked full-time. Recruited as workers, they were not assigned the tasks of bearing children, being available to care for them, making homes or servicing men, nor did the government seek to protect or support their family life. The recruitment of migrant women facilitated the position of indigenous women as primarily wives and mothers.

Chapter Two

&

Unbelongings

In June 1948 the *Empire Windrush* brought 492 men from Jamaica to Britain and a woman stowaway – Averilly Wauchope, a dressmaker from Kingston.[1] Its arrival could be seen as part of the history of demobilization and of return. Most of those on board had served in the British armed forces during the war and were returning to Britain where they had been stationed.

A letter sent by 11 Labour MPs to the Prime Minister, Clement Attlee, on 22 June 1948, the day the *Empire Windrush* docked, stated:

> The British people fortunately enjoy a profound unity without uniformity in their way of life, and are blest by the absence of a colour racial problem. An influx of coloured people domiciled here is likely to impair the harmony, strength and cohesion of our public and social life and to cause discord and unhappiness among all concerned.
>
> In our opinion colonial governments are responsible for the welfare of their peoples and Britain is giving these governments great financial assistance to enable them to solve their population problems. We venture to suggest that the British Government should, like foreign countries, the dominions and even some of the colonies, by legislation if necessary, control immigration in the political, social, economic and fiscal interests of our people.
>
> In our opinion such legislation or administrative action would be almost universally approved by our people.[2]

In its construction of national identity through an opposition between "immigrants" and "the British people" as "our people", the letter to Attlee offers a characteristic view of the way in which questions of who was British, who could become British and who could be seen as belonging in Britain were addressed in the post-war period. As it indicates, these questions received raced answers.[3]

Within the empire black British subjects were represented as part of "our people" in a pattern of familial imagery where colonizers and colonized were seen as members of one imperial family. The colonies were represented as England's daughters, the colonized as children of empire, and England as their motherland or mother country. British monarchs frequently figured as the fathers or mothers of this family. Phillip Gibbs, for example, celebrating the first radio broadcast made by George V on his silver jubilee in 1935, conjured up a father speaking to members of his family throughout the empire:

> Something happened on the night of the King's jubilee which had never happened before in the history of mankind. A human voice – the King's – spoke to the whole world. . . He was speaking to the peoples of the British Empire as the Father of the Family, and these sincere and simple words were heard by men and women of every creed and colour, eager to show their allegiance to the British Crown and their affectionate loyalty to the man who wore it.[4]

The familial ties which the image of a motherland suggested could also be represented in the figure of a queen in celebrations of Empire Day – Queen Victoria's birthday – or in the 1950s in Queen Elizabeth II's extensive tours of empire and Commonwealth, and her broadcasts at Christmas time as well as on Empire Day.

As the letter to Attlee makes clear, these constructions of the colonized as part of "our people" depended on them being outside Britain – contained and controlled elsewhere. Before the Second World War differences between colonizers and colonized had been constructed in terms of metropolis and colonies. Between the wars there was some identification of a "colour problem" in seaport towns such as Liverpool and Cardiff, and in 1929 the Chief Constable of Cardiff proposed a legal ban on "miscegenation", modelled on the South African Immorality Act of 1927.[5] However, as the letter to Attlee argues, Britain was seen as a country "blest by the absence of a colour racial problem". This was a common view, with the "colour problem" generally seen as something that troubled other countries – usually identified particularly with the American "colour bar". The letter, reiterating this view, seems to bear no trace of irony as it represents Britain as a country which has no colour bar in the same breath as it proposes to legislate against the entry of "coloured people".

Reaction to the arrival of the *Empire Windrush* expressed the fear that the boundaries between colonizers and colonized might collapse. The empire no longer offered a secure image of control of the colonized elsewhere, as signalled by Indian independence in the previous year. The *Empire Windrush* brought the colonized into the metropolis. The concern to maintain boundaries was manifested in the immediate proposal for controls on entry in the letter to Attlee, "by legislation if necessary" – a concern which culminated in a series of Immigration Acts from 1962.

As the letter also suggests, constructions of the "colour problem" in Britain reversed the pattern of familial imagery. "Coloured people" are not here "our people" in a common membership of one imperial family, but "their people" for whose welfare colonial governments are responsible. It is in the interests of "our people" to exclude "their people" from Britain, and such an exclusion will be almost universally approved by "our people". In making the passage from Jamaica to Britain, those on board the *Empire Windrush* had also made a passage to the identity of "immigrants" who brought with them a "colour problem". The reversal of familial imagery is perhaps nowhere more apparent than in the phrase which came to be commonly used about "immigrants" in the 1950s, when "our coloured brethren", with its parody of the way the colonized were portrayed within the colonial civilizing mission, became a common term of racist abuse.

These constructions of national identity and "immigrants" addressed the question of who belonged in Britain by developing a hierarchy of belonging which was not only raced but also gendered. According to their place within it women were allotted very different relationships to home and family.

Our people

In the aftermath of war, the question of who were "our people", with a place in Britain, emerged in the context of concerns about maintaining British power in the world. In 1943 Winston Churchill said that for Britain "to maintain its leadership of the world and survive as a great power that can hold its own against external pressure, our people must be encouraged by every means to have larger families".[6] In a broadcast in 1947, however, he blamed "two years of socialist rule" for "half-a-million of our . . . most lively and active citizens in the prime of life" having applied to emigrate. Addressing those who might still intend to apply for emigration, he said, "We cannot spare you . . . at a time when we are scouring Europe for 20,000 or 30,000 or more of the unfortunate displaced persons of the great war to come in and swell our labour force."[7]

Maintaining British power was a major preoccupation of post-war reconstruction, although few would have put their ambitions as high as Churchill's "maintaining world leadership". It was sharpened by Indian independence, by the rise of the United States and the Soviet Union as super-powers, and by Britain's parlous financial position and dependence on American loans. Pronatalism, as Churchill's speech in 1943 suggests, was a common theme in this. In the light of Churchill's encouragement to "our people" to have larger families, the role of women as mothers was seen as their most important contribution to national life. As the Beveridge Report argued in 1942, ". . . in the next thirty years housewives as Mothers have vital work to do in ensuring the adequate continuance of the British race and of British ideals in the world".[8] Despite Churchill's reservations, however, the dominant answer to the problem of maintaining Britain's power also favoured emigration of "our people" in the late 1940s, including "our . . . most lively and active citizens in the prime of life". In schemes for emigration to Australia, Canada and New Zealand promoted by the Labour government, the dominions were constructed as part of "our people", and the schemes were fuelled by a concern to maintain their Britishness as a strategy for maintaining British power. The displaced persons to whom Churchill refers were seen as "suitable immigrants" who could help to make up the numbers who had left for the dominions.

In Eva Hubback's pronatalist concerns in 1947, British influence takes on a religious dimension as, quoting Victor Gollancz – "there are in this country reserves of moral leadership that can still save the world" – she offers prescriptions for women to have more children:

Should the Mother Country . . . fade out of existence or become too greatly outnumbered by peoples with different characteristics, or should Britons become so few in number that we no longer had the influence and prestige of a great Power, our country could no longer be in the position that she is in today – as the centre of a great Commonwealth – to spread the ideals in which we believe, and the world would inevitably be very much the poorer. . . If this threatened decline materialises, so that in a few centuries our numbers have shrunk to a population a third of its present size, it is hardly likely that this green and pleasant land would be left unoccupied. . . Pressure from the Near and Far East – where it may take generations before the planned small family becomes the accepted pattern – may well mean that an emptying Britain would be largely occupied by people from nations with very different traditions and ideas from our own.[9]

In defining Britain as a great power primarily in terms of its position at the "centre of a great Commonwealth", Hubback drew on the connections which had been made between motherhood and imperialism since the mid-nineteenth century. In the long history of concerns about declining birth rates there had been frequent reference to national and imperial interests and the fear that if the British population did not increase fast enough to fill the empty spaces of empire, then others would.[10] Empty spaces in the post-war period were identified mainly as the dominions, whose populations were seen as contributing to Britain's power. Hubback argued, for example, that "it is largely because our own 47 and a half millions can combine with the Dominions that we are still a great Power ourselves". Where the West Indies and Asia were seen as over-populated, the dominions were regarded as sharing the British problem of population decline, and Hubback was concerned that they, like Britain, would experience pressure from the over-populated countries of Asia, whose people would eventually flow into Canada, Australia and New Zealand.[11] In constructions of national identity where the dominions were part of "our people", women's capacity to bear children could form part of the solution to the problem of population decline not only in Britain but also in the dominions. The language in which their task was couched drew on biological racism, with veterinary and agricultural imagery featuring prominently in metaphors of stock, blood and breeding. In these definitions of "our people", policing national boundaries was not just about ports at Dover and Liverpool, but also about Sydney, Wellington and Vancouver.

The emigration of children from Britain to Australia was one outcome of these concerns. Child migration had a long history although before the war children were mainly sent to Canada.[12] In 1938, the Archbishop of Perth, welcoming a group of child migrants, had argued that:

> . . . if we do not supply from our own stock we are leaving ourselves all the more exposed to the menace of the teeming millions of our neighbouring Asian races . . . those boys who had landed that day, and others who would follow in time to come, would be Empire builders in the truest sense of the world; they would be a credit to the land of their birth and a credit to the land of their adoption.[13]

The urgency of "adopting" more children was canvassed at an Australian government conference called to discuss child migration in January 1945:

> There are special and urgent reasons why a major effort should be made immediately in the field of child migration. The peculiar circumstances of the war have created in Europe a greater number of orphans, stray children, "war babies" et cetera, than ever before. This makes the present a time of potentially unparalleled opportunity for Australia to build up her population with child migrants. . . It is proposed that the Commonwealth seek out in Britain and Europe, in each of the first three post-war years, at least 17,000 children a year (i.e. about 50,000 in three years) suitable and available for migration to Australia . . .[14]

"Adopted" by Australia, few of the 2,500 children who were sent from Britain between 1946 and 1952 were adopted by families there, because, as Margaret Humphreys argues, "many of their parents had not, and would not, have given permission for their children to be sent overseas in the first place".[15] Told that they were orphans, many child migrants had parents in Britain, who in their turn were told that their children had been adopted in Britain or had died. The "seeking out" of children proposed by the Australian government was done with the co-operation of British children's homes in the voluntary sector. Although local authorities in Britain were reluctant to send children in their care, children were "sought out" by voluntary societies, including Dr Barnardo's, the Fairbridge Society, the National Children's Home, the Children's Society and the Salvation Army, and by child care agencies run by the Catholic

Church, the Church of England, the Church of Scotland and the Presbyterian Church.[16]

Another outcome of these concerns was the Free and Assisted Passages Schemes of 1946 and 1947, which led to the emigration of 140,000 people from Britain to Australia between 1946 and 1951 and of 47,815 to New Zealand.[17] Given the pervasive official concern with declining population in Britain, the acute labour shortage, as well as the acute financial crisis of 1946 and 1947, the decision to continue with inter-war policies whereby emigration was financially assisted, facilitated and encouraged is extraordinary. Under the Australian Free and Assisted Passages Agreements, funded jointly by the British and Australian governments, which came into operation in March 1947, ex-service men and women were given free passages, temporary housing and assistance in finding employment. Civilians had to pay £10 as a contribution towards their passage; £5 for children aged between 14 and 18. The scheme cost the British government over £5.5 million. Under the New Zealand scheme, announced in 1947, New Zealand paid the entire cost of resettlement.[18]

The extent to which schemes drew on raced definitions of Britishness is apparent from the intentions both of the British government and of governments in the dominions. Australia had established a Department of Immigration in 1945, and Arthur Calwell, Minister of Immigration, was a proponent of the White Australia Policy, anxious to recruit migrants of European origin, but favouring "our people". "It is my hope," Calwell stated, "that for every foreign migrant there will be ten people from the UK."[19] In an arrangement made by Australia and Britain in 1945 it was agreed that Polish people who had served in the war with the British forces and were living in Britain should be eligible for emigration to Australia, but that West Indians who had done so should not be eligible.[20] Thus, black British subjects were excluded, while white people who were officially aliens were granted honorary Britishness to enable them to participate in the scheme. The New Zealand government wanted application forms to specify that only applicants "wholly of European race" were eligible. The British government, afraid of the "embarrassment" such a public announcement would cause, commented that "the rejection of a coloured applicant after interview without any reason being given was not open to the same objections".[21]

As Kathleen Paul has persuasively argued, government policy promoted the migration of "our people" in part because it feared that the dominions would otherwise recruit mainly from displaced persons camps in Europe. Rival recruiting terms were in operation at these camps at different times from Australia, New Zealand, Canada and Britain, as well as France, Holland, Belgium, and the United States.[22] To maintain the Britishness of the dominions the government was therefore prepared to encourage emigration there while themselves recruiting from displaced persons camps to make good the shortage. The Royal Commission on Population was quite explicit about this in 1949, arguing that encouragement of emigration could be combined with a policy of selective immigration to ensure that "the needs of the rest of the Commonwealth for manpower were met as far as possible from people of British stock and that Great Britain, with its much larger population, would take on as much as possible of the problem of assimilating people of other than British stock". But, it added, "we have to keep in mind that . . . the sources of supply of suitable immigrants for Great Britain are limited . . ."[23]

"Suitable immigrants"

In the letter to Attlee prompted by the arrival of the *Empire Windrush*, MPs stated: "This country may become an open reception centre for immigrants not selected in respect to health, education, training, character, customs and above all, whether assimilation is possible or not."[24] The notion of "suitable immigrants" – the phrase used in the report of the Royal Commission on Population – recurs here in the idea that some of those arriving in Britain *were* selected in respect to health, education, training, character and customs and *could* be assimilated.[25] It was particularly people who were recruited under government-sponsored schemes who fitted this definition. Although many regarded themselves as refugees, the government, arguing that "displaced person" was a pejorative term, renamed them EVWs. They were welcomed in a parliamentary debate as full of "the spirit and stuff of which we can make Britons" and "first class people" who would be "of great benefit to our stock".[26] Thus in a reversal of the legal definitions and of those which were embodied in the British Nationality Act of 1948, MPs depicted EVWs who were formally aliens as people who could become Britons, and the men who arrived on the *Empire Windrush* who were formally British subjects as aliens.

In identifying "suitable immigrants" as white, the notion of "assimilation" – highlighted in the letter to Attlee – was central. Assimilation was used in a variety of ways, but in definitions of "suitable immigrants" it was frequently about sexuality and reproduction, hinging on notions of intermarriage. As Sir Harold Wiles, a Deputy Permanent Under-Secretary at the Ministry of Labour, expressed it in a letter to M. A. Bevan, a senior civil servant, in 1948:

> [EVWs] . . . are coming definitely for permanent settlement here with a view to their intermarrying and complete absorption into our own working population. Whatever may be the policy about British citizenship, I do not think that any scheme for the importation of coloured colonials for permanent settlement here should be embarked upon without fully understanding that this means that coloured elements will be brought in for permanent absorption into our own people.[27]

The fear of the collapse of boundaries between colonizers and colonized was not confined to national borders which needed to be policed and controlled – whether these were in Dover, Liverpool or Sydney. The policing of sexual boundaries was seen as central to the maintenance of the nation, and "miscegenation" became a major theme of race discourse in the late 1940s.

The Royal Commission on Population produced similar definitions. Noting in its Report, published in 1949, that "the main source of immigrants under the present schemes are the European Volunteer Workers", it commented that "Eire is likely to be a continuing source of emigrants to Great Britain", but that there was unlikely to be much migration from Eastern Europe, Scandinavia or most other European countries. Both Holland and Italy might also supply migrants, it suggested, because their own high birth rates had recently given rise to fears of over-population. Generally it welcomed the possibility of migration from elsewhere in Europe, although making it clear that this would not be sufficient to provide Britain with the numbers it needed to prevent a decline in the young adult population. The possibility of black or Asian migration from colonies or former colonies was dismissed in one sentence:

Immigration on a large scale into a fully established society like ours could only be welcomed without reserve if the immigrants were of good human stock and were not prevented by their religion or race from intermarrying with the host population and becoming merged in it.[28]

In practice, many first-generation European migrants did not marry "the host population". Some were already married on arrival in Britain. Some married other European migrants in a variety of partnerships – Italian–Polish, Ukrainian–Polish, Italian–Ukrainian, Irish–Italian.[29] Inter-marriages, however, like the 4,000 British–Polish marriages recorded at the end of the war, did not generally attract official concern, although they could lead to hostility at a local level and calls for a British-born wife to go and live in Poland.[30]

In constructing its raced hierarchy the Royal Commission's primary purpose was to rule out the possibility of large-scale immigration from whatever source. The "problems of immigration" which it noted – the dearth of available "suitable immigrants" and the dangers to the family of those who were not deemed suitable – led it to conclude that "continuous large scale immigration would probably be impracticable and would certainly be undesirable, and the possibility – it can be regarded as no more than a possibility – that circumstances might compel us to consider or attempt it is among the undesirable consequences of the maintenance of family size below replacement level".[31] However, the other problem which the Royal Commission and the government were addressing in debates about population and the "problems of immigration" was the labour shortage. As Churchill had argued, displaced persons were being recruited in order to "swell our labour force". The definition of "suitable immigrants" also focused on capacity to work. Government schemes for EVWs defined suitability particularly in terms of age, able-bodiedness and health.

In the 1960s Asian men were recruited into dirty, low-paid jobs in the textile industry which white women were abandoning.[32] But the general pattern in the recruitment of labour in the late 1940s was to reinstate the sexual division of labour in the workplace as it had been before the war, recruiting migrant women into occupations which had been feminized before 1939. This pattern is particularly apparent in the textile industry. Its labour problems became a focus of government concern in 1945, since the textile industry was the subject of a major export drive. The Evershed Commission of 1945 and the 1946 Report of the Working Party on the Cotton Industry canvassed one solution, which was that men should do jobs previously done by women, but with male rates of pay.[33] There followed the extensive campaign in 1946–8 to recruit indigenous women. At the same time representatives of the Cotton Board approached the Board of Trade with a proposal to recruit women from displaced persons camps into the cotton industry.[34]

Out of 21,434 women who came to Britain as EVWs, the majority were concentrated in the textile areas of Lancashire and West Yorkshire, and were recruited into the textile industry, both wool and cotton. Bulk recruitment schemes from Italy were also organized, and in 1949 the first workers under these schemes arrived: 2,000 Italian women, who were sent to industrial work, particularly in textiles, and to service work in hospitals.[35] Antonietta Zelenczuk was recruited to work in a cotton mill in Oldham from a small town near Naples, together with three friends. She records:

> I went to Milan for a medical check. I didn't have much schooling. They asked me which is the capital of England, and I say London. I have to have medical check, blood test. In a couple of weeks he writes to say, you pass to go to England. I went to Milan before Christmas 1950. I came here in January 1951. Some girls didn't pass, because they couldn't read or write.[36]

Zelenczuk intended to return to Italy after two years – the length of her contract – but for her first 26 years in England visited Italy only three times, and spent her entire working life in employment in Oldham textile mills.

In textiles the recruitment of European women was favoured over those from the colonies. A government working party looking into the possibility of recruiting colonial labour in 1948 reported that it was "unlikely that West Indian women could stand up to the Lancashire climate for any length of time . . . [and] . . . it was understood that most of the women available were illiterate and thus unlikely to make suitable textile operatives".[37] Lack of accommodation was a further reason put forward, and the presence of EVWs was used as an argument against recruiting women from the Caribbean because it was seen as impracticable to expect Europeans to share lodgings with black people.[38]

While shortages in textiles were a post-war phenomenon, there were also shortages of womanpower in hospitals, as there had been pre-war. Irish women had been recruited into nursing and midwifery before the war and by 1951 they comprised 11 per cent of all nurses and midwives in Britain.[39] The first stage of the EVW scheme was the "Balt Cygnet" of 1946 which recruited single Balt women aged 21 to 40 to staff tuberculosis sanatoria in Britain. In hospitals, however, there was also recruitment of women from the colonies as nurses and ancillary workers. Discussions about recruiting nurses had begun in 1944, and by 1948 local selection committees had been set up in 16 countries including Jamaica, Nigeria and Trinidad.[40] In the 1950s women were also recruited from the Caribbean by the British Hotels and Restaurants Association to work as chambermaids and in kitchens.[41]

Post-war concerns about rebuilding family life did not extend to migrants, whose families were split up in various ways. J. A. Tannahill, writing of the EVW scheme in 1958, noted that "it even proved necessary to separate family groups who were all workers for the undermanned industries (eg. husband and wife, mother and daughter, brother and sister) and who had asked to be sent to Britain together".[42] Recruitment also led to the separation of married partners. Resistance to such separations, where women were wanted mainly in textiles, and men in mining and agriculture, led to inclusions of a clause in recruitment procedures in 1947 where couples signed that they agreed to separation after arrival.[43] In contrast to the way in which demobilization arrangements in the British armed forces in 1945 had given priority to married women, and created a B category for the construction of houses for British families, priority in shipment in the EVW scheme was given to those without dependants and, despite some workers' efforts to have hostels adapted for married couples, accommodation remained for single people only.[44] Concerns about the numbers of EVW dependants entering Britain meant that from July 1947 recruitment was confined to single persons.[45]

Black people's migration also commonly involved the splitting of families. In the process of migration, although often joining family who had arrived earlier – including aunts, cousins, siblings and husbands – women were usually separated from parents, and often from children. Caribbean families were commonly split in this process, in various ways. While women might leave some children back home, bringing others with them, others bore children in Britain whose siblings were in the Caribbean. A sample survey in 1953 found that 63 per cent of women who had migrated to Britain from Jamaica were mothers, but of these more than 90 per cent had left children in Jamaica, of whom 95 per cent were left in the care of their grandparents.[46] Families were split up particularly along lines of age and disability. The criteria of age, able-bodiedness and health in the EVW scheme meant that those who were recruited often had to leave older relatives behind, especially since the denial of refugee status allowed for a very narrow definition of dependants who could be brought to Britain. Many potential recruits were deterred by reluctance to leave dependants and to undergo separation, and it was sometimes pointed out to recruiting officers that even Nazi Germany had not always split up families in labour camps.[47] A particular reluctance among women to leave older dependants is attested by the way in which, to encourage more female volunteers, the government temporarily widened its definition of dependant to include a widowed mother, but only so long as she was "reasonably healthy".[48] Leaving older relatives was an experience common to many migrants. Anglo-Indian migration to Britain in the late 1940s, for example, was mainly of younger people leaving older Anglo-Indians feeling lonely and abandoned.[49] While disabled and older people were also frequently overlooked in concerns to rebuild indigenous family life, labour shortages did lead to their greater visibility as workers through encouragement to older people to work beyond retirement age, and the Disabled Persons (Employment) Act of 1944. The temporary need to recruit disabled people as workers sometimes extended to disabled European migrants.[50]

The denial of a familial identity to migrants was in strong contrast to their own concerns about their responsibilities for family and dependants from whom they were separated.[51] Gail Lewis writes that:

> . . . it was more often than not the case that early black women migrants had financial responsibilities for dependants in the Caribbean or elsewhere. The number of Caribbean-born young women and men who remember the departure of their mothers for England while they were left with a grandmother or aunt, is eloquent testimony to this.[52]

Margaret Prescod-Roberts refers to the money sent back to the Caribbean by women who migrated to Britain or America as "crucial to your survival and the survival of the immediate family", and argues that in decisions about who would go the "lucky families [were] where women went, because women would send back money. . . When men went by themselves . . . you didn't know what you were going to get."[53] Supporting family back home was also a major concern of European migrants. Hundreds of parcels were sent from the "hostels" where the Polish Resettlement Corps were housed to relatives and friends in Poland.[54] In the 1950s emigrants from the Republic of Ireland contributed a large sum to Ireland's gross national product through moneys they sent home, and money sent by female migrants in Britain were part of this history.[55]

The construction of female migrants as workers is particularly evident in arrangements made for housing recruits. The accommodation in which they found themselves on arrival in Britain ranged from army camps to hostels, to private lodgings, to accommodation attached to their place of work. Balt women who worked in tuberculosis sanatoria were recruited because of the difficulties of getting indigenous women to take up work where residence was usually a requirement, and where sanatoria were sited in remote places.[56] Migrant women who were recruited as nurses were often accommodated in hostel-type nurses' homes. Those recruited into residential domestic service had to live in their employers' homes. The Polish Resettlement Corps was housed in vacated British, American or Canadian barracks, which were renamed "workers' hostels".[57] It was generally under this name that ex-barracks and former prisoner-of-war camps were also used to accommodate EVWS, Italian women who came to Britain under bulk recruitment schemes, and some Irish migrants. Many migrants therefore lived in Nissen huts in the late 1940s, ate communally and slept in dormitories. Genowefa Dziewanda had been deported to Germany from Poland when she was 14, and at the end of the war was recruited from a displaced persons camp to work in the Lancashire textile industry and housed in a "workers' hostel" in Oldham. She records:

It was where they used to keep prisoners of war, the Germans used to be there. And afterwards they used it for the displaced persons – we used to say Poles, Ukrainians, Czechs, any nationality stay there. . . When we came we had nothing. We need shoes, we need clothes. So some girls said, "I give you a pound so you can get a coat. You save your pound and the other three girls will give you a pound, so you've got four pounds and can buy a coat." So she has a coat this week, and the next week it's another girl's turn. So we keep sharing so that we could buy something when someone really needed something. You help each other, that's how we managed.[58]

Migrants generally shared common conditions of accommodation, regardless of gender. The most obvious distinction between them was that while provision was made for the Polish Resettlement Corps and EVWs in "workers' hostels", none was made for black migrants. In certain areas black men did share hostel accommodation with white migrants, but hostility between them caused by the racism of white migrants led to hostel organizers demanding that the number of black residents be restricted to 12.[59]

The relationship between migrant women and indigenous women was thus characterized by a division of labour between them. Within a situation of full employment, many indigenous women were able to move upward in the occupational hierarchy away from domestic service and unskilled factory jobs into retail and office work. Their upward mobility was facilitated by the recruitment of migrant women into British industry and services at the bottom end of the occupational hierarchy. Migrant women recruited as workers were not constructed as economic dependants of men, nor were they associated with motherhood, family or domesticity. While the possibility of their future family life hovered over the discussion of "suitable immigrants" in the notion of assimilation and its connections with inter-marriage, this was generally a concern about "miscegenation" which foregrounded the figures of black men. Motherhood and family work were assigned to indigenous women, whose most important job was defined as bearing children and maintaining family life.

Although both indigenous and migrant women were recruited to the labour market, the basis of their participation was different. Part-time work was one of the major ways in which the two requirements for indigenous women – that they should be primarily wives and mothers, and that they should also be paid workers – were squared, enabling them to subordinate their employment to the needs of family. There was no corresponding notion of dual roles for migrant women, who were wanted as full-time workers, with a strong preference for single women in recruitment schemes for European migrants. The development of part-time work after the war has been seen as representing "the new form of the compromise between patriarchal and capitalist interests", where "women's labour was made available to capital, but on terms which did not threaten to disrupt the patriarchal status quo in the household, since a married woman working part-time could still perform the full range of domestic tasks".[60] But migrant women's availability to care for children, manage homes or service men was not a concern, whether of patriarchal or capitalist interests.

Unbelongings

Unbelonging is a main theme in many women's accounts of their arrival in Britain as migrant workers or as refugees. The meaning of home is a place from which they are in exile or a place which has been destroyed by war in the loss of family and community. Sometimes it is a place to which they long to return. The number arriving as refugees was masked by the renaming of displaced persons as EVWs. As the political map of Europe was redrawn some faced the possibilities of permanent exile.

It is possible that some war criminals gained entry to Britain under official schemes.[61] But only a very limited number of Jewish Holocaust survivors were allowed into Britain. Few Jewish people were among the displaced persons recruited as EVWs.[62] Under the Distressed Relatives scheme, procedures were designed so that the numbers who could qualify "would be in 100s rather than 1000s".[63] Kitty Hart, a survivor of Auschwitz who came to Birmingham after the war, records:

> . . . everybody in England would be talking about personal war experiences for months, even years, after hostilities had ceased. But we, who had been pursued over Europe by a mutual enemy, and come close to extermination at the hands of that enemy, were not supposed to embarrass people by saying a word. . . People didn't understand. In some ways the suffering I endured in the early post-war years were worse than it had been in the KZ [concentration camp]. Personally, I certainly found that time more traumatic.[64]

Multiple racisms in the period produced a variety of constructions of different groups. Tony Kushner argues that in 1945 "the two basic Jewish images of Shylock and alien had still not been overcome".[65] Anti-semitism persisted during and after the war. As early as 1947 Mass Observation reported that "people are no longer moved by the thought of Jewish suffering in concentration camps", and in the same year there were anti-Jewish riots in many British cities following the hanging of two British sergeants in Palestine by the Irgun group.[66]

Despite the way in which within official definitions EVWs were seen as "suitable immigrants", many also faced hostility. Mrs P, who was recruited from a displaced persons camp in Germany and arrived in England in 1947 to work in a Lancashire textile mill, records that the first words she learnt in English on arrival were "bloody foreigners". The phrase "bloody Pole" and particularly the question "why don't you go back to Poland?" recur as themes in accounts by Polish people of their reception in Britain in the late 1940s.[67]

The sense of Britain as a place of exile is very apparent in the case of black migrants. Sarah Thompson, who came to Brixton from Jamaica in 1955, records, "It's my heart's desire to say bye bye Britain. . . I never felt I belonged here. It's not my home. Jamaica is my home, it's in my blood."[68] The longing for return is sharp in most accounts by black migrants, with racism producing one dominant meaning of home – back home. Mary records:

It was a terrible way to live. I wanted to go back as soon as I came here. I was really angry at how I had to live after the sort of life I knew in the West Indies. But I just had to see it through, there wasn't the money to go back.[69]

As Mary's account suggests, while Britain was a place of exile, many black migrants also foresaw the permanency of this. Mrs B records, "We couldn't walk it home, walk it back to Jamaica, so you had to cope."[70]

Black migrants sometimes made the journey to Britain with optimism, as a journey to a place of belonging. England as the "mother country" recurs in many accounts by men and women who migrated from the Caribbean in the 1950s. Vi Chambers records:

When we were in school, we were taught that England was the mother country, it supports its own, it looks after us. I never wanted to go to America, because when I was a girl I had pen-pals here and I had quite a lot of family who came up in the RAF – my cousins and so on. So I corresponded because I had a cousin who sent me all these addresses of schoolgirls, and all I wanted to do was to come here.[71]

Another woman records:

There were adverts everywhere: "Come to the mother country! The mother-country needs you!" That's how I learned the opportunity was here. I felt stronger loyalty towards England. There was more emphasis there than loyalty to your own island. . . It was really the mother country and being away from home wouldn't be that terrible because you would belong.[72]

As these accounts suggest, constructions of empire in the colonies tended to translate British empire into English empire and portray Englishness in very different terms from the opposition between "immigrants" and "our people"/British in the metropolis. "Brought up as we were under a faraway flutter of the Union Jack," Beryl Gilroy records, "I believe that at that time we West Indians did think of ourselves as English."[73]

Many accounts of arrival record a sense of shock about England which is to do with particular constructions of Englishness in the colonies. Discoveries took a number of forms. The realization that there was a white working class in England who did menial jobs is a theme in many accounts.[74] Vi Chambers records a different sense of shock:

I expected to see white people doing menial jobs because this was a white country, so it had to be the white person who did these jobs. But it was still a shock to see the way they lived. . . You didn't expect to see white men and women as tramps. You'd think that it was only in a black country that you'd see that. When I came here first, I'll never forget this thing – it's imprinted on my mind. I used to live in Kensal Rise, and I was walking down Queensway, and I saw this white woman walking into a pub. I was so shocked. She had a scarf on her head, knotted at the front, and she had a cigarette hanging down out of her mouth. The thing that imprints it on my mind is that I looked down at her feet, and she had sandals on, and her toenails were so dirty. And some of these people, they were so, so backward. This old man used to live two doors from me, and I used to see him on the way to work and he used to empty his teapot in the toilet outside. For some reason it was a big, big shock.[75]

Mrs H records her discovery that in England received pronunciation was not the only way in which people talked:

It was funny coming to England and meeting those people in Sheffield first, because they say "ta". And I was so shocked. I said, "This is England? These people speak different." I was amazed until I realised the different accents of different places.[76]

Constance Nembhard records a number of different aspects to her discoveries:

When I came here I really was shattered, because I had based my opinion of life as portrayed in the novels of Jane Austen, and though I had read Dickens, I suppose I didn't want to think they were real. So coming and seeing the houses was a real shock to me. . . There were English people living upstairs, whom I now know to be cockneys. I couldn't understand a word they were saying, and I got really worried. . . We grew up under the colonial system, and we knew everything about England, everything. And we came here, nobody had ever heard of Jamaica. I mean few, few people. And it was funny, the few who had heard of Jamaica treated you differently. Those who had never heard, they all had the opinion that we lived in trees. . . When I was in the LCC, I was in one of the offices one day in Westminster, and one of the chief executives from County Hall came down and took a tour of the building. The telephone rang, and I was the nearest and answered. And I gave him the message. And I was asked afterwards where I learned to speak English. Can you imagine, somebody in that position, and doesn't know. He didn't know that English was our only written language in Jamaica.[77]

Buchi Emecheta was almost 18 in 1962 when "my dream finally came true" and she arrived in England from Nigeria:

Whenever my father pronounced the word "UK" it sounded so heavy, so reverential. It was so deep, so mysterious, that my father always voiced it in hushed tones wearing an expression as respectful as if it were God's Holy of Holies. Going to the United Kingdom must surely be like paying God a visit. . . I thought people in England lived like they did in Jane Austen's novels. . . England gave me a cold welcome . . . If I had been Jesus I would have passed England by and not dropped a single blessing. It felt like walking into the inside of a grave. I could see nothing but masses of grey, filth and more grey.[78]

This view of England as the "mother country", which "supports its own, looks after us" or as "God's Holy of Holies", was one which many black migrants did not hold. But those who did rarely sustained a sense of being "its own" for very long. On arrival, often within hours, a main discovery about different constructions of Englishness in the colonies and the mother country is recorded by Mrs C:

When we came here we swore we were English because Guyana was British Guiana. We were brought up under the colonial rule. Queen's birthday, if you don't have a new uniform to go and sing "God Save the King", you hurt. When you come here, you discovered it's a different thing. If you're English, you have to be white.[79]

Chapter Three

₰

Home and colonialism

In 1964, in a chapter entitled "Blacks next door" in her *Back street new worlds*, first published in *Punch*, Elspeth Huxley wrote:

I have seen immigrants living in revolting slums in Stepney, Balsall Heath in Birmingham and elsewhere, but far more in substantial Victorian houses, with names like Blenheim Villas and Cadogan Mansions, in Leeds, Bradford, Birmingham and Southall, as well as in London. These are the sort of houses that would once have had a maid-of-all-work in the attic, a mistress in her decent bombazine mending pinafores in the parlour, and the master in his striped trousers, black coat and wing collar going off to his city office every morning on the dot.

Almost everywhere, the pattern's been the same: into these middle-class, nineteenth-century houses, maybe with a little front garden and a yard at the back, go the immigrants, often with broods as ample as their predecessors had . . . To live hugger-mugger with one room for each family, and plenty of communal life within the larger inter-related group – the extended family – is just what they were used to back home and what many of them like.[1]

Huxley's portrayal of black life as "hugger-mugger" marks a particular moment in race discourse in the post-war period, when in the early 1960s attention began to turn to black reproduction and black family life, which was represented as domestic barbarism in opposition to Englishness. Her reference to black life as "hugger-mugger" was echoed by Tom Stacey in the *Sunday Times*: "I have heard few complaints about this hugger-mugger life: it was a lot better than Kingston's *Back o' Wall* and seething numbers provided cosiness and security in a strange land."[2] Huxley's reference to "broods" was part of a concern with the "immigrant" birth rate, where "immigrant" was defined as black. While the deficiencies of government statistics on "immigration" were frequently deplored in

45

the early 1960s, an array of figures on this birth rate were still produced, embellished, interpreted and widely reported in the press.[3] By the mid-1960s black women's visibility focused on their role as mothers, and on the need to limit their reproduction.

In the 1950s, however, black femininity was largely invisible within cultural representations of "immigrants" and black motherhood particularly so. In a gendered construction of race, oppositions between Englishness and "immigrants" foregrounded the figures of the white woman and the black man. The white woman embodied Englishness as domestic and familial life, and the notions of belonging, attachment and settlement this suggested. The black man was seen as rootless and adrift, or wild and untamed. Black male sexuality was seen as a threat to white femininity.

Cultural representations of race in Britain in the 1950s were not confined to oppositions between Englishness and "immigrants" in the metropolis. Differences between black and white were also constructed in terms of colonizers and colonized in empire. Few connections were made between the two. Invoking Britain's imperial history did not fit easily with representations of "immigrants" as alien and strange. In Huxley's account "immigrants" became a symbol of national decline, but she makes little reference to the dissolution of the British colonial empire, which was well advanced by 1964. Portraying them against scenes from domestic British history, it is the social order of Victorian middle-class domestic life with its mistresses and servants which becomes the embodiment of Englishness to which black life as "hugger-mugger' – now in occupation of the substantial houses embodying that social order – is contrasted.

In other contexts, however, Huxley was also concerned with differences between black and white in terms of colonizers and colonized. The daughter of coffee plantation owners who had settled in Kenya, she wrote extensively about the country where she spent much of her childhood. Her admiring biography of Lord Delamere was called *White man's country*. It traced the history of the "British effort to establish an outpost of civilisation in eastern Africa" and its subtitle attributed to Delamere "the making of Kenya".[4] After the war she wrote extensively in defence of this outpost, championing the cause of white settlers in Kenya, and calling Jomo Kenyatta "a small-scale African Hitler".[5] Margery Perham in a letter to Huxley referred to *White man's country* as "the best apologia for white settlement that has been written".[6] It is perhaps not coincidental that *Back street new worlds* was published in the year after Kenyan independence.

In her biography of Lord Delamere, Huxley represents imperial history mainly as a story of white masculinity and its pioneering adventure in bringing untouched land under cultivation and untamed people under British rule. This is a heroic and public enterprise, signifying power and adventure in wide and unexplored territory – a characteristic narrative of national imperial identity, as produced in a range of genres, including films, novels, poetry, boys' comics and children's literature. As British colonial rule ended, this story faded.

The relationship between Englishness and "immigrants" in the metropolis was generally constructed differently from the relationship between colonizers and colonized, but in the context of anti-colonial resistance – as in Kenya – a common theme emerged. Englishness was represented in images of family and home which were portrayed as white. Black was not associated with domestic and familial life except through its connections with this white family – connections which were usually seen as threatening. As themes of powerlessness, vulnerability and decline were developed, in threats from "immigrants" in the metropolis and resistance to colonialism in empire, the story of nation that was told put at its centre the figure of the white woman.

Wanting one thing

After the war, ideals of companionate marriage emphasized women's "sex fulfilment" and "sex happiness" and outlined a democratization of sexual pleasure between husband and wife. Heterosexual intercourse was generally understood as the most natural of all human activities, so long as it was within marriage. The Church of England, discussing the way in which religion had ceased to be the main "driving force" in society, argued that "it is inevitable that sex should take its place – inevitable because sex is . . . the great *natural* means of fulfilment, completion and union for human beings".[7] In Freudian discourse heterosexual intercourse was seen as the sign of emotional maturity, with other forms of sexuality as "deviations from this standard", and as "substitutes for inter-course".[8] Thus, although women and men were seen as having different characteristics, traits and roles which were rooted in their biological difference, the mixing of these differences in heterosexual relations signified completion and maturity.

Heterosexual relations and maternity were regarded very differ-ently when they were between men and women who were seen as biologically different not only in terms of gender but also race. The concept of "miscegenation" – widely used in race discourse in the 1950s – signalled not only the idea that races were biological categories marked by difference, but also that the mixing of these in heterosexual relations was deeply problematic and unnatural. As *Glamour* magazine advised its readers in 1951:

> Many coloured men are fine people, but they do come from a different race, with a very different background and upbring-ing. Besides scientists do not yet know if it is wise for two such very different races as whites and blacks to marry, for some-times the children of mixed marriages seem to inherit the worst characteristics of each race.[9]

Fears and warnings about miscegenation, as in *Glamour's* advice, addressed relationships between black men and white women. Characteristic questions were the one posed by *Picture Post* in a special edition on marriage in 1954: "Would you let your daughter marry a negro?", and the one posed by Colin MacInnes in 1956: "What of these tales of coloured men corrupting our young girls?"[10] A general silence surrounded sexual violence in the period and black men's relationships with white women were rarely seen in this way. The most common answers to these questions used images where white women were rendered either as black men's whores, or as victims of their incapacity for familial and domestic life – pregnant and then abandoned.

The notion of white women as victims of black men's incapacity for family and domestic life is apparent in Edith Kirton's account of her marriage to St Clair Kirton in 1958. Her husband had migrated to England from Barbados in 1955. She records:

> I sent out invitations for my wedding, and none of them came. Because he was coloured – that was the only reason. Because my uncle Jimmy and his wife travelled round with the army, and he had coloured servants. So I was degrading the family

with going out with St Clair, and there was no way they were coming to my wedding. So I didn't have any of my aunties and uncles at the wedding. . . . Aunty Mary came to the church, but she didn't come to the reception. . . She just came to see me get married, because they didn't believe I was going to get married. They said that he'll never marry you. They only want you for one thing, and that's what we had to put up with. They only want you for sex, they don't want you for anything else. He'll get you pregnant and leave you. And I didn't accept that at all, because I loved him, and I thought, well, whatever we do, we're still going into church. . . And when I went to ask permission to get married in church, "No". It was right out. "No". He didn't believe in mixed marriages, therefore he could not marry me in church.[11]

The Methodist minister's refusal to marry them meant that the wedding eventually took place in a local Anglican church.

The verdict of uncles and aunties – that she was degrading her family – is about the place of the colonized as servants, not as family members. But the aunt's judgement is also about black men's incapacity for relationship and family life – "he'll get you pregnant and leave you". The portrayal of black men as rootless and adrift was characteristic. In *A taste of honey* the black man depicted is a sailor, his presence in the film always foreshadowing his departure as he wanders from place to place. In Colin MacInnes's 1957 novel *City of spades* the main black character – Johnny Fortune, a young Nigerian – is characterized as a drifter, and is also constantly on the move, although in his case this is also a movement from one white women to another.[12] In both texts, black men get white women pregnant and then leave them, just as Edith Kirton records as the expectation of her aunt.

The aunt's judgement is also about black male sexuality: "they only want you for one thing." This was a notion which applied to white men too, in the common idea of a male sex drive depicted by Barbara Pym in *Jane and Prudence*:

"They say, though, that men only want *one thing* – that's the truth of the matter". Miss Doggett again looked puzzled: it was as if she had heard that men only wanted one thing, but had forgotten for the moment what it was . . .[13]

However, this notion was much more developed in relation to black men, whose sexuality was regarded as primitive, insatiable and uncontrollable. While in one version, white women were the victims of the "black buck" who interrupted their smooth progress towards maturity where their sexuality was predominantly the route to motherhood and family, in another version white women were seen as corrupted by black men, as their whores or "kept women". In this version they too "only wanted one thing" and were seen as sharing black men's incapacity for relationships.

The strength of themes about the "black buck" and the deviance of white women who married black men is also apparent from oral testimony. One white woman records, "People didn't understand why I married him and at work people were shocked. The first thing that came to their minds was sex – that's the only reason why I married a black man as far as they could see."[14] Dorothy Prosper married David Prosper in 1960, and records:

> It got as nasty as two women I worked with, and they were talking one day, and they asked me such a horrible question – about why I wanted, why I went out with coloured people. And I just told her, I said, "well you go with one and find out". They said to me, the things that were going round then were they were a lot bigger than white lads, and I said that I wouldn't know about that, but I said, "if you want to know, go with one and find out". And walking up town one day, just after we'd got married . . . there were two old women: "Disgusting, disgusting, shouldn't be seen, shouldn't be seen, we don't want that here". . . You were looked on as being low and knockabouts in those days.[15]

In 1964 Clifford Hill interviewed 34 white women married to black men. He found that:

> Most of the wives said that they were made to feel "low class" because of their association with a coloured man. They were looked upon as "sluts" or prostitutes, because it was generally thought that no nice girl went with a coloured man. "People don't even bother to enquire whether or not you are married," complained one girl. "They see you walking down the street with a coloured man and they stare at you and you can tell from the look they give you that they think you're a cheap prostitute with a poor pickup".[16]

In some accounts, white women's relationships with black men were explained in terms of their nymphomania.[17]

Fears of miscegenation were associated with alarms about prostitution and venereal disease, which also foregrounded black men and white women, with black men said to be "preyed upon by native prostitutes", or alternatively "living off the bodies of white women".[18] Although other migrant men, including Italians and Maltese, were sometimes associated with pimping, while black and Asian men were attributed a role in the spread of venereal disease, in both cases it was Caribbean men who were usually seen as particularly culpable.[19] The notion that white women who had relationships with black men were prostitutes had been common between the wars, when Muriel Fletcher asserted in her *Report on an investigation into the colour problem in Liverpool and other ports* that "90% of the white women in Liverpool who consort with coloured men . . . are said to be prostitutes . . . the white women . . . are mentally weak, prostitutes (or) younger women who make contacts in a spirit of adventure and find themselves unable to break away".[20] Sydney Collins found that this identification remained common in the 1950s, and suggested that allegations of prostitution against white women were among the reasons for their marriages to black men.[21] Some black women also objected to black men's relationships with white women on the grounds that the white women involved were of low class and dubious morals.[22]

In an article in the Birmingham *News Chronicle* in 1956, white women who had relationships with black men were characterized as "good-time girls". Under the headline "Evils of Birmingham: problems of good-time girls and coloured men in overcrowded lodgings" Councillor Joan Tomlinson argued that:

There is a steady growth of drug-taking and something akin to, but legally different from prostitution – the "kept woman". . . White girls live with coloured men. Many don't marry them and change to another man when they get bored.[23]

In *City of spades*, Montgomery Pew journeys into a black male world which is characterized not only by prostitution, but also by illicit drinking, gambling, drugs and violence.

Alarms about "miscegenation" were nearly always about reproduction as well as sexuality, urging the dangers of producing "half-caste" children. In Birmingham in 1954, the *News Chronicle* asked,

"Is Birmingham going to become a coffee-coloured town?"[24] While maternity was generally seen as a woman's main biological drive and a sign of her maturity, completion and fulfilment, it was regarded very differently when it was associated with miscegenation. People of mixed parentage had been associated with moral decline, disease, unemployment, homelessness and prostitution between the wars, and this continued. In *City of spades* these characters are Arthur and Barbara. Arthur is in and out of jail. Barbara is a prostitute.

The end of empire

The construction of differences between white and black in terms of home, family and domesticity is common to two films made by Rank in the 1950s and early 1960s. *Simba* (1955) has a colonial setting. *Flame in the streets* (1961) represents relationships between black and white in the factories and streets of the metropolis. Both are of a genre favoured by British cinema in this period – films intended to treat serious issues of the day.[25]

Similarities between the films are not immediately apparent. While the Mau Mau in *Simba* are portrayed as primitive, irrational and violent, this is reversed in *Flame in the streets*, where the respectability of the main black characters – Peter and Gabriel – is carefully delineated.[26] Both films end with images of conflagration, but where in *Simba* this is the destruction of a white farm at the hands of a black mob, in *Flame in the streets* a mob of white teddy boys attack black men with torches lighted from a Guy Fawkes bonfire. In representing the colonized in empire and "immigrants" in the metropolis, however, a common theme is their threat to home. Both films represent home and family as white, and share a preoccupation with the ways in which black is related to home through its connections with white life. Both also represent black life as lacking any familial or domestic dimension. In so far as black is connected to home, this is through black men's relationship to white women.

The main theme of *Simba* is the threat to white homes, families and settlement in Kenya from the Mau Mau. This is the theme which provides the film with its opportunity to treat serious issues, as white characters adopt a variety of positions on what is to be done and the nature of Africans. It is also what provides the narrative interest, as the relationship between Alan and Mary, the white hero and heroine, develops through their own conflicts over these questions to the final resolution where they come together as – in a *Pietà*-like image – Mary cradles the dead body of her black friend, Dr Peter Karanja, in her arms.

The film opens with a range of images of white life in Kenya. A panorama of the land, shot from the air, signals Alan's arrival by plane in Nairobi from England on a visit to his brother, with a brief glimpse of the city as the plane comes in to land. Mary then drives Alan through this landscape, identifying it as white in her naming of the farms they pass. The moment of arrival at Alan's brother's farm – Mary blowing the horn in anticipation of their welcome – is disrupted by the sight of police outside, and the movement into a white home becomes a revelation of the Mau Mau, who have ransacked the house and killed Alan's brother. The scene then shifts to Mary's home – another farming family – and a domestic scene as her mother pours coffee, and Mary argues with her father over the nature of Africans. It is here, over the coffee cups, that Alan announces his intention of staying in Kenya to take over the running of his brother's farm.

Domesticity and family are thus established from the outset as images of white civilization which the Mau Mau are intent on destroying. They also work to suggest whites as settlers – people who belong to Kenya through a network of attachments to their families and to the land which they own and farm. It is this settler identity which Alan takes on. His decision to stay is about maintaining his brother's farm, and so joining the struggle against the Mau Mau, as well as suggesting the possibilities of a growing attachment to Mary. The way in which white is associated with home and family, and the struggle to maintain these in the face of the Mau Mau threat, are reinforced by the domestic interior and imagery of family life and coffee cups that surround Alan's announcement.

There is no portrayal of black family relationships in the film. Apart from Peter and the "houseboys", black men are shown either alone, as sinister figures with criminal or murderous intent, or as a rampaging mob. Where domesticity, home and farming serve as images of white order and cultivation of the natural world, blacks are not shown in domestic interiors, apart from in their role as the tamed and domesticated "houseboys" of the English, or as Mau Mau who invade white homes to ransack, steal and kill. A central question the film poses concerns the relationship between white civilization and black nature, as "houseboys" and Mau Mau are juxtaposed in white debates about Africans. Here two versions of primitive are at issue, with "houseboys" produced as evidence that blacks are like children – "one of the family" as Mary's mother describes them – who can be tamed through their relationship to a white family. The Mau Mau evoke a different version of primitive as savage. Should whites trust "houseboys" as evidence of their ability to tame and domesticate blacks, or are all blacks like the Mau Mau?

While "houseboys" and Mau Mau represent contrasting versions of black masculinity and different relationships between black and home, in both cases the connection is through white families. "Houseboys" serve white farming and domesticity by tilling the soil, driving the cattle, and providing domestic order and comfort. Mau Mau wreak havoc as they invade, ransack and burn white farms, slaughter cattle and kill white people in their own homes. These two relationships are juxtaposed in a number of sequences. In the Mau Mau raid on Mary's house, their violence disrupts a scene where "houseboys" serve food to Mary's mother and father, and the latter is killed as he goes to minister to a wounded "houseboy" in the kitchen. After the Mau Mau meeting, where black is evoked as a dark primitive threat, the dissolve is to "houseboys" tilling neat rows of cultivated soil.

It is Peter Karanja who stands outside these versions of black masculinity as tamed/domesticated and wild/savage. Richard Dyer has argued that he represents the possibility of a black person becoming "white", and that the anxiety surrounding this is the foundation of the narrative.[27] Through his British education and his work as a doctor, Peter is associated with rationality and order – a product of the colonial civilizing mission who is deeply distrusted by most of the white characters. This work provides his only point of contact with blacks in the film, who come to him as patients. Otherwise he is shown with whites – with Dr Hughes, his colleague, with Mary as both his colleague and friend, with Alan who, after initial hostility, begins to trust and champion him. The film ends with his journey with Mary to rescue Alan from the Mau Mau.

In the final sequence, however, Peter is shown shifting from this white world, as he moves from Alan's home to confront the Mau Mau – a movement which is also towards his death at their hands. As he stands alone between the mob on one side, and Mary and Alan on the other, the shot is from Alan's and Mary's perspective, as they watch him, and it is Mary's voice, interpreting what he is saying to Alan, which speaks his message to a white British audience. The possibility of a black person becoming "white" is extended here to the possibility of a black man taking on the civilizing mission of whites, the film's final images suggesting the demise of this mission. Mary, the main white character who believes in such a possibility, cradles Peter in her arms as he dies. They are surrounded by the wreckage of Alan's farm, burnt by the mob. It is the white militia, not Peter or Mary, who succeed in rescuing Alan at the last moment.

The final image is of a young black boy. The boy's familyless state has been carefully established in an early scene, as he wanders alone around Alan's farm. The final statement of the film is Peter's dying words as he looks at the boy: "He's done nothing wrong." Peter could be pronouncing his own epitaph, as a slaughtered innocent, reinforcing the Christian imagery, which is also suggested by the Pieta-like image of Mary holding Peter's dead body. The camera then moves to a close-up of the boy as he walks alone, and apparently aimlessly, stepping over guns that are strewn about the havoc of the farm. The image seems to suggest the consequences of the demise of colonialism. Black – previously associated with notions of home and family through connections with white families – is now rendered familyless.

Like *Simba*, *Flame in the streets* portrays family and domesticity as white and is preoccupied with questions about black relationship to this white domain. Set in London, "immigrants" are represented through the figures of black men, whose respectability is emphasized. In exploring questions about black relationships to domesticity and family, the film foregrounds relationships between white women and black men: Judy, who is married to Gabriel, and Kathie, whose plans to marry Peter provide a main conflict of the film. A central question posed is whether Kathie can bring Peter home and incorporate him into white family life through marriage.

White femininity is constructed in the film through the contrasting figures of Kathie and her mother, Nell. Nell is first shown in her kitchen with a paintbrush in her hand working to improve her home. Throughout the film she is characterized by her aspirations for a better home in a better district – one with a bathroom – which are frustrated by her husband's indifference to symbols of affluence. Apart from one shot at the boundary of the private – standing at the gate anxiously looking out for Kathie's return – she is shown within her home, either alone or with members of her family. She leaves it only once, in search of her husband, Jacko, to enlist his support against Kathie's plans to marry a black man, but immediately returns, and spends much of the rest of the film lying down in a darkened bedroom to recover. Of the main characters in the film it is only Nell who sees nothing of the flame in the streets, either as celebrations of Guy Fawkes or as the violence of white teddy boys against black men.

Nell's immurement in her domestic world is associated with neurosis which finds expression in her reaction to Kathie's plans:

> I'm ashamed of you, when I think of you and *that* man sharing the same bed. It's filthy. Disgusting. It makes my stomach turn over and I want to be sick. You can't wait can you. You're no better than the whores in the high street. You can't wait to be with him, that's the truth. All you want is one thing. Go with him then, make your bed and lie on it. Go to your nigger, go to your nigger.

This reaction is seen as hysterical – a product of her own repression. The contrast between Nell's position and Kathie's is associated with their different relationships to home and domesticity, where "housewife" signifies a neurotic identity, preoccupied with materialist aspirations.

Jacko also opposes his daughter's plans. In contrast to Nell, Jacko is constantly in public, in a crush of people, as he transacts his business as a shop steward, and when shown at home is always on the verge of going out. His neglect of home and family is one point of conflict between husband and wife. In his public role as shop steward, Jacko embodies a liberal position, successfully opposing white members of the union who would deny Gabriel promotion to a supervisory job on the grounds that he is black and that "the men don't want to take orders from spades". Later he helps to rescue Gabriel from white attackers who have pushed him into the Guy Fawkes bonfire in the streets. In his opposition to Kathie's plans to marry Peter, the film represents this liberalism, apparent in the workplace as well as in the streets, stopping at the gate of the family home.

As in *Simba*, there is no portrayal of black family relationships. "Immigrants", portrayed mainly in the streets and the workplace, are rendered as familyless. In so far as they are connected to the world of domesticity and family, this is through black men's relationships with white women, especially in scenes inside Gabriel's and Judy's home. In contrast, Kathie's home and family are portrayed in detail, across the generations, highlighting not only mother–daughter and father–daughter relationships in the conflict with Kathie, but also the relations between husband and wife as Jacko and Nell argue over how to respond to Kathie's plans, and the relations between father and son and daughter-in-law as Nell enlists the support of her father-in-law against Jacko. The continuity of white family life suggested in these relationships, and their connections with settlement and attachment, are emphasized by Jacko, who still lives in the house where he was born, and takes on the mantle of his father – a founder of the union – in his work.

The contrasts between white family and black familylessness are particularly apparent in the closing sequences of the film. In the face of her parents' opposition, Kathie wanders the streets in search of where Peter lives. Kathie's virtue is never in question – she has not become like "the whores in the high street". But in her entry into a black world she is adrift and homeless, asking her way from black strangers, entering the territory of black housing where she stumbles inadvertently into the wrong rooms. This is the one place in the film where black domestic interiors are briefly represented, but they are framed through Kathie's eyes – made visible through her opening and shutting of doors. As Kathie becomes a voyeur, standing on the thresholds of rooms, surveying scenes into which she has intruded, black life is associated particularly with sexuality as she disturbs a black man and woman in bed together and the black man invites her to "come on in and join us".

In a reverse movement at the end of the film Peter enters the territory of white family and home. Jacko has brought Kathie home, and she has brought Peter with her. This mission to "go and find Kathie, bring her home" is set by Nell, and followed scrupulously by Jacko who goes after her to warn Peter off and reclaim his daughter: "I've come to take you home, Kathie." As violence erupts in the streets he keeps reiterating, "Come back home, Kathie."

However, it is in the end that Jacko who comes home, trailing Peter and Kathie behind him. The one resolution which the film offers is Jacko's reconciliation with Nell. As Nell challenges him that he had no time for her, treated her like part of the fixtures, turned the front room into an office, even made love to her as though he were taking a quick drink, Jacko is reduced to tears. The lesson Jacko learns is about the need to give his family more time and attention, and his mission to reunite the family, disrupted by Kathie's relationship with Peter, is the sign of his repentance and of his reunion with Nell.

The camera lingers briefly on the final image of Nell and Jacko standing on one side of the white familial hearth, with Kathie and Peter on the other, separated by the whole width of the room. Kathie's brief excursion into black life is over. As the credits come up over this scene, the question remains whether Peter can be incorporated into a white family. As he and Kathie confront Nell and Jacko they symbolize the ways in which the focus on miscegenation in race discourse in the 1950s constructed black relationship to family and home. When black is associated with home and domesticity it is as intrusion and disruption. Whether this is conceived in terms of black men abandoning or corrupting white women, or even when the possibility of their incorporation into family life is acknowledged, home and family are constructed as white.

Despite their many differences, *Simba* and *Flame in the streets* share a gendered construction of race. Femininity, highly visible in representations of white life, is almost completely missing from black life. In both films, black femininity can be glimpsed only fleetingly – on the margins, in the background. Black women say nothing. Domesticity and family which in *Simba* are images of white civilization could be seen as more problematic in *Flame in the streets*, where – through Nell – they are associated with materialist aspirations, neurosis and hysteria. At the same time the film undercuts this association through the detailed attention given to Nell's point of view and Jacko's acknowledgement of the error of his ways. The constant sense of tension in the film reinforced by the imagery of fireworks going off and bangers being thrown, the conflict on the streets as white teddy boys attack black men, the fate of Gabriel who is badly injured in these attacks – all these remain unresolved. Nor does the uneasy image with which the film ends resolve the questions surrounding Peter's relationship with Kathie. Peter may be about to acquire familial relationships as an in-law in Kathie's home, or there may be further confrontations. In offering reunion and reconciliation between Nell and Jacko as its only resolution, the film heightens its use of family and home as emblems of white life, and of Englishness.

Black female sexuality

In her autobiography, *Black teacher*, Beryl Gilroy comments that "black women were enigmas, especially to white men . . . we were mysterious to them and they cloaked their fantasies about us in derision and denunciation."[28] Black women's sexuality was generally seen in more complex ways than black men's. Sometimes black female sexuality was constructed as entertainment and titillation for white voyeurs, and this could affect black women, as Amanda Murphy records:

> I was a virgin until I was married. But somehow or other, it was as if because you were black you were loose. . . My friend and I were out and someone said, "there's a wog", and something about "being laid", and she just turned round and hit him in the nose. She was English, and she just biffed him one, and he was on the ground. And he just got up and said, "I didn't mean anything!" But that's the kind of remarks you used to get – it was always as if you were supposed to be an easy catch. The other kind of remarks that were being made were, "We would like to know what it was like with a black woman", and they used to say that to you straight in a conversation. People that you'd think you were having a conversation with, like a group of students, and they would make that remark. . . They didn't see anything wrong with saying, "Well, we've never had it with a black woman". . . And I said, "Where is she?" and that took the wind out of their sails. And I'd look around pretending it didn't have anything to do with me, because I didn't feel it had.[29]

In a number of popular images – singers like Shirley Bassey, the girl from Tiger Bay – black women were constructed as exotically sexual.[30] In *Sapphire*, voted best British film of the year by the British Film Academy in 1959, a red taffeta underskirt is the sign that Sapphire, who had passed as white, was really black.

Generally, however, black femininity was invisible within cultural representations of "immigrants". The focus on miscegenation meant that it was white rather than black femininity which was highlighted. This focus also meant that when black femininity was made visible – usually quite sketchily – it was constructed in terms of its relationship to white masculinity/femininity as well as black masculinity. Black women came to be seen in part as a solution to the threat posed by black male sexuality to white femininity and to the problem of shifting, transient black men. The role assigned to them was to tame and domesticate black men, by settling them down. By furnishing black men with sexual partners, they were to ensure that black men kept away from white women. Within this construction, it became apparent that black male sexuality was seen not only as a threat to white femininity; white masculinity was also implicated. In anxieties about miscegenation white women were seen as belonging to white British men – "our women".

This construction of black femininity began to appear in the late 1950s. In the autumn of 1958 the Eugenics Society printed a broadsheet by G. L. C. Bertram which called for research into the degree and results of miscegenation which he already likened to "the over-late bolting of the stable door". Bertram, like many others, blamed miscegenation on the uprootedness of male migrants arguing that their arrival, without an appropriate proportion of their own womenfolk, had produced frustrations, temptations, prostitution and half-caste children.[31] This inferred that an "appropriate proportion" of black women would provide some solution to his fears.

In the same autumn the *Daily Mirror*, in an article entitled, "Introducing to you . . . the boys from Jamaica", asked the question "Are they stealing our women?" Reassuring its readers, it noted that half of those arriving in Britain from Jamaica were wives and their children "coming to rejoin their husbands".[32] This was the only reference to Jamaican women in a piece about "the boys", and portrayed female migration from the Caribbean as a matter of dependants coming to join husbands. Shifting away from the view of black women as workers in the late 1940s, it announced a confidence that black women would ensure that Jamaican men did not steal "our women".

The previous year, Sydney Collins had also reported this view of black women. The arrival of West Indian women "immigrants" was, he said, particularly welcome to the British male, "who feels that she will provide a companion for the coloured male immigrant, who will keep away from British women". This reassuring effect on the white male population, "whose fear of sex competition is partly allayed by the presence of coloured women", was also promoted, he argued, by the way in which white men themselves sought the friendship of coloured girls, and were consequently more friendly towards coloured men.[33]

White men's relationships with black women generally received little attention in the period. They could also produce hostility from families. Although Amanda Murphy was reconciled with her husband's family before her marriage, there was initial conflict:

> We decided to get married . . . and he told the family about it and they were just absolutely livid, really quite appalled. . . They said they would not be coming to the wedding and they tried to persuade him that he was making a mistake, and that coming from a middle class family, it would be very difficult to have me alongside him in any society of any kind.[34]

Generally, however, white men's relationships with black women attracted less hostility than white women's relationships with black men.[35]

In darkest England

During the late nineteenth century and into the twentieth, explorers who did not venture as far as the colonies found a rich seam of social exploration closer to home, in darkest England. Their journeys took them mainly to urban areas in Northern England and in London's East End, which like the colonies were seen as uncharted territory – in Mayhew's phrase "the undiscovered country of the poor". The analogy between colonial and urban British exploration was often made explicit. William Booth's *In darkest England and the way out* drew on Henry Stanley's *In darkest Africa*:

As there is a darkest Africa is there not also a darkest England? Civilisation, which can breed its own barbarians, does it not also breed its own pygmies? May we not find a parallel at our own doors, and discover within a stone's throw of our cathedrals and palaces similar horrors to those which Stanley has found existing in the great Equatorial forest?[36]

The urban poor, like the journey into the unknown, were depicted in the language of colonial discourse, described by William Booth as "colonies of heathen savages in the heart of our capital".[37] George Sims began *How the poor live*:

In these pages I propose to record the result of a journey into a region which lies at our own doors – into a dark continent that is within easy walking distance of the General Post Office. This continent will, I hope, be found as interesting as any of those newly-explored lands which engage the attention of the Royal Geographical Society – the wild races who inhabit it will, I trust, gain public sympathy as easily as those savage tribes for whose benefit the Missionary Societies never cease to appeal for funds.[38]

What Peter Keating calls the "nearness–farness paradox" – the extent of the social gulf which separated the explorers from scenes located so near at hand – was always signalled by pronouns as "we" (the explorer and their audience) made "them" (the urban poor) visible. The region which Sims proposes to record is one which lies "at our own doors" and he invites the audience to accompany him – "set out with me on the journey" and "be brought face to face with [the] dark side of life" – an invitation which means that "we walk along a narrow dirty passage", and then "we knock at the door" to get a view of the inhabitants.[39] The "them" becomes a sight which, normally invisible, "hidden from view behind a curtain", as Charles Booth expressed it, explorers unveil for their readers through their scrutiny, even though "we shrink aghast from the picture".[40]

After the war the "nearness–farness paradox" was reworked in a range of social explorations concerned with "immigrants". The "dark continent within easy walking distance of the General Post Office" with its "wild races" and "savage tribes" was an image of the contrast between two nations – rich and poor, known and unknown, civilized and savage. In post-war social explorations of "immigrants" these two nations were merged into one category of unitary respectability as white.

The way in which texts on "immigrants" structure differences between white and black is apparent from the shift in the meaning of pronouns. "We" becomes the white author and their white audience, and "they" no longer a white category which is as strange and alien as "heathens and savages" but "blacks next door". White neighbours figure repeatedly in these texts and become part of their "we". Indeed, the audience is no longer seen as a stranger to the scenes that will be recounted but as a group whose own vision and expectations structure the text. The observer/explorer acts as a mediator of the vision of the white neighbour rather than a guide to the reader who offers to lift a curtain. What this observer has to say about "immigrants" is presented as already familiar to this white audience. White thus becomes one nation, uniting writer, audience and white neighbours in a common respectability and civilization in opposition to black as alien, strange and primitive.

In pre-war social exploration, scrutiny of domestic life and arrangements had focused particularly on the boundaries between the public and the private. These became the markers of the rough–respectable divide within the working classes. As Judy Giles argues:

> Certain streets could be identified as "rough" or "respectable" according to a range of visual signifiers. According to these codings, "respectable" areas were characterised by quiet streets, closed front doors, clean doorsteps, shining brasswork and a lack of *public* interaction either between family members or between neighbours beyond social civilities. In contrast "rough" areas revealed themselves by noise, dirty windows, lack of curtains, children playing in the street, women "popping" in and out of each others' homes, gossiping in the street, and arguments between neighbours, between family members and between mothers over children.[41]

In studies of "immigrants", however, these boundaries disappeared as markers of differences in white urban life. Instead white was characterized as respectable in opposition to black.

Sheila Patterson's book *Dark strangers* exemplifies these shifts. The "dark" and "strange" of the title no longer refer to white urban life and the analogy with the "wild races" of a "dark continent", but to "a sociological study of a recent West Indian migrant group in Brixton". As the title also suggests it represents migrants as aliens in the metropolis:

> Brixtonian mores are on the whole those of the respectable upper-working class, or even of the more status-conscious lower-middle or white collar class. . . What then do these respectable residents expect from their street and their neighbours? They expect a tolerable and at least superficial conformity to "our ways", a conformity to certain standards of order, cleanliness, quietness, privacy and propriety. Clean lace curtains are hung at clean windows, dustbins are kept tidy and out of sight, front steps are washed, front halls are like band-boxes, and house fronts are kept neat. . . No immigrant group has in the mass so signally failed to conform to these expectations and patterns as have the West Indians.[42]

White here is a unitary group whose respectability makes them into "residents". Black as a category which is neither respectable nor "resident" is constructed through the expectations of white neighbours about conformity to "our ways".

In Elspeth Huxley's work the opposition between Englishness and "immigrants" draws particularly on private–public in a catalogue of boundary objects and markers:

> West Indian tenants tend to have their failings like everyone else. One is to be as careless and untidy outside their own family circle as they are clean within it. Stairs, landings, shared lavatories, yards, front steps, are often filthy; windows unwashed and cracked; un-emptied dustbins stink, children pee in the gardens and it's the old story – everyone's property is no one's responsibility. Amongst white neighbours, feelings of resentment breed as copiously as flies among the garbage; and those feelings nourish and sustain colour prejudice.[43]

As in Patterson, the text is structured around the expectations of white neighbours, and black life disrupts the boundaries between public and private. Huxley uses images of "a man who lies in bed every weekend with his feet sticking out of the window", and of "the way they keep their hats on indoors". Characteristically these are not her own observations – she is mediating the complaints of "Brixtonians". In Huxley these white neighbours become part of the "we" of the text:

Other Caribbean domestic habits and customs collide with our own. Most West Indians . . . like loud music, noise in general, conviviality, visiting each other, keeping late hours at weekends, dancing and jiving. . . Most English prefer to keep themselves to themselves and guard their privacy. Ours is a land of the wall, the high fence, the privet hedge – all descendants of the moated grange.[44]

"Our own" here, as Englishness, unites explorer, audience and "white neighbours" as one nation, transforming the two nations of rich and poor in earlier social exploration into two nations of white and black. National identity is domesticated, and defined against the "other" of black domestic barbarism. The emblems of Englishness become the quiet street and the privet hedge.

Chapter Four

෯

This new England

After the austerity of the immediate post-war period class discourse, like race discourse, began to focus on Englishness as a unitary category based on a common private and domestic life. By the mid-1950s home was identified as the site of a new affluence in a discourse about class which spoke of classlessness. Charles Curran, for example, writing in 1956, characterized the development of a "new estate" of affluent workers as a "classless zone, neither proletarian nor bourgeois" which had "turned its back on the first, but . . . does not wish to assimilate to the second".[1] It was an estate whose affluence was associated especially with new housing estates, sometimes in new towns, and the array of television aerials decorating these estates. In Curran's view these developments were of enormous significance – "the most far-reaching change since the coming of industrialism".

Celebrated as a progressive story about national life, ushering in a more egalitarian and prosperous society, as in the Conservative Party's election slogan in 1959 "You've never had it so good", imagery of England as two nations could be reworked into an opposition between a common Englishness of well-kept homes and "blacks next door". Much writing about the "new England" confidently proclaimed the demise of divisions of class and region, rich and poor, employed and unemployed which had been embodied in images of inter-war hunger marches and dole queues. However, while the inter-war period was invoked to point up the significance of change, it could equally serve to symbolize a time of working-class community and solidarity, in a story about new developments which expressed concerns about the threat they posed to working-class culture. In Richard Hoggart's *Uses of literacy* (1969), for example, poverty is a constant feature of the "older order" of working-class community that he describes, drawing on his own inter-war childhood in Leeds. But the weight of his account is on its vitality, pleasures and humour rather than on deprivation. The contrast is not so much between pre-war poverty and post-war affluence as between the vitality of the "older order" and the way in which it has been sapped and weakened by post-war commercialization, although Hoggart associates this with mass publications, especially the tabloid press, rather than with television.

Stuart Laing has shown how far working-class culture became a focus of attention across a wide range of texts in a proliferation of representations in the period 1957–64.[2] At the same moment that Curran and others were writing its obituary, images of Northern working-class life flooded cinema screens, novels and stages. Although many texts were written in the tradition of social exploration and presented the social mobility they noted from the point of view of an outsider, an increasing number were produced by men like Hoggart who identified their background as working-class, but themselves experienced social mobility to an identity as writer, often through education.

Ostensibly about class, and generally exploring themes about social mobility, many texts also foregrounded anxieties about white masculinity, which took a variety of forms. The increasingly home-centred and family-centred life of the worker, while in some respects seen as progressive, was also identified as a process of feminization – one in which he was drawn away from public meetings, trade unions and the male solidarity of his work-mates.[3] He had more leisure and better wages, but was spending both on mass culture and entertainment, which drew him into a "candy-floss world" offering him a diet of pap in place of the more solid and robust fare of the traditional working man and culture "of the people" – brass bands, pigeon-fancying, working men's clubs.[4] The television aerial as a main symbol of affluence was part of both anxieties – seen as a major reason why men's lives were increasingly home-centred, which at the same time made them into passive spectators of trivia. The social mobility of those who wrote of working-class life from a working-class background could also arouse anxieties about masculinity through the London literary world that the identity of writer suggested, and its associations with notions of the effete and effeminate – the literary and the South.[5]

As in race discourse, the context for much of this anxiety was national decline. The fear that men were becoming feminized drew on the contraction of Englishness through the loss of imperial power, symbolized particularly by Suez. The fear that a robust culture was giving way to "candy-floss" drew on anxieties about the Americanization of cultural life, which, Harry Hopkins argued, suggested that Britain was becoming "merely one more offshore island".[6] Both found expression in the intense homophobia of the 1950s, in which gay men were seen both as a symptom and a cause of national weakness – fears which were reinforced by the disappearance of Guy Burgess and Donald Maclean in 1951.[7]

The pervasive misogyny of many texts associated with working-class realism in films, novels and plays has often been noted. White femininity, which as "our women" was seen in race discourse as in need of protection from the threat of black male sexuality, was more likely in these texts to be subjected to white male abuse and contempt. Humiliation could be meted out to the woman of a higher social class desired by a working-class man, despite the way in which she facilitated his upward mobility or served as a marker of it, especially in marriage. When women were themselves associated with aspirations to social mobility, this was often represented as neurotic, materialistic or acquisitve, like Nell in *Flame in the streets*. In some texts women were seen as confining men within a life centred on consumption and domesticity, or as threatening the male solidarity and traditional values of working-class community. In both cases a central thread in the portrayal of women was the notion that they drained men of vitality.

Thus anxieties about masculinity were frequently worked out in relation to women, who attracted a range of punishments. The assertion of heterosexuality as male power over women was a theme in much working-class realism, and many texts claimed the power to humiliate and degrade women as a male entitlement. In this way there could be some resolution to male anxiety, however uneasy, distancing the hero from associations with feminization, homosexuality or loss of potency and vitality.

Workers at home

The appearance in England of "people of indeterminate social class" was noted in 1941 by George Orwell and dated, not to the 1950s, but to the period between the wars in the emergence of a new way of life:

There are wide gradations of income but it is the same kind of life that is being lived at different levels, in labour-saving flats or council houses, along the concrete roads and in the naked democracy of the swimming-pools. It is a rather restless, cultureless life, centring round tinned food, *Picture Post*, the radio and the internal combustion engine.[8]

J. B. Priestley had articulated the emergence of this England even earlier, in 1934, using a similar litany of imagery in identifying:

the England of arterial and by-pass roads, of filling stations and factories that look like exhibition buildings, of giant cinemas and dance-halls and cafes, bungalows with tiny garages, cocktail bars, Woolworths, motor-coaches, wireless, hiking, factory girls looking like actresses, grey-hound racing and dirt tracks, swimming pools and everything given away for cigarette coupons. If the fog had lifted I knew that I should have seen this England all round me at that northern entrance to London, where the smooth wide road passes between miles of semi-detached bungalows, all with their little garages, their wireless sets, their periodicals about film stars, their swimming costumes and tennis rackets and dancing shoes.[9]

This way of life was identified especially with the South and its new suburban housing and light industries. The contrast Priestley makes is explicitly between this England and what he calls "nineteenth century England", the world of industrialism in the Midlands and North, which at the time of his 1933 journey he described mainly as "dole country". Orwell makes the same association, locating the England he describes in Slough, Dagenham, Barnet, Letchworth, Hayes – the new townships that were a result of "the southward shift of industry".

After the war what in Priestley and Orwell had been a development confined to the South was seen as spreading across England more generally. T. R. Fyvel commented on the growth of suburbia:

A generation ago, the English suburban house – and garden – still belonged largely to a middle-class way of life beyond the reach of the mass of the workers. Today the whole nation feels entitled to this privilege: hence you have the sprawling suburban housing estates.[10]

Wayland Young noted the patterns of consumption in northern towns:

> Since George Orwell published *The Road to Wigan Pier* in 1936, Wigan has changed from barefoot malnutrition to nylon and television, from hollow idleness to flush contentment. The landscape is the same all right, but as soon as the figures come on you are clean out of Orwell-land.[11]

Used to denote a social and geographical divide in Priestley and Orwell, the "new estate" became an image of one nation uniting different regions and social groups in a common way of life. What generally disappeared from view was the northern working-class masculinity associated with heavy industry – the point of contrast with the England of cocktail bars and swimming costumes in Priestley's account. Its demise was seen as contributing to the rise of the new estate by Curran, who attributed this to geographical and occupational mobility away from coal, cotton and shipbuilding, assigning Northern masculinity to a vanished world of the past. In its absence, the working class was still identified as male in the figure of the worker, but themes about his feminization in post-war England became more explicit.

These were submerged themes in Priestley writing between the wars, when, as Alison Light has argued, there was a movement away from public imperialist rhetorics of national destiny to a more private and domesticated version of Englishness.[12] In his account of the England of bungalows and giant cinemas, factories look like exhibition halls and in them are factory girls who look like actresses. Sally Alexander argues that this suggests "the fear that England and the English are in danger of being feminized by their wirelesses, movie-star worship, silk stockings, and hire-purchase; not only is the new working class in these new industries female, but the wants and needs which the new industries supply are feminine."[13]

It was especially in the contrast between the North as the world of work and the South as the world of leisure and consumption that the fear of feminization was expressed. Some of the imagery Priestley used for leisure suggested masculinity – greyhound racing and dirt tracks – but most was associated with a more feminized world and the main symbol of a male world of leisure was absent. Instead of pubs, there were dance-halls, cinemas, swimming costumes and tennis rackets, and there were also suggestions of home-based leisure in the references to wirelesses and cocktail bars.

Anxieties about white masculinity were articulated more clearly in the 1950s, when distinctions between the North as the world of work and the South as the world of leisure disappeared in favour of a common emphasis on the worker's relationship to home. Accounts of the new England not only identified home as a main site of affluence, but also wrote of the worker's life as increasingly centred on his home and family. In his transition to post-war affluence from pre-war unemployment and poverty, the worker had become a "new man".

It was in the context of identifying a newly "home-centred" society that, in 1959, Mark Abrams proclaimed the advent of this new man:

The good husband is now the domesticated husband. . . The new man stays at home, and he is likely to find burdensome and repugnant any activities or interests that force him to leave the family circle and to forgo part of his domestic privacy and comfort.[14]

The article was illustrated with one picture of a smiling housewife in her kitchen surrounded by a paraphernalia of labour-saving devices – vacuum cleaner, food-mixer, washing machine – and another of a bow-tied man watching television from the comfort of an armchair while his wife shared a sofa with three children.

Despite the bow-tie, Abrams did not associate these images with middle-class life. In tracing the growth in ownership of refrigerators, vacuum cleaners, washing machines and televisions, his argument was that "for the first time in modern British history, the working class home, as well as the middle class home, has become a place that is warm, comfortable and able to provide its own fireside entertainment".[15] The home was constructed as a site of leisure and consumption in opposition to work, in images which led to the almost complete erasure of domestic work. The wirelesses which had figured prominently in Priestley and Orwell gave way to televisions, and *Picture Post* to the tabloid press, but cafés, dance-halls and cinemas were absent, or appeared only in references to the way in which television ownership had led to the decline of cinema attendance.[16]

The new man was an ambivalent figure. His family and

home-centredness were generally seen as progressive – a change in manners through which the overbearing patriarch was replaced by an understanding husband and father, the mainstay of companionate marriage and family life, coaxing his wife to acknowledge the possibilities of sexual pleasure, and treating his children to guidance rather than bullying. Within the ideal of companionate marriage there was an emphasis on a new equality of relationship between husband and wife, variously conceived as companionship, team-work or role-sharing.[17] Images of young fathers pushing prams proliferated in studies of working-class families; John and Elizabeth Newson in their study of child care depicted a father who "chooses to sit at his own fireside, a baby on his knee and a feeding bottle in his hand".[18] Michael Young and Peter Willmott reported that working-class fathers in Bethnal Green were not only pushing prams at weekends, but also taking their daughters for a row on the lake and their sons to the putting green.[19] Working-class fathers who had moved out to new estates, they argued, were even more home-centred:

> When they watch the television instead of drinking beer in the pub, and weed the garden instead of going to a football match, the husbands of Greenleigh have taken a stage further the partnership [which is] characteristic of modern Bethnal Green. The "home" and the family of marriage become the focus of a man's life, as of his wife's, far more completely than in the East End.[20]

Ferdynand Zweig reported that the father was stepping into the mother's place or occupying an equal place beside her in caring for the children.[21] The father, he argued, had undergone a process of change from the strict or bullying patriarch whose authority was used as a bogey to the role of older brother to his children, giving help, assistance and guidance.[22]

Even women's part-time work could be seen as part of the democratization of the family. It was in the context of discussing "working wives" that the Church of England produced a classic picture of companionate family life:

> Doubtless there are families in which family life is gravely impaired by the absence of the mother, but there are others where the contrary may be true. There is evidence to suggest that the greater comfort of the home made possible by the

mother's earnings serves to draw the family together. Husbands are prepared to spend their time on painting and decorating; better domestic equipment makes it simple for the whole family to share the home duties; the home, in fact, becomes a joint enterprise in which the whole family takes a pride.[23]

Sharing the home duties, within a sexual division of labour where the male role was DIY was a common image of the companionate family.

Despite the general welcome extended to what was seen as a change from an authoritarian to an egalitarian family, there were also considerable anxieties about men's home-centredness. These were usually expressed in terms of class in a concern that the privatization of social life led to a decline in men's participation in public life, whether in working-men's clubs, pubs, politics or trade unionism. The ethos of class solidarity, Zweig noted, was weakened, "as a man thinks primarily of himself and his home", with even Communist workers affected "by the general mood and tendency towards domestication".[24] Curran argued that "the public meeting has all but died out".[25] Reduced attendance at meetings of trade unions, Friendly Societies and voluntary associations was a common concern.[26] This could be figured as a decline in politics or a decline in working-class community. It was also figured as a decline in male solidarity:

> . . . the worker is moving away from his mates. His home and family-centredness brings in its wake the tendency to keep aloof from his mates. Formerly he used to congregate with his mates, to "knock about" with them, to scheme with them, and there was a great deal of mutual aid. Now he sees his mates outside the works only occasionally. . . There are no campaigns to wage, as little mutual help and assistance are needed. The Unions are taken for granted, and do their work without his help.[27]

The passivity suggested by television-viewing also troubled many commentators who saw the television aerial as the emblem of the new England. No one was troubled by the passivity of the female viewer. Television, Abrams argued, kept the man indoors away from all outdoor mass entertainment and activity, reducing him to "a detached, isolated observer".[28] Curran called the new man "apolitical man", in tracing the effects of the boom in television, which he saw both as "the most significant social event of the decade" and as a development which brought withdrawal into a private universe of fantasy.[29] Zweig also identified passivity and privatization as marks of the new man's home and family-centredness as he and his family kept themselves to themselves, linking these developments to a process of softening in the worker:

> The workers' world was formerly known for its masculinity. The worker had little to do with children or womenfolk. He was a hard-working, hard-swearing and hard-playing man. His manners were often rough. His voice was often loud, his manner of speaking blunt and harsh. Now he has mellowed considerably.

"I would," he said, "venture to call it his feminization."[30]

Avoiding the fate of mothers

Ambivalence about the new man, where his home-centredness was welcomed, but there were anxieties about the impact this had on working-class community, illustrates the extent to which many texts defined working-class as male. Joining women at home, men were seen as abandoning class as community and solidarity. Many texts about the working classes focused on what was happening to men and characteristic figures were the affluent worker and the working-class hero.

Other texts, however, foregrounded women, who could figure as central to the working-class community which was threatened by new developments. Richard Hoggart who saw domesticity as the main quality of traditional working-class life, and identified home and neighbourhood as the main aspects of "the older order", foregrounded the figure of "our mam" as one mainstay of working-class community. As the pivot of the home, our mam held community together, with responsibility for most aspects of familial life, proud in the knowledge that so much revolved around her.[31] Hoggart's perspective was of a particular kind of inter-war childhood, that of the "scholarship boy" who had moved away, and who looked back to a community not only from adulthood, but from the social distance that education had produced, writing for an audience who were assumed to be completely unfamiliar with working-class speech, manners and life. There is some suggestion in the text that, as a scholarship boy, Hoggart had experienced his own place as outside the world of northern masculinity, secluded from pubs, streets and the workplace by the need to do his homework, and to stay in education past the school leaving age. The scholarship boy, he argues, "sits in the women's world . . . quietly getting on with his work whilst his mother gets on with her jobs – the father not yet back from work or out for a drink with his mates", while "the man and the boy's brothers are . . . in the world of men".[32]

Hoggart's female heroine, described by Terry Lovall as "middle-aged, shapeless and asexual" and "a stolid and immobile figure from Hoggart's memory-washed streets", has attracted considerable criticism.[33] The fate of working-class mothers, Hoggart suggested, was:

> a steady and self-forgetful routine, one devoted to the family and beyond proud self-regard. Behind it, making any vague pity irrelevant, is pride in the knowledge that so much revolves around them. This can make the most unpromising and unprepossessing young woman arrive at a middle-age in which she is, when in the midst of her home and family, splendidly "there" and, under all the troubles, content.[34]

As Lovell argues, what is missing is the perspective of a daughter. For the adult son, as Hoggart's text shows, this figure might call forth admiration. But she was likely to be more ambivalent for a daughter whose own inter-war childhood involved the possibility of becoming our mam rather than admiring her from afar, especially for a daughter who had absorbed very different ideals of femininity via Hollywood.

The daughters, when discussed, were usually assumed to be the main beneficiaries of men's home-centredness. Young and Willmott saw companionate marriage as a development which brought greater equality between the sexes and a rising status for the young wife which they described as "one of the great transformations of our time".[35] Ronald Fletcher argued in similar vein that the position of the woman in the family had been fundamentally changed, and characterized this as "moral improvement".[36] Women were also assumed to be beneficiaries of the new affluence as they made the transition from the role of housekeeper – serving a man who spent his money and time outside the home – to a role where they became the choosers and the spenders as Mrs Consumer.[37] Young and Willmott, however, while enthusiastic champions of companionate marriage, argued that the movement out to new estates disrupted the close ties between mother and daughter that were so strong a feature of life in Bethnal Green.

Accounts by women of inter-war childhoods suggest that many were more concerned to avoid the life of their mothers than to celebrate it from a distance, as Hoggart does, or to mourn the disruption of close proximity to their mothers that Young and Willmott highlight. Sally Alexander, writing about the lives of women who grew up in working-class households in London in the 1920s and 1930s, traces themes about what they saw when they looked at their mothers: "economic hardship, hard work, and neglect from husbands who were often unemployed, who drank, or who abandoned them".[38] Their refusal of their mothers' lives in their "yearning to escape the domestic treadmill" could take a number of different forms, she argues, expressed in desires for education, literature or a skilled trade. A desire for glamour was often prominent among these, influenced by images of labour-saving devices and film stars' dress and hair-styles as "advertising and the cinema, playing on fantasy and desire, enabled women to *imagine* an end to domestic drudgery and chronic want".[39]

A desire to avoid the fate of mothers was not confined to daughters of our mam. Ideals of femininity from advertising and the cinema are prominent in Maria Woods's account of her desire to escape suburbia:

How handsome they [GIS] all looked in that crisp blue uniform, with those flashy Rolex watches (which were usually hocked half way to pay-day or wagered in a crap game), and the sexy way those peaked hats were worn down over their eyes reminded we girls of Alan Ladd and Robert Mitchum. Our suburban lives seemed so boring in comparison, and as for the local boys in their baggy shiny flannels and with their Bryl-creemed hair, they might as well have emigrated to Australia, for all the notice that we took of them. Their shouts of "Yanks' meat" were met with disdain, as we walked past them in our tight pencil-slim skirts and our drop ear-rings. We were travelling on a cloud of glamour, and endless good times stretched ahead of us in America, the land of milk and honey. I thought it would be a better life, I did think I was going to have all the latest gadgets in the kitchen, and I was going to have this little white picket fence round this lovely house. Mum would be pleased – my daughter in America has got something called a mixer. And that's what I really thought.[40]

Other women have recorded the influence of an inter-war childhood on their desire to avoid their mother's lives. Margaret Thatcher, for example, records that "I loved my mother dearly, but after I was fifteen we had nothing more to say to each other. It wasn't her fault. She was weighed down by the home, always being in the home."[41] Most women of this generation did not make such a spectacular journey away from their mothers' lives as Thatcher, who by 1959 had already entered Parliament as MP for Finchley. Even those who made the journey to America or Canada as war-brides could find the reality of domestic life there compared unfavourably with their mothers' lives in Britain. When she left suburban England after marrying a GI, Woods found herself not only without the white picket fence or the mixer, but also without a bathroom or a home of her own, living in an American small town with her mother-in-law.

One perspective from a daughter of our mam suggests a further way in which refusal of mothers' lives might be expressed – through women's desire to give their own children, including daughters, a better childhood and better opportunities than they themselves had experienced. Win Kewley was born three years after Hoggart, like him into a working-class community in Leeds. Her father was a coal-miner, and she was the eldest in a family of six children. A main theme in her account of her childhood, like Hoggart's, is the poverty, hard work and drudgery of her mother's life and includes the impact on her own childhood of her mother's employment:

It was a struggle. My mother had the kids. She went out cleaning. She used to get up at 6 o'clock to go cleaning in town, scrubbing stone floors on her knees. She had to do this because we were so poor. And so I was the oldest, I was in charge of getting all the others ready for school. Make sure they were ready and the youngest one, putting him in his pushchair and taking him down to this elderly lady who looked after him 'til my mum came home from work and picked him up, and then making sure the others all got to school. I don't know how I did it. I know once I went to school in such a rush with them all, I'll never forget the embarrassment. I should have been having a little skirt on and a jumper, and I put the jumper on and forgot the skirt, so my underskirt was what I had on at the bottom. And the shame of finding out when you get to school that you've got an underskirt on, and I walked about all morning with it, trying to cover it, and they were all making fun of me. You know those things that stand out, the embarrassment.

Boots for the bairns – that was the 1930s. The council brought this thing out that they would supply boots for the kids, so that they'd have something on their feet. And my mum was dead against this, because they had this pride you see. Charity, you didn't want to accept charity. But my sister was really down on her uppers, so with much heart-searching my mother took up a pair of these boots. They had three holes punched in the top so people couldn't sell them. . . . Everybody knew you'd got these boots, and you were looked down on as someone that's accepted charity. But my sister came home crying in hers with great big blisters on her heels, and she couldn't wear them. . . And my mum wept. My mother bore her hardships stoically. She didn't weep. But she wept when my sister came in.

Unlike Hoggart, Kewley did not take a route away through education:

You were straight into work, straight into a tailoring factory. I don't think my mother thought about education, because she'd been so poor and had such a struggle. All she was thinking about was being able to earn some money and live. When I started work, my 8/- a week, less 4d stoppages, that was a godsend to her – it was money in her purse. Because we were working class, factory work was the expected thing. I didn't know anybody who went to work in an office. There were a few places for scholarships, and it would work out one person – two at the most – in each school would get a scholarship. I was an ailing child. I was taken out of school and sent to an open-air school. So when I got back to school again, in the final exams I'd no chance. Even when someone won a scholarship, people were mostly too poor to let them go to high school, because they had the expense of the uniforms – so wonderful if they'd gone, and then to get an office job after that, because they'd had a better education than us. It was just something out of our reach. We'd no choice, just get into a factory. It was expected, so you did it.

Bringing up her own children, born between 1948 and 1959, Kewley identified education as the way in which they could avoid the social exclusions that her own mother's life had involved her in:

I wanted to make things easier for my kids. . . I wanted them to have a chance, a better going-on than I'd had. Get out of this, don't be like I was, don't be like my mum was. I thought my kids are not going to come straight out of school into a factory, they're going to have something better, and especially when they were bright. . . And my husband expected that they would leave school and go into a factory. We rowed over that. "They're not going", I said, "they're staying on to do A levels". "What for, they're girls" he said, "they'll only get married". I nearly went berserk. So I stuck it out. I thought no way am I going to give in to this.[42]

Eventually her eldest son and her two daughters all went to teachers' training colleges.

Looking back

In the late 1950s and early 1960s cinema screens, novels and stages were flooded with images of working-class life, and television took up the trend with the screening of the first episode of *Coronation street* in 1960. At the moment when northern working-class masculinity was assigned to a vanished past in new England literature, working-class realism often put this at the centre of its story.

The preoccupation with traditional working-class culture in general, and northern masculinity in particular, did not mean that working-class realism ignored the new estate. Of the themes elaborated in the new man literature – working men as passive spectators of television and their disengagement with trade unions and politics – it explored the former, and a common thread in many stories was the effects of affluence on working-class communities, as well as the commercialization and Americanization of culture. In reinstating northern masculinity, it reverted to Priestley's and Orwell's analysis where this was the point of contrast with the new England of consumption and home-based leisure, but in most accounts this new England was now part of northern life. Some texts explored the story of men who moved away from the traditional working class through education, occupation or marriage. Others portrayed the new estate threatening traditional working-class culture on its own territory.

The main subjects of these texts was ostensibly working-class life, but, as John Hill has argued of New Wave films:

> The narrative patterns adopted in such films not only revolve around characters who are working-class but who are also male and whose progress "along" the narrative is characteristically worked out in terms of their relations with the other sex. Questions of the hero's identity in relation to a class thus never appear "pure", but are crucially "overdetermined" in relation to questions of sex. . . . [The films] share a particular way of working out their heroes' sexual involvements – according to what might justifiably be called the patriarchal principle. By and large, women function either as elusive objects of desire or as threats to the conventional social/sexual order (mainly via adultery), and, either way, must be brought under some kind of male control.[43]

In bringing women under male control, however, texts did not always find an easy resolution to the anxieties they raised.

A comparison between *Look back in anger*, first staged in 1956, and *A kind of loving*, the 1962 film based on the novel by Stan Barstow, suggests some of the uneasiness of resolutions to anxieties, which in both texts centre on the threat of a loss of vitality. In *A kind of loving*, as in Hoggart, vitality is associated particularly with traditional working-class community, and the contrast is with the new estate whose main representatives in the film are women. As Vic, the hero, finds himself living on the new estate he is cut off from the traditional working-class culture symbolized by his father's membership of a brass band. Loss of vitality in *Look back in anger* is associated with the passing of a number of worlds, and although some reference to traditional working-class community is included, the emphasis is particularly on national decline in the loss of imperial power and Americanization. Both texts, however, translate these concerns into a central image: women emasculating men.

The images of traditional working-class life with which *A kind of loving* opens establish from the outset its associations with vitality and community. In the first shot, children are playing in the street, a recurrent image in the film where their noise is a constant backdrop to scenes of working-class life. As the camera tracks the children running up the street to an ice-cream van, it arrives at a crowd who are gathering to see a wedding. Christine – Vic's sister – and her bridegroom emerge to a hubbub of noise and bustle, orchestrated by a photographer who ushers different groups in and out of the frame. As the appreciative crowd watches and comments, their position as audience heightens the sense of action which is interspersed with stills on the photographer's command to "hold it". The credits come up over shots which suggest the life of the community in the knowledgeable comments of the crowd about the characters within the frame, the different generational groups who are posed there for the camera, and the series of stills which make up the wedding pictures with their suggestions of framed photographs on mantel-pieces. The crowd then joins in the action, advancing with confetti, and cheering the wedding car on its way.

In contrast the new estate is devoid of life. There is little movement in its streets, and its characteristic noise is the barking of dogs, not children playing. The only shot of a child shows her alone, on her tricycle, contained within her front garden under the watchful eye of her mother. In contrast to the race discourse of the period, where the quiet street and privet hedge were emblems of a common Englishness invaded by "immigrants", in *A kind of loving* they signify the sterility of the new estate in contrast to the life of the traditional working class.

This public–private contrast is central to the portrayal of the hero. In tracing Vic's progress the film shows him moving from one world to the other. In the first section his own exuberance matches the vitality of the children as he races through allotments, cobbled streets and parks, hurling himself down steps and onto buses. Moving into the new estate through his marriage to Ingrid, he lives on the outskirts of the city in his mother-in-law's semi-detached house in a quiet street. In this section of the film the new estate is shown mainly as a domestic interior, which confines and contains

Vic's activities, reducing him to a feminized and domesticated life where his main duty is to watch the television.

In representing the new estate as female, *A kind of loving* features women as the main threat to traditional working-class community, a characteristic of New Wave films more generally. As Terry Lovell argues, ". . . this cycle of films persistently portrays the status-conscious woman as the vulnerable point of entry for seductions which might betray a class and its culture".[44] Ingrid and her mother, Mrs Rothwell, are united in their shared obsession with television and shopping. Like the new England literature, the scenes of domestic interiors which dominate Vic's married life construct home as a site of leisure and consumption erasing domestic work. Mrs Rothwell is animated about television programmes and the purchase of carpets, curtains and clothes for Ingrid. Her domestic work is represented mainly as a possessive pride in maintaining these objects. She occasionally bestirs herself to get someone in to mend the television, reprimand the window-cleaner on a shoddy job, or harrass Vic about his domestic habits. Mostly the women watch television from the sofa in the front room.

Vic's movements provide the narrative structure of the film, but it also sketches in some other movements which suggest how far the traditional–new estate opposition is superimposed on a much more conventional story. After the wedding with which the film opens, Vic's sister Christine moves into a modern flat, built on land where traditional working-class housing has been demolished. Vic himself has moved into a white-collar job as a draughtsman. Vic's workmate, Conroy, moves into a job as a salesman where he gets a car. None of these movements are seen within the film as problematic. Although Christine is associated both with the new estate and domestic interiors, she is portrayed as a threat neither to working-class community, nor to masculinity. Conroy's car, a sign of successful masculinity, is treated quite differently from Mrs Rothwell's new carpet. Vic is quite happy to be ferried about in Conroy's car on a pub crawl. It is on his return that he vomits all over the new carpet.

The conventional story told in *A kind of loving* is about female sexuality, which is defined through the male characters. It is constructed within the film both as a means by which men control and dominate women, and as a problem for men whose desire may lead them into submission to women. The problem of the new estate is a thin gloss on a much more time-worn theme about men's containment and domestication by women through marriage. In the suggestion of an angel–whore opposition between Christine and Ingrid, and in Conroy's description of Ingrid as a praying mantis who eats men alive, there are suggestions of a more generalized fear of female sexuality. The film resolves these problems in a variety of ways. Ingrid's pregnancy is represented in conventional terms as the means by which Vic becomes trapped in a marriage that he does not want, but Ingrid is then punished through miscarriage. Miscarrying through falling down the stairs in Mrs Rothwell's house, the loss of her child becomes associated with the sterility of the new estate. In the final resolution of the film, women are defeated through the restoration of male solidarity, which Ingrid has earlier repeatedly broken.

Vic's first reassertion of his masculinity after his marriage is prompted by the notion of his sexual rights over his wife, and their frustration in her refusal. It takes him on the pub crawl with Conroy, with whom he had earlier fought over Ingrid, reversing her earlier disruption of male solidarity. When he leaves Ingrid and seeks help from the women in his family he finds no support. Female solidarity crosses both boundaries of generation, and of new estate–traditional working class. As they refuse to comply with his version of events, Vic tells both Ingrid and Christine that they sound like their mothers. His own mother, like Ingrid's, refuses him entry to the family home. The female solidarity with Ingrid is general, and is based around a common view of the importance of marriage and childbirth.

Visiting his father's allotment, however, Vic finds a different response as his father, advising him on what to do with Ingrid, tells him "she'll live where she's bloody put" and they plot the defeat of women. The reassertion of male control comes through solidarity against women, and at least partially resolves anxieties about masculinity. Ingrid, already punished by miscarriage, is portrayed at the end submitting to Vic's terms, which include the restoration of sexual access to her, the break-up of the mother–daughter relationship and a curtailment of her desire to live like the new estate. The patriarchal family is reinstated. Secured in the face of the female solidarity surrounding Ingrid, northern working-class masculinity reasserts itself not only against the new estate, but against women generally. Like the middle sections of *A kind of loving, Look back in anger* could be read as a portrait of a man confined and constrained within a domestic world – in this case not the new estate with its television and new carpets, but a bathroomless one-room attic flat with old furniture. However, the vocabulary used by the female characters in the play for this setting – "menagerie", "zoo" – aptly suggests the way in which it is dominated and masculinized by Jimmy Porter in his role as a caged animal. In beating against the bars, his violent energy is different from the vitality associated with traditional working-class culture in *A kind of loving.* Jimmy's noise is a constant feature of the play in his lengthy verbal, psychological and sometimes physical assaults on others when he is on stage, and his jazz trumpet which acts as a reminder of his presence for much of the time that he is off. He objects to all other noises, associating them particularly with women in "the eternal flaming racket of the female".

Even when off-stage, Jimmy remains the dominant presence in the play as other characters obsessively discuss him, recalling in his absence what he has said to them about himself. His noise drowns out all other voices and most other stories. In so far as characters in the play are given pasts, these are mainly the histories of their relationship with Jimmy, who is both their present and their past. Jimmy, in contrast, has a history whose losses are a main theme of the play – his childhood loss of his father, his loss of relationship with his friend Hugh, his loss of Hugh's mother through her death within the action of the play. This past is offset against the present, the latter represented particularly by the news. Newspapers dominate the domestic scene, attracting far more attention than the ironing board behind which the female characters in the play are usually positioned, and through their association with Jimmy serve as one indication of how far the domestic world is masculinized by his presence. As he reads out fragments of the day's news, treating his companions to a critique of the papers' contents, the present is portrayed as superficial by comparison with the weight of the past. Jimmy mocks other stories when they are in newspapers. In drowning out the stories and pasts of his companions, what he demands of them is an understanding of his own.

Jimmy's origins are sketched quite vaguely in his own account of them, and in the contributions of other characters who discuss him when he is off-stage. They are those of "working people", Jimmy's friend Cliff tells Alison, "he gets on with me because I'm common". He has been to university, Alison tells her friend Helena, but "according to him, it's not even red brick, but white tile". Jimmy's own identification with the working class is represented particularly through his bond with Mrs Tanner, Hugh's mother, whose story and past he does to some extent acknowledge. Mrs Tanner, Alison tells her father, is "what Jimmy insists on calling working-class. A Charwoman who married an actor."[45] Jimmy's insistence on the language of class where Cliff refers to "working people" is character-istic of a number of his speeches. His fooling in the play with Cliff provides another association with traditional working-class culture as in their double-acts they perform versions of music-hall sketches. These double-acts, which follow the reading of newspapers, sug-gests not only Jimmy's loyalties to the traditional working class but also how far that world is of the past, a theme which is reinforced by Mrs Tanner's death.

Many readings of the play have noted the transposition of questions of class onto those of sex.[46] The opposition between working class and "old estate" in *Look back in anger*, like the opposition between traditional working class and new estate in *A kind of loving*, is worked out in terms of misogyny. As Jimmy attacks Alison, ostensibly on the grounds of her class and family, it is her sexual and maternal power that he wants to break. His image of Alison burying him alive is linked with his recurrent references to women as "butchers" and expresses his disgust and fear of female bodies and of heterosexuality:

> She has the passion of a python. She just devours me whole every time, as if I were some over-large rabbit. That's me. That bulge around her navel – if you're wondering what it is – it's me. Me, buried alive down there, and going mad, smothered in that peaceful looking coil. Not a sound, not a flicker from her – she doesn't even rumble a little. You'd think that this indigest-ible mess would stir up some kind of tremor in those distended, overfed tripes – but not her.[47]

Jimmy's desire to break Alison's maternal power is expressed in similar imagery of disgust at the female body. "If you could have a child, and it would die. Let it grow, let a recognisable human face emerge from that little mass of india rubber and wrinkles."

As in *A kind of loving*, the death of Alison's child is a chief means by which women are defeated in the play – a common punishment meted out to them. It is through this loss that Alison, who has defied Jimmy by leaving him to return to her parents, comes back to him grovelling. At the end of the play, abasing herself before Jimmy from the floor where she has fallen, she makes herself into a version of the woman he has desired – humiliated, degraded and tortured:

> I thought: if only – if only he could see me now, so stupid, and ugly and ridiculous. This is what he's been longing for me to feel. This is what he wants to splash about in! I'm in the fire, and I'm burning, and all I want is to die! It's cost him his child, and any others I might have had! But what does it matter – this is what he wanted from me![48]

This is the first time in the play that one of the characters tells Jimmy her story, rather than listening to his. Jimmy's reaction is characteristic. "I don't exactly relish the idea of anyone being ill, or in pain. It was my child too, you know. But (*he shrugs*) it isn't my first loss."[49] Jimmy's obsession with his own history is set here against Alison's suffering, subordinating her story to his own, her present to his past.

Male solidarity against women – the main way in which masculinity is reasserted in *A kind of loving* – is treated differently in *Look back in anger*. Jimmy breaks up female solidarity without difficulty. The brief interlude when Alison's friend Helena supports her against Jimmy is quickly ended as Helena replaces Alison in Jimmy's bed and at the ironing board, smoothing his shirts. Helena, however, also breaks up Jimmy's and Cliff's double-act. Although Jimmy's disgust at heterosexuality seems undiminished, and he tells Cliff that "you're worth half a dozen Helenas to me or anyone", homo-eroticism remains a submerged theme within the play, and does not disrupt its associations of tough assertive masculinity with hetero-sexuality. Male solidarity, however, does disrupt Jimmy's antagonism to the old estate through his identification with Alison's father, Colonel Redfern.

Redfern is the only character in the play who is given a history which is not centred on relationship to Jimmy. As Jimmy looks

back, in an extraordinary speech in the opening act, he is as obsessed
with Redfern's past as he is in later speeches with his own:

> I hate to admit it, but I think I can understand how her Daddy
> must have felt when he came back from India, after all those
> years away. The old Edwardian brigade do make their brief
> little world look pretty tempting. All home-made cakes and
> croquet, bright ideas, bright uniforms. Always the same
> picture: high summer, the long days in the sun, slim volumes of
> verse, crisp linen, the smell of starch. What a romantic picture.
> Phoney too, of course. It must have rained sometimes. Still,
> even I regret it somehow, phoney or not. If you've no world of
> your own, it's rather pleasant to regret the passing of someone
> else's. I must be getting sentimental. But I must say it's pretty
> dreary living in the American Age – unless you're an American
> of course. Perhaps all our children will be Americans. That's a
> thought isn't it?[50]

Jimmy's interest in Redfern's story here, in a complete reversal of
his normal practice, extends to an attempt to understand the feelings
of another person. In the context of his railing against the establishment in general, and Alison and her family as its representatives in
particular, this is an extraordinary identification. Jimmy's championship of the working class against the old estate in the metropolis
is not matched by any championship of the colonized against the old
estate in empire. In his picture of colonizers, the colonized are
absent, and the imperial romance is disrupted only by rain. His
identification with Redfern suggests that when Jimmy laments that
"there aren't any good, brave causes left", such causes encompass all
those that he associates with masculinity – not only his father's
struggle in the Spanish civil war, but also Redfern's imperialism.
Good causes are masculine causes, and there are none left because of
national decline, which through its association with the decline of
empire and with men's emasculation by women is rendered as the
emasculation of England. As Jimmy says later, "There's nothing left
for it, me boy, but to let yourself be butchered by the women."

One symbol of decline is American power, and the speech ends
with the prospect that "all our children will be Americans". The end
of the play, however, is the loss not only of Alison's child but of her
future fertility. Since Alison is a main representative of the old estate
this could be read as a punishment on them as well as women, but, as

both Alison and Jimmy remind the audience, this is the death of Jimmy's child too. Male solidarity cannot bring about a resolution to anxieties in *Look back in anger* because, through national decline, English masculinity is no longer potent. Through all his rantings Jimmy, like his vision of the England that he inhabits, is impotent. Despite the association of empire with the Edwardian period, Colonel Redfern's speech about his feelings about the loss of imperial power are dated very precisely in the play – to 1947 and Indian independence. They could be read as expressing Jimmy's feelings about his own present, and both the present and the future of England:

> I think the last day the sun shone was when that dirty little train steamed out of that crowded, suffocating Indian station, and the battalion band playing for all it was worth. I knew in my heart it was all over then. Everything.[51]

Chapter Five

Chapter Five

✍

Good homes

In 1964 Pearl Jephcott, in a study of Notting Hill in London, wrote of a West Indian woman:

> She has furnished [her room] by the most lush of Edwardian tastes. But the (cracked) window with skinny, dirty curtains is never cleaned, while the "front" on to which the room looks and for which she is one of the people responsible, is a shambles. . . Considering the primitive conditions to which some, if a minority of West Indians have been accustomed – the poverty and yaws of certain of the rural areas of Jamaica, or the mud and mosquito-ridden villages of much of the coastal plain of British Guiana – they have adapted themselves remarkably well to city life.[1]

Jephcott called the lives she found in Notting Hill "anachronistic" by comparison with "the pride of possession, the 'nice home' that is a characteristic of the working-class family of today". Among the anachronisms she identified were large families, which she saw as an indication of the "survival of byegone patterns" and basement homes where the health visitor's comment was: "a terrible place for a baby".

"Primitive", "anachronistic", "byegone patterns" all suggest some of the ways in which the notion of a "good home" was reworked after the war around an opposition between the modern and the primitive. Black is associated with a rural which is very far from the English pastoral – defined in terms of poverty, disease, squalor and backwardness rather than plenty, health and simplicity. Jephcott's study included white households, particularly Irish, so that it was not only black women who were identified as "anachronistic". At the same time the "nice home . . . of the working-class family of today" which Jephcott contrasted with the squalor of Notting Hill suggests the extent to which the white working class were seen as respectable citizens who could be incorporated into the idea of nation.

The good home was a central image of national progress, well-being and health, and at its centre, in most accounts, was the good mother. She was a figure who, in her post-war incarnation, was concocted from an extraordinary mixture of reason and emotion, culture and nature, science and intimacy. Women, generally constructed as one among many "others" of a modernity characterized by individualistic, rationalist and instrumental impulses, were offered a route to their own particular post-war feminized version through becoming ever more emotional and subjective, a process of becoming which involved learning from experts how to be more natural and accepting guidance on how to behave instinctively.

Listening to scientific expertise was prescribed as one of women's central tasks in creating a good home. Advice was available from a range of sources including advertisements for household products and tampons, sex and child-care manuals, women's magazines, clinics, doctors, health visitors, social workers, home advisers, marriage guidance counsellors and psychiatrists. Sex education was also targeted mainly at women, in childhood, adolescence and adulthood. The importance of listening to advice was central to the definition of "problem families" – not just any family which manifested inefficiency and squalor, but those which resisted "the well meant efforts of social agencies" to combat these conditions.[2] Women in "problem families", one study found, might deliberately never go near a clinic at any time.[3]

An emphasis on emotion, intimacy and instinct is particularly apparent in child care literature. Some need for rationality was implied in an emphasis on the need for women to control their bodies, and the construction of science as their aid and guide in doing so, through the use of modern sanitary protection during menstruation, birth control to facilitate "voluntary parenthood", medical treatment for infertility, and hospitalization of childbirth. After childbirth, however, the most modern scientific expertise on child care advised them to do what came naturally to them, an emphasis particularly apparent in the work of Donald Winnicott, who made a series of broadcasts on BBC radio during and after the war to disseminate his advice – that mothering grew naturally out of being a mother and mothers themselves knew best. The recognition that such a view left little role for child-care experts surfaces in these broadcasts, where Winnicott sometimes portrays his own role as a substitute for what he really desires – to be a mother. His argument that mothers' devotion to their babies was the basis of a healthy society made what he saw as an intensely intimate relationship, embodied in the act of breast-feeding, into a sign of public welfare. John Bowlby, taking up similar themes, also emphasized the need for intimacy in the importance of the emotional work of a mother. In these accounts what Winnicott usually characterized as "devotion" and Bowlby as "mother-love" became the basis of national stability and health.

Domesticity was also a theme in the dissemination of scientific advice. The emphasis on emotion produced in health discourse was taken up in advertisements for household products which represented women mediating the latest scientific research in order to provide love for their families. Tasks like doing the washing and cleaning the lavatory were invested with emotional significance, as women were shown protecting the family from dirt, disease and danger through products whose capacity to kill all known germs or to produce a shining radiant whiteness were guaranteed by men in white coats.

The emphasis on the natural in literature on motherhood sometimes meant that the "primitive woman" was offered as a role model to teach the "civilized" woman how to behave and to revert to the natural state from which civilization had distracted her. Tess Cosslett's analysis of natural childbirth and the primitive woman traces the way in which the figure originally invoked in Grantly Dick Read's work in the 1930s – "a 'native' woman leaving her work to give birth painlessly and joyfully in a thicket by herself" – was extended in his *Childbirth without fear*, published in 1954, and although originally a male construct, was taken up and appropriated by women advocating natural chilbirth in the early 1960s.[4] A similar figure may also lurk in the way in which Bowlby, identifying maternal deprivation as a western problem, reflected on "the astonishing practice which has been followed in maternity wards – of separating mothers and babies immediately after birth", and contrasted "this madness of Western society" to practices in "so-called less developed countries".[5] At the same time, Bowlby's formulation challenged the opposition between western as civilized and "so-called less developed countries" as primitive. Cosslett writes:

The primitive woman is . . . not nearly so primitive as she seems: she is a cultural construct, incorporating the maternal ideals of a particular society, and, paradoxically, her instinctive wisdom has to be learnt from books by "civilised" women. She begins as very much a male ideal, allowing domination of the birth-scene by the charismatic male obstetrician; taken over by women writers, she is used to assert female power and autonomy.[6]

As this cultural construct she is a timeless figure, living in no particular place. Black women in Britain, although often seen as primitive and closer to nature than white women, were never held up as role models. As the good mother at the centre of the good home became a symbol of national health and stability in images which emphasized intimacy, emotion and relationship, black women were excluded. In the 1950s, they were generally invisible in race discourse and were not associated with motherhood or domesticity. The construction of black incapacity for relationship or familial life foregrounded the figures of black men. But when black women's motherhood became a focus of race discourse in the early 1960s, it was in Pearl Jephcott's terms – as over-fecund, and as a threat to the health of the nation.

Hygiene, neurosis, intimacy

After the war there was a general shift from the language of hygiene as a term which encompassed concerns about reproduction, sexuality and disease to a concern with neurosis, with many definitions of health – like Winnicott's – drawing on Freudianism. Even those who remained impervious to this influence dropped the term "racial hygiene" from discussions of reproduction and eugenics, with the British Social Hygiene Council, whose concerns had encompassed all aspects of what it called racial and sexual hygiene, renaming itself in 1950 the British Social Biology Council.[7] Sex education was less likely to be called hygiene, although this name survived in at least one girls' grammar school in the late 1950s.[8] Motherhood manuals were no longer likely to be called *The hygiene of life and safer motherhood* – the title of an inter-war advice book.[9]

These shifts were apparent in child-care literature, where the influence of Freudianism meant that the mental health of children increasingly replaced hygiene and physical health as the sign of good homes – although Bowlby sometimes called his preoccupations "mental hygiene". Motherhood was emotionalized as Bowlby, like Winnicott, emphasized the quality of women's relationship with children, their mother-love expressed particularly through intimacy. Arguing that "mother-love in infancy and childhood is as important for mental health as are vitamins and proteins for physical health", and that children who were deprived of this love were "the source of social infection as real and serious as are carriers of diptheria and typhoid", Bowlby advocated a programme for the prevention of family failure, to which he wanted to recruit not only marriage guidance and child guidance workers, but also physicians, nurses and social workers, stressing the need for widespread training and retraining, and for radical changes in outlook among professional personnel.[10]

The hygiene approach, so prominent in the work of the Hygiene Committee of the Women's Group on Public Welfare during the war, generally remained dominant in the literature on "problem families" of which the central feature, according to Blacker, was "the failure to provide a home fit for children".[11] As in *Our towns*, a much-quoted picture of this family catalogued deficiencies in hygiene in considerable detail:

From their appearance they [the children] are strangers to soap and water, toothbrush and comb; the clothing is dirty and torn and the footgear absent or totally inadequate. Often they are verminous and have scabies and impetigo. Their nutrition is surprisingly average – doubtless due to extra-familial feeding in schools. The mother is sub-standard mentally. The home, if indeed it can be described as such, has usually the most striking characteristics. Nauseating odours assail one's nostrils on entry, and the source is usually located in some urine-sodden, faecal-stained mattress in an upstairs room. . . The bathroom is obviously the least frequented room of the building. There are sometimes faecal accumulations on the floors upstairs, and tin baths containing several days accumulation of faeces and urine are not unknown. The children, especially the older ones, often seem to be perfectly happy and contented, despite such a shocking environment. They will give a description of how a full-sized midday meal has been cooked and eaten in the house on the day of the visit when the absence of cooking utensils gives the lie to their assertion. One can only conclude that such children have never known restful sleep, that the amount of housework done by the mother is negligible and that the general standard of hygiene is lower than that of the animal world.[12]

This view of mothers' negligence was not about mother-love. Theodore Tucker, for example, acknowledged that "the mother may be genuinely fond of them [children] and loathe to face the pain of separation – and the children themselves will almost certainly wish to remain with her". Neglect in his account was signalled by broken furniture, uncleaned windows, torn blankets and vile smells.[13]

Bowlby's work challenged this hygiene approach. He regarded deprived children as the products of maternal deprivation, rather than the absence of adequate standards of hygiene. Bed-wetting and soiling, he argued, were characteristic of children in institutions, however good their standards of physical care – a result of the separation of children from mother-love. Dirt, at least in moderation, might mean care rather than neglect, as in his contrast between "a docile group of physically well-cared-for children" in an institution and "the same children, rather more grubby perhaps, happily playing in their own or foster-homes". In his emphasis on "the absolute need of infants and toddlers for the continuous care of their mothers", it was the mental health of children which signalled a good home, with maternal deprivation producing a range of disorders, from depression and anxiety, through apathy and aggressiveness to deliquency.

The hygiene and mother-love approaches both emphasized the importance of mothers' work but, as Bowlby makes clear, their requirements frequently conflicted. Winnicott's anxieties that "administrative tidiness, the dictates of hygiene, a laudable urge towards the promotion of bodily health" might "get between the mother and her baby" found expression in a range of settings.[14] A speaker at a 1960 conference was satisfied that professionals were getting less obsessional about standards of hygiene, but was still concerned that "you may prevent dysentery and produce neurosis". In hospitals, it was argued, "nursing administrative techniques and rules of hygiene prevented emotional contacts with the children to a devastating extent".[15] There was increasing concern by the end of the 1950s with hospitals' attitudes towards the mothers of young children, and the Platt Report in 1959 recommended that an obvious way of preserving continuity between the child's hospital and home life was by admitting the mother with the child.

The range of advice available to mothers in mothercraft manuals also developed increasingly child-centred approaches influenced by Freudianism. Most advice was still formulated by men in the 1950s, although manuals by Sir Frederick Truby King's daughter, Mary, and by Mabel Liddiard were available. Truby King, whose work was a major source of expert advice between the wars, had emphasized the importance of sticking rigidly to a feeding schedule – a routine which was hampered by too much mother-love – and mothers were warned of the risk of spreading germs by too much hugging and kissing.

After the war, however, experts developed advice which was in direct opposition to this. Winnicott advocated what he called "natural feeding", which he defined as feeding "given exactly when the baby wants it", and where "a mother naturally follows the desires of her infant".[16] His extraordinary image of devoted motherhood could not have been further from the emphasis on regularity and order and the dangers of enuresis highlighted in the hygiene approach:

> Sometimes the urine trickled down your apron or went right through and soaked you as if you yourself had let slip, and you didn't mind. In fact by these things you could have known that you were a woman, and an ordinary devoted mother.[17]

Psychoanalytic approaches were popularized through Winnicott's broadcasts on BBC radio, a popularization also apparent in Benjamin Spock's texts, imported from America.

Many women who became mothers after the war remained immune to modern child-centred approaches. Some paid little heed to any expert advice, preferring to rely on what their mothers told them, or their own judgements. Gladys Petty records:

> I stopped taking babies to the clinic. I thought I was better off doing what I thought. I found that whatever they said at clinics, babies are different. You just learn from trial and error.[18]

Others record adopting advice which still stressed regularity and discipline. Wynn Nixson gave birth to three children between 1948 and 1960:

Ante-natal exercises were like a military exercise . . . the pre-war ethic of discipline, routine and firm control still ruled . . . you were meant to leave them [babies] outside in their pram . . . if they cried for attention you didn't give it, because that would spoil them.[19]

Pam McKinlay's children were born between 1957 and 1961. She records a memory of Dr Spock, which she either read about or looked at, but she felt that its advice did not apply to her. Instead she adopted a regime similar to Wynn Nixson:

The child had to go into the garden whether it was raining or not, because it was considered the thing . . . fresh air would make them sleep. . . Only in the most inclement weather were they brought indoors, and then they went into the play pen . . . you went from room to room shouting to get them used to your coming and going . . . but you would never take them with you because that would be spoiling, and they had to learn how to behave. Looking back I sometimes think I was quite cruel.[20]

Thus, despite Spock and Winnicott, emphasis on regularity and discipline by no means disappeared in the 1950s. Even as late as 1970, Good Housekeeping's *Home encyclopaedia* had still not revised its advice, first published in 1951, that women should spend their mornings attending to cleaning and cooking, while their babies spent most of their time in a pram or playpen.[21]

Freudian influences drew on American sources, which were prominent in the bibliographies of British writers who disseminated this approach. The shift of attention from bodily to mental health involved accounts where bad wives and mothers were seen as women whose psycho-sexual development had gone awry. In foregrounding the importance of an intimate relationship between a mother and her child, they pathologized gay men and a range of women – lesbians, "frigid women", "neglectful mothers" – in terms of their relationship with their own mothers. Defects in a daughter's development were attributed to her childhood experience of a dominating, weak, neglectful or over-protective mother which in turn made her into a bad mother.

These developments are particularly evident in constructions of unmarried motherhood in the 1950s. Bowlby quoted American and Canadian studies which attributed pregnancy outside marriage to "a

strong unconscious desire to become pregnant", sometimes moti-
vated by the desire "to use the shame of an illegitimate baby as a
weapon against . . . dominating parents".[22] Christine Cooper's
analysis, originally published under medical auspices in *The Prac-
titioner*, was reprinted by the National Council for the Unmarried
Mother and her Child (NCUMC) in 1955:

> Contrary to the common view, the mothers of illegitimate
> children are seldom promiscuous "good time" girls or prosti-
> tutes, for these individuals usually avoid having babies. Whilst
> the social and economic circumstances of the mothers vary
> widely, her illegitimate child is commonly a symptom of her
> neurotic character, resulting from disturbances in her own
> family background. In many cases this disturbance is obvious,
> for instance in the broken or unstable home, but in others more
> subtle emotional factors are found, such as dominance or
> rejection by one or other parent, or early disturbances in the
> parent–child relationship.[23]

This is a watered-down version of the analysis Leontine Young
had developed in an American text published in the previous year
cited by Cooper, which reiterated the view that unmarried mothers
became pregnant not as a result of immorality or free choice but
because of an unconscious wish to bear a child. The "pathological
drama" in which they were absorbed was to do with their past,
homes and childhoods, and particularly with their relationships with
their mothers. "The great majority of unmarried mothers," Young
averred, "come from homes dominated by the mother," although,
she added, some were "father-ridden" rather than "mother-ridden".
In her account, girls who claimed to be pregnant as a result of rape
were merely finding a convenient cover for behaviour instigated by
their unconscious wishes.[24]

This was a very different view of the unmarried mother from that
embodied in the Magdalene regime, which, surviving into the 1950s,
was virtually at an end by the 1960s. Magdalenes, both Catholic and
secular, had incarcerated unmarried mothers, with no contact with
the outside world, to wash the stains of their sin away through
unpaid laundry work. Although many of their inmates had been
transferred from children's homes, and were not unmarried
mothers, they were regarded as "wayward girls" by association.
Regimes stressed the importance of protecting girls in danger of

99

being led astray, and Catherine Fairley, who was in Lochburn Magdalene in Glasgow from 1956 to 1958, records that they were not allowed newspapers except on Sundays, when they were provided with years-old copies of *People's Friend*, from which any references to sexuality had been cut. It was at this Magdalene that the inmates staged a mass escape in 1958, and their allegations of ill-treatment, starvation and beatings produced demands for an inquiry. Lochburn was closed, and its building demolished in 1961.[25]

The NCUMC had already challenged the penitentiary regime between the wars in its intention to provide a "modern home, full of air and sunlight".[26] Like many other agencies it had been committed to keeping illegitimate children and their mothers together whenever possible, and this policy had been endorsed by the Ministry of Health.[27] Christine Cooper, however, drawing on Leontine Young's work, recommended more encouragement to unmarried mothers to have their babies adopted.[28] John Bowlby made the same recommendation, arguing that because a high proportion of unmarried mothers were psychologically disturbed, they were unfitted to give children emotional stability.[29] The NCUMC reached no conclusion on changing its policy in 1953, but took the question seriously, as their reprinting of Christine Cooper's work shows. Although only a minority of unmarried mothers gave birth to their babies in unmarried mothers' homes in this period, those who did were frequently encouraged to have their babies adopted.[30] Not all social workers went along with the Freudian view of the unmarried mother, and Moral Welfare workers employed by religious organizations were particularly resistant, although this did not necessarily mean that they resisted an emphasis on adoption.[31] But, paradoxically, the influence of the Freudian view of unmarried mothers as neurotic could produce a similar outcome to the old penitentiary emphasis on their sinfulness – at least as far as separation from their babies was concerned.

Many British writers and professionals remained immune to the influence of Freudianism and continued to frame their accounts in a medico-moral language with a much longer history, focusing on bodily rather than mental health. Within this white female bodies were pathologized in a variety of ways according to class, race, age, disability, sexuality and marital status. Elizabeth Arthur records that marriage featured on her doctor's prescription pad:

> When I went to a doctor and complained of any ill-health, I was always told it was because I wasn't married and hadn't children – that was what was wrong with me. And when I went to tell the doctor I was getting married, he said, "well, you'll be much better now". In those days although some women had sex outside marriage, I think there were still a number of women who didn't. I wouldn't be a frustrated woman. Presumably that's what he meant. I mean I didn't ask.[32]

As Arthur's account suggests, illness was sometimes associated with spinsterhood, and this was in part connected with the assumption that all spinsters were celibate. Among the illnesses that Blanche Smith listed were 'hysteria, epilepsy, obsessional neurosis, depression, manic schizophrenia, and nervous breakdown". However, marriage did not necessarily effect a cure. "Frigid women", often defined as those who did not have vaginal orgasms, were associated with an even longer list of illnesses including "fatigue, insomnia, backache, headache, including migraine, respiratory infections, indigestion, constipation, dizziness".[33]

Older women were still seen mainly in terms of the menopause. While doctors provided reassurance, stating "categorically that the menopause as such does not cause insanity", keeping themselves healthy was seen as predominantly a matter of coping with hot flushes, giddiness, loss of memory, skin disorders, facial hair, weight gain, mood swings and much else besides. The strategies they were advised to adopt included strict attention to a reducing diet, knitting and crocheting, and learning shorthand or Russian.[34] Older women were reassured that the menopause would not be the end of their marital "sex happiness", but where their husband's sexual pleasure was diminished by the slackness of their vagina, they were advised that plastic repair of the slack supports could restore sexual gratification to both partners.[35]

Literature on disability had its equivalents to learning Russian. Taking up parish work or joining an orchestra were two strategies which were mooted as potential "compensatory activities" for what Joan Clarke defined as normal adult biological experience – "courtship, mating and procreation". Although she did not rule out "normal experience" for all disabled people, sexuality was seen as possible only so long as "physical attraction is unimpaired". The main strategy she suggested was dependence on the advice and guidance of able-bodied confidants and counsellors.[36] Generally, disabled bodies, whether male or female, were not associated with sexuality or reproduction.

Black bodies were pathologized as primitive, animal and dirty in ways which made no distinctions of sex, class, age, disability, sexuality or marital status. Nor did the emphasis on psychology generally extend to groups who were regarded as primitive, and so lacking an inner life, psychological complexity or the capacity for emotional development. The literature on "problem families" was dominated by the hygiene approach, although Bowlby stressed the importance of psychological factors.[37] The literature on black life in Britain also emphasized dirtiness. Black people resisted this construction through a reversal of the modern–primitive, clean–dirty oppositions in their own attribution of backwardness, dirtiness and ignorance to whiteness.

The view of black people as primitive and dirty emerges as a main theme in the stories that black women and men tell. A chapter in Beryl Gilroy's autobiography is called "Keep your hands off me". These are the words a white colleague uses to her when she attempts to help her get rid of a wasp. "Don't touch me, don't ever touch me." But the colleague does not protest when a tramp goes to her aid, and whacks the wasp away. "Rather the tramp and his filth, rather the wasp, rather even the sting of the wasp, than the slightest touch from me."[38] Vi Chambers records, "Shortly after I came here, I was coming down Oxford Street, rushing to catch a bus, and this white lady came up, she was walking, and my hand caught hers, and she brushed her hand like that. 'You bloody nigger', she says."[39] "Did you notice that speck of wet on the floor in the loo, Mrs Ril? . . . Dribs and drabs all over the place! . . . There never used to be specks of wet on the floor in the loo. . . Disgusting I say it is. There must be gremlins with foreign habits in this school." This was another response that Beryl Gilroy records from a white fellow-teacher in a school. Another colleague examined her on questions of health and hygiene, seeing her as "a carrier of fearful tropical diseases".[40] In a different job a white female colleague inquired what "natives" did about their "monthlies", and Gilroy replied with mock seriousness, "We swim! We jump into the nearest river and swim and swim for miles."[41]

A question that was posed to many black people in this period was whether they had lived in trees in Africa, and whether they had tails, a question addressed to migrants from the Caribbean as well as Africa. Elsie George, who was recruited in Nigeria to work in nursing in Britain in the 1950s, records:

The patients wouldn't let you touch them. They get nervous – "ooooh". The children on the children's ward, one day when it was visiting time and this mother came to see her son and her son said, "Mum, will you call nurse?" The mother said, "Well, what for?" He said "Just call that nurse I want to see her, call her". That little boy was three or four. What he said was, "Mum, why is her hand – outside it's black and in there is white". And she said, "Ssh, don't say that, that's how God made her". He said, "No, no, no, she's dirty, she's dirty". The mother said, "No, don't say that any more". After him, one of my colleagues, she was from Wales, a Welsh girl. And after the lecture one day:

"Nurse G, Nurse G," she said.

I said, "Yes, Nurse N."

"Did you live in the jungle?"

I looked and I said, "Oh yes, Nurse N."

"Nurse G, Nurse G" she said.

I said, "Yes, Nurse N."

"Were you living top of the tree?"

I said, "Yes, Nurse N."

"Nurse G, Nurse G. Have you got a tail?"

"Yes, Nurse N."

"Were you wearing a grass skirt?"

I said, "Yes, Nurse N." And believe me, I was really upset, and wondering, what a country. Why, a lot of them had come over to Africa, and they're welcome, they're happy. But what's going on, I thought. So the next morning I picked up a picture from home, I had a lecture, we had a break:

"Nurse N."

"Nurse G?"

I said, "I've got to tell you something, I've got to show you something."

We went to the toilets.

I said, "Now Nurse N., come into this toilet compartment."

"Why?"

I said, "You just go in, I'm coming with you."

We went in and locked the door.

"You know what, you want to see my tail don't you?"

"Yes."

I said, "Alright, you take your pants off, I'll take mine off, and show you the tail."

She said, "No, no."

I said, "Alright", and I got out the photograph and said, "Look at this photograph. You see anybody living on top of the tree?" It was the school children at this Catholic school where I taught last.

She said, "No, Nurse G."

I said, "Are there any grass skirts?"

She said, "No, Nurse G."

"Do you feel I look like a monkey with a tail?"

She said, "No."

I said, "Right, I don't know what made you think that."

She said, "No, no, no. It's what they taught us in school. I will never again."

I said, "Well what sort of education system is this? Why should they discriminate?" But it still carries on. In the '50s, you go on a bus, you can't find a seat. You sit there, and they don't want you to sit near them.[42]

Even in ostensibly favourable images of black people in Britain, where their spontaneity was routinely contrasted to British constraint they were constructed as primitive and animal. In *Sapphire* there is an opposition between black bodies as rhythmic and sexual, and white bodies which do not respond to the beat of the bongo. Montgomery Pew, the main white character in Colin MacInnes's novel *City of spades*, constructs the same opposition in reflecting on black migrants: "And I say thank goodness they've come into our midst . . . because they bring an element of joy and fantasy and violence into our cautious, ordered lives."[43]

In many black women's narratives the meanings of clean–modern and dirty–primitive are reversed. Dirtiness and backwardness are major characteristics of white life. Mrs H records:

Now I buy fish and chips, but in those days I wouldn't because they have this big newspaper to wrap it in, and we in our country say newspaper is not clean. Those things amazed me when we come here. I see how they had the bread not even wrapped up.[44]

In Vi Chambers's account, English life is marked by lack of hygiene:

I would not readily have a glass of water from any and every white person as I do not feel that all white people are necessarily clean. For example, I once had a neighbour whose little girl I used to look after. She also had a son and one evening the little boy had a wee on the floor, and she just took the dish rag and wiped the floor and just dropped it back in the kitchen sink. I was so shocked. . . I went in the pub with my husband one day, and a man came in the pub with his miniature poodle, and he had his beer glass, and the little poodle is lapping the beer out of the glass. Animals are animals, not human beings. . . Can you have a dog sleeping in your bed?[45]

In *Black teacher* Gilroy portrays her encounter with the white working class in her work as a teacher in London schools as an encounter with dirt, disease, backwardness and ignorance.

Sexuality and home

The home emerges as an ambiguous place within health discourse. As a private sphere it was seen as the place where needs for intimacy should be met through monogamous life-long marriage and parent–child relationships. Defining the "ordinary good home" in terms of "ordinary good parents" and particularly of "the mother's tremendous contribution, *through her being devoted*", Winnicott set this in opposition to the bad home where parents were psychiatric cases, immature, anti-social, unmarried, in an unstable relationship or separated, identifying a need to ensure that while these parents got attention from society, there remained as little interference as possible – he recommended "organised non-interference" – with the ordinary good mother–infant relationship.[46] Winnicott's preoccupations suggest a strong impulse to keep a separation between public and private, where only "bad homes" were subject to public scrutiny and intervention.

However, there were also many concerns about the adequacy of homes to secure stable and happy family life. Where Bowlby saw juvenile delinquency as a product of maternal deprivation, other accounts identified failures in parental control as the cause of delinquency and of increases in venereal diseases among young people. In campaigns for sex education even what Winnicott saw as the "ordinary good home" was identified as deficient and most of those who urged the establishment, improvement or reform of sex education recommended public intervention. They deplored the harmful effects of ignorance on family life and marriage and affirmed that instruction should ideally be given within the family by parents. Recognizing that they were contesting the view that sexuality belonged to the sphere of intimacy and privacy, they justified public initiatives precisely on the grounds that "far too many parents were unable to talk freely to their children about sex".[47]

A strong theme in accounts by women who grew up between the wars is the shame and secrecy surrounding sexuality, which extended to menstruation, contraception, divorce, sexual violence and sexual abuse of children as well as to many aspects of mother-hood, with not only abortion, but also pregnancy and childbirth, whispered. Hoggart, arguing that working-class girls were not as promiscuous as boys, attributed this to their "ignorance about the facts of sex", and saw this ignorance as their protection from danger, enabling them to "walk through the howling valley of sex-approaches from the local lads and probably of sex-talk at work, and come through to the boy they were going to marry quite untouched mentally or physically'.[48] In accounts by women, however, the language of lowered tones, whisperings, mutterings and silence which surrounded sexuality and most aspects of the body were productive of much misery and fear. This is a common and major theme in accounts across differences of class, race and sexuality.

Writing in 1973, Mary Stott recorded her inter-war adolescence as a time of misery and shame about her body. Among the words that she did not have in her vocabulary were puberty, pubic hair, womb and vagina. Among those which she rarely heard or used were periods, pregnant and childbirth. "The period of the development of my bosom and pubic hair is a total blank to me," she writes, "probably because the embarrassment of this unexplained phenomenon was so acute that I had to thrust it out of consciousness." What she minded most about adolescence was that childbirth itself was a taboo subject: "I was twenty-one when my brother's wife became pregnant, and my mother whispered it to me as if it were a secret not very nice to talk about." Menstruation was not even whispered, for her mother only supplied her with a bag of towelling diapers, with no explanation and no word to use for what they were for. Discussion of sexuality was proscribed as dirty. "Copulation, conception and childbirth were kept hidden under impenetrable wraps."[49]

In oral testimony, many women see their ignorance of sexuality when young as a product of a narrow-minded background or their own naïvety, but accounts from a range of women suggest that ignorance was not a product of any particular background, and that impenetrable wraps covered many women, regardless of their race or class. As a black woman, Pauline Crabbe experienced the birth of her first child in ways which were similar to Mary Stott. Her family had migrated to Britain from Jamaica in 1919 bringing two servants with them. When her first child was born in 1936, "having G was a terrible experience, I knew nothing about it. My mother had never told me anything. For quite a long time I thought it came through the navel."[50] In Evelyn Haythorne's depiction of her childhood and adolescence in a working-class mining village in Yorkshire, a language of whisperings, mutterings and silence is a main theme. Secrecy extends not only to sexuality, pregnancy and childbirth, but also to the rape of her brother's girl-friend. There is a particular silence about lesbianism until her mother uses the word during the war:

As I had never heard of the word lesbian before I did not know what she was ranting and raving about so I asked her what was wrong. . . She bent over me and with a finger pointing nearly up my nose said, "You listen and listen good. You don't have anything to do with that sort. They are sick, they are a pack of dirty buggers and no decent persons have owt to do with them".[51]

Lesbian remained one of the dirtiest words of all after the war. Film-goers did not often see overt representations of lesbians or gay men, since, until 1961, American production codes forebade this.

When *The killing of Sister George* was staged in London in 1965, it was passed by the censors only because the word lesbian was never used. There was an almost complete absence of lesbians in women's fiction.[52] Dilys Rowe complained of this lack of attention in 1962, noting that while public awareness of male homosexuality was beginning to put parents on their guards against the emotional traps that turned boys into inverts, "the possibilities hardly ever occur to most parents of girls". She wanted some democratization of homosexuality, arguing that lesbians should receive as much attention as gay men, for, she averred, "the fact is that lesbianism may be no less pitiable, no less sexually repulsive and no less destructive of lives than much male homosexuality".[53]

Lesbian as a dirty word features in the autobiographies of lesbians in the period – and for some this dirtiness meant that it was a word they did not use to define themselves. Pat G. had never heard the word, "and when I finally did hear it I couldn't say it for years. It seemed such an ugly word – I didn't mind the word 'homo', somehow that was more acceptable." Richel Pinney bracketed lesbian with "slime, muck, the devil – all the other dirty words you can think of. . . I even find it difficult to use now. I will use homosexual anytime, rather than lesbian."[54] For black lesbians, there could be additional difficulties. Marie migrated to England from Barbados in 1960, where the word she used was *wicca*, and had been in England for several years before she first heard the word lesbian.[55]

The wraps under which heterosexuality was hidden were not usually completely impenetrable, but they were much more likely to be lifted in the workplace than in the home. The workplace was where women could find out about contraception as well as joke and banter about sexuality, although this was not usually true of occupations like domestic service.[56] Winifred James, who left school at 14 in 1933, stayed at home to do the housework on her father's farm, while he dispensed with the live-in maid, thus saving on her wages and her food. Bitterly resenting the injustice of waiting on her brothers for sixpence a week, she went into service. Her mother, who had been in service herself, suggested she applied for a job at Marks and Spencers:

Nobody tells you anything. I didn't learn about all that goes on until I went to Marks and Spencers. And then I got my eyes

open. I was naive. All these girls who worked on the counters –
well! My mother never told me anything – never. She used to
make us cloths from sheets – we didn't have sanitary towels or
anything – she made them, and they went in a bucket and then
they were boiled. I don't remember what my mother told me
about it. Not much.[57]
War service is also seen by many women as a time in their lives when
their eyes were opened, and bodies and sexuality explicitly acknowledged in the language of everyday conversation.[58]

Health discourse mounting a challenge to this shame and secrecy
identified sex education as the main solution. Campaigns were
orchestrated by a wide range of professionals working across
education, health and social services, with professional women
prominent among campaigners. The Women's Group on Public
Welfare, for example, recommended in 1962 that "While parents
. . . if possible, should help their children to understand about sex
relationships, it is clear that all parents cannot be relied upon to do so
– hence there must be some sex instruction for all girls and boys
before they leave school."[59] The British Medical Association,
investigating increases among venereal disease in young people in
1964, had as one of its aims the promotion of co-operation between
the religious bodies, the medical profession and the social services.[60]
It reported that "witnesses repeatedly emphasised to us that far too
many parents were unable to talk freely to their children about sex.
Sometimes the barrier is an emotional one, sometimes it is merely
that the parents cannot find suitable words." In answer to the
question who should give sex education, the answer that was
increasingly offered was the members recruited by the British
Medical Association to serve on its committee – teachers and nurses,
church workers and social workers as well as doctors.

The Wolfenden Report of 1957 might be read as flowing in the
opposite direction from sex education campaigns with their emphasis on the need for public interventions. In relation to male
homosexuality the recommendation was for a decriminalization of
homosexual intimacy between adult men, so long as it was in private.
The function of the law, it was argued, should not extend to
intervention in the private life of citizens, nor be used as a means of
enforcing any particular pattern of behaviour further than was
necessary to ensure the preservation of public order and decency.

"We do not think it is proper for the law to concern itself with what a man does in private unless it can be shown to be so contrary to the public good that the law ought to intervene in its function as the guardian of the public good."[61] Privacy thus became the yardstick for judging the appropriateness of legal intervention, with "what a man does in private" exempted. Among other grounds for the argument here was the notion of a democratization of sexualities which were disapproved. Lesbianism and adultery, the Report argued, were not criminal offences even though they earned widespread condemnation – male homosexuality should be brought into line with these.

Wolfenden, however, also included a section on therapeutic measures for gay men, which marshalled a range of health and other professionals to the cause of treatment, including not only doctors and psychiatrists, but also clergymen, psychiatric social workers and probation officers. Although arguing that homosexuality should not be regarded as a disease, the Committee nevertheless saw it as a matter which belonged to the discourse of health. Treatment was seen as appropriate regardless of whether homosexual acts were public, and, within their recommendations, criminal offences, or "what a man does in private" and, within their recommendations, outside the scope of the law. Thus, rather than privatizing sexuality, the need for public intervention was shifted away from the law towards health.

Sex education campaigns did not write off the pre-war generation as a lost cause, but they did target the post-war generation particularly, and especially girls. Michael Schofield, interviewing teenagers in the early 1960s, found that 86 per cent of girls compared to 47 per cent of boys had received some kind of formal sex education in schools, and that the amount of sex education given to girls did not vary among different types of school. More girls than boys also received parental advice on sex at home, he found, but in the majority of cases this was unspecific and mainly a matter of "moral exhortation" – for example, "no one wants soiled goods".[62] Much sex education was also confined to vague moral warnings or animal biology. At a number of schools, some minimal knowledge of reproduction was imparted, framed around the activities of the rabbit or the frog. When it went beyond this, sex education for girls always focused on the importance of marriage, and could be confined to advice about how to stop men "going too far".[63]

Jean Grant was born in 1945, but her account of growing up in the 1950s reflects as much misery and shame about the body as Mary Stott's from an adolescence nearly 40 years earlier:

As soon as I started feeling conscious of my body changing, I didn't take a bath any more in front of the fire because it was too public. So I started doing what they call strip washes by the fire. . . I made a great big nightie at school when I was eleven, and it was like a big tent with long sleeves and a high neck and it went down to the floor and it was massive. I would stand at the sink so nobody could see the front of you, and I would always turn the mirror the opposite way round so that anybody looking in the mirror wouldn't be able to see me. I would wash myself underneath the nightie without taking it off, and then I would thread the clothes underneath, take my arms out of the nightie and put my clothes on underneath and get dressed. Because nobody actually said to me that you had to be ashamed of your body, but the general feeling I got was that it always should be covered up – you never exposed it to anyone. I got the impression that if you did, you were bad.

When I started my periods, I didn't know anything at all about them. I know a lot of girls at school had periods, but I didn't know what they were. And you didn't ask, well you didn't know what to ask, you didn't know what it was to ask a question about it. But I can remember that the first time I was bleeding, I called my sister – we had an outside toilet in the yard – and I said to her that I was bleeding, and was all my inside going to come out. I was frightened. I didn't know why I was bleeding. And she just said "No, I'll just go and tell mum and then I'll come back".

So I expected my mum to come back, and stayed on the toilet – it was dark and I hadn't taken the torch with me. . . My sister came back and she brought this long Winceyette sheeting. I recognised it as being from my mum and dad's bed. . . And I had to roll it up into about six, and I was told to put that there to catch it. But I didn't know what you did about when it was full, so I just kept rerolling it as many different ways as you could to always get a clean bit by you, and each night washed it in the sink under the cold water, and then in salt water. That was the most embarrassing thing. We had an old pan with a lid on, especially to soak them and it was kept in the back kitchen. And it was always in the corner of the scullery and I used to absolutely hate this thing, because somebody would always lift the lid off it. I just was so embarrassed about it. I actually went for years not knowing what menstruation was. I was fourteen when I started but very naive. I didn't know that you could have babies once you'd started periods. I didn't know any of that. You were just naive about it. And then when I was sixteen at the chemists there was a little booklet on the counter, and it said about menstruation. So I bought this little book and read it, but I didn't dare tell anyone that I'd got the book. Because I felt like it was a dirty book.[64]

Like Mary Stott, Jean Grant had no words for adolescent body changes:

Sex before marriage was dirty, periods were dirty. I would even cringe now at the f word. You didn't know anything about homosexuality and lesbianism. You didn't talk openly in a group about anything. They called everything below the waist the bottom. Breasts were your chest. Women in dirty magazines had breasts.[65]

Jean Grant's experiences were particularly common among girls who grew up as Catholics, through church teachings about the female body, although Jean Grant was not herself a Catholic. They were shared by other women of her generation. Barbara Marsh, a black woman who migrated to England in 1962, had spent her post-war adolescence in Jamaica:

I had my period at fourteen – my mother didn't tell me anything, she never said nothing until this day. . . We didn't get any biology lesson. I wasn't frightened owing to the fact that I used to read . . . grown-up books. They mention periods – they call it "menstruation", they didn't say "period". . . The only thing that worried me, true, was my mother wasn't very friendly. I didn't know how to go and tell her: "Well, it's started". For instance people was so silly, if you start having breasts, they start telling you off, as if it's something wrong you done, and it's nothing wrong, it's not your fault, it's something natural, but they didn't treat you as if it was natural.[66]

As these accounts suggest, silence and secrecy remained common among women in the post-war generation, handed on by mothers from inter-war childhoods, who in their turn found a refusal of this aspect of their mothers' lives difficult in the 1950s. As Jean Grant records:

> The rules weren't said, they were just there. I suppose you got the feel of them by how mum or dad spoke about things – about what they heard on the wireless, what happened to somebody down the road who got pregnant out of wedlock as they would call it then, which was a major sin at that time. So, you got all these vibes and because you were never asked your opinion you took on board all this information, and then you lived your life by it.[67]

Health discourse was one way in which women could resist shame and secrecy, enabling women who entered professions like social work, or who volunteered to be marriage guidance counsellors, to acquire a vocabulary for sexuality which usually centred on the importance of marriage. Other women's resistances came through experiences of workplaces like factories, offices and shops, although these provided a different, much less formal language and knowledge, often through jokes and banter. In 1963, a group of lesbians formed the Minorities Research Group to help those who felt guilty or isolated, which led to the first all-lesbian publication in 1964.[68] In 1962 Doris Lessing provided the first fictional account of menstruation in *The golden notebook*.

Encountering women

"I thought he was so very different from all the other fellows; he didn't bring the body into it."[69] This is the voice of one of the women interviewed by Moya Woodside in her study of patterns of marriage. Reviewing her book in 1952, J. H. Robb commented, "One would like to know if the girl who said [this] of her husband's behaviour during courtship was frigid, had unhappily married parents, a dominating mother, and married one of the 'introverted' types referred to earlier in the book."[70]

This encounter captures one of the many ways in which women were represented in health discourse. The reviewer may be objecting to the voice because it is not enthusiastic about heterosexuality, or because it reflects the view that the body and sexuality are problematic and difficult for women. In either case, disinclination or shame about sexuality that is to do with marriage – "her husband's behaviour during courtship" – are seen not just as mistaken, but as a symptom of pathology, couched here in terms of a popularized Freudianism.

Encounters like this became common after the war, were by no means confined to the pages of journals and were often between women. With the decline of residential domestic service, the welfare state, through its provision of health, education and social services, replaced domestic service as a key place where women met across differences. Since both the recruitment of women as workers in health and social services and the range of women who used these services crossed differences of class, race, sexuality, age and disability there was a rich diversity of such encounters in clinics, schools, welfare centres, hospitals, doctors' waiting rooms and surgeries and, through home visits, in the home. It was motherhood that was a main reason for many of these encounters which focused especially on pregnancy, childbirth and child care, with the paid and unpaid work of women as mothers overlapping in many ways, both in the tasks and the women involved. A woman might find herself at different moments in her life in a labour room giving birth to her own baby and delivering someone else's as a midwife, collecting welfare orange juice and distributing it, feeding another woman's baby and feeding her own.

The institutions and agencies of the welfare state were not only places where women met across differences. Their policies and processes also played a part in constructing such differences. This is particularly apparent in the recruitment and training of women to employment whose major purpose was to teach other women how to be better mothers and to create better homes, and in the differential way in which the provisions of the welfare state were available to women on the basis of how far their motherhood and homes were socially approved.

The need to foster the good home was a main aim of agencies who dealt with "problem families". Although "problem family" mothers' neglect sometimes led to intervention to remove children, the post-war emphasis on keeping them in their own homes involved the increasing recruitment of women to train and encourage mothers to improve their standards both as paid and voluntary workers. The

Woman health officer saw health visitors as the best-placed of all social workers to ascertain the potential problem family, and in some areas they specialized in work with those they had identified. The work of the Women's Voluntary Service (wvs) included home visits, "to show the mother how to clean her home, care for her children, shop and cook", while in some local authorities women were paid to do such work as home advisers or home helps. The National Society for the Prevention of Cruelty to Children (nspcc) appointed women visitors for the same purpose. Schemes were developed to give home-training in prison to mothers who were convicted of child neglect, but there was also support for putting them on probation, with a requirement that they should reside in a home "where they are trained in the care of their children and the management of their homes". Residential homes opened to give instruction in child care, hygiene, family budgeting and cooking recruited women to provide this training.[71]

Child care was a main task in which women participated both as paid workers and mothers. Although mainly formulated by men, expert advice on child care was disseminated by women, as midwives, health visitors and social workers. The extent to which employment in child care was feminized is illustrated by the history of children's departments. The person qualified to fill the new post of children's officer recommended by the Curtis Committee was referred to as "she". "We use the feminine pronoun," they reported, "not with any aim of excluding men from these posts, but because we think it may be found that the majority of persons suitable for the work are women."[72] Two-thirds of the children's officers appointed by 1951 were women. By 1961 women also comprised more than 90 per cent of those who had received training as child care officers, and almost 90 per cent of those who received a certificate in the residential care of children.[73]

Through this recruitment, encounters between women could involve extensive intervention and scrutiny of mothers' work – most common for those judged "unfit", a category which included unmarried mothers who kept their children as well as "neglectful mothers". Such mothers could also come under scrutiny from female researchers. One research project, undertaken by a woman, tested the intelligence of 100 "neglectful mothers" between 1948 and 1954, administering a Stanford-Binet test.[74] Research on unmarried mothers found them vacillating in their attitudes to their children: alternatively neglectful and over-protective.[75] Health visitors collected information for Blacker's inquiry into the "problem family" and in the notes about how they were received reported considerable resistance to their project. There were three classifications: "those who felt themselves to be in need of help and who took the investigator into their confidence . . . those described as 'plausible', 'glib' or 'untruthful' who seemed to mistrust the investigator . . . and those who were openly hostile, offensive and rude".[76]

Training in health and social services was uneven in the period, with the Younghusband Report in 1959 deploring the "long history of failure to take the vigorous action necessary to provide trained social workers", but it was developed in the period for many occupations.[77] It often provided reinforcement for the view that women should abandon their professional work when they bore children themselves, at least while children were young. Elizabeth Arthur served in the Voluntary Aid Detachment (VAD) during the war, studied social science at Glasgow University in the late 1940s and went on to do professional training for social work in the 1950s:

> I went back to college, to the London School of Economics where I did what was called a generic course to follow my social science diploma, so I could become a medical social worker – an almoner as it was called then. My greatest wish was to marry and have children. I felt very strongly if you had children, you shouldn't dream of work while you had them. On the course with me was a woman who had a child of two which she left in the care of a baby-minder, and I and another woman of my age on the course thought that was dreadful. We thought she shouldn't be doing the course, or that she shouldn't have had the child. And now of course I don't think that. Later on I appreciated you could like children without wanting to spend every minute with them. I just remember being shocked by this woman, and how could she be a social worker and tell other people how to bring up children when she was leaving this two-year old.[78]

The view that employment when children were young was incompatible with being a good mother and a good social worker was sometimes reinforced by professional training. Among questions set in examinations for health visitors and nurses in the early 1950s was: "How in any particular family could a young mother be saved from going out to work?"[79]

Elizabeth Wilson who was employed in psychiatric social work in the 1960s, records reservations about the way in which her training structured her differences from other women:

> as defined by my colleagues, my work was to help women to be better mothers – not an aim with which I had much sympathy, or for which I was appropriately equipped. What I'd wanted from psychoanalysis was to understand myself, not police other women.[80]

The history of encounters between women in the welfare state includes resistance by many women both as providers and users of services to the way in which such differences were structured, including the influence of class and race.

Class is a strong theme in anxieties about ignorance, which were often attributed by professionals to working-class women. Moya Woodside found that they regarded treatment for illness as a last recourse, and that gynaecological conditions caused particular shyness and reluctance to undergo examination and treatment. Even women who had had several children, she reported, disliked the idea of discussing menstrual or sex difficulties with a doctor, especially when the doctor was male. "They also have a fear," she added, "sometimes justified, that their complaints will be dismissed with scant sympathy." She defined the main bar to measures for combatting ill-health as working-class women's "ignorance of hygiene, of the care of the body, of the simple principles of physiology and nutrition".[81] At the same time her account suggests some of the ways in which working-class women resisted the construction of their ignorance as "old wives' tales" – one of which was to avoid contact with middle-class professionals.

Class and race infused encounters in complex ways. Although black women often encountered white patients who did not want them to touch them, a theme in some accounts is the way in which white working-class women sought them out as confidants. "I've 'eard say that black people don't harp on the rights and wrongs of things," Beryl Gilroy reports as the reason she was sought out by a white woman who had borne twins by her father.[82] Pauline Crabbe, who worked for the NCUMC in the 1950s, records that some white working-class women told her they felt easier with her than with a white counsellor. "One woman said, 'you speak like us'."[83] Both accounts seem to suggest a white view that black women could provide what Gilroy calls "black consolation" regardless of class differences, a view which was reinforced by the way in which white people rarely saw black people as middle-class whatever their occupational identity.

One example of the way in which the welfare state constructed differences between women and children is a theme in Pauline Crabbe's account of her work at the NCUMC. Counselling black women as well as white, she found that while white working-class women might seek her out in preference to a white counsellor, this did not mean that she could give the same advice to both groups:

There were two options discussed in counselling – which were to continue with the pregnancy and keep the baby, or to continue with the pregnancy and part with the baby via adoption. Black women couldn't do this though, because there was no adoption for black babies. All adoption societies were run by white people and occasionally mixed race children could be placed if they were not very black, but they were difficult to place.[84]

As Crabbe's account suggests, black children were generally seen as "unadoptable", despite her own resistance to this in her work. As the recommendations of the Curtis Committee embodied in the 1948 Children Act were developed and reinforced in subsequent legislation, through to the 1963 Children and Young Persons Act, the view that attempts should be made to find foster or adoptive parents for those in institutions was increasingly emphasized, but this approach did not extend to black children.

Gilroy's work as a teacher brought her into contact with a rather different version of black children's adoptability. "Once a year," she records, "without fail, the children 'saved Black Babies'. They paid half-a-crown each, chose a name for the child, and were given a photograph as a token." One seven-year old boy voiced to her his view of this scheme – "Yeh! Nah the poor little bleeder won't be a pagan no more."[85] This view of white Christian duties did not apply to black children and children of mixed parentage in the metropolis, whose construction as "unadoptable" was shared by white disabled children. A 1958 study of adoption commented that "a very large number of children of mixed races are unadoptable. . . It is encouraging that, in spite of prejudice, many of these picanninies manage to make their way in the world quite well." In 1966 another study stated that "it will never be easy to place babies who are deaf, crippled or coloured".[86]

As Crabbe's account also suggests, this view of children as "unadoptable" could reflect the attitudes of potential adoptive parents, but was particularly a product of the policy of adoption agencies. Some foster-mothers were also reluctant to care for black children, while others said that they would take a coloured child "if he [was] not too dark".[87] At the same time agencies did not include blackness in their definitions of the good homes where they sought to place children – either in relation to the recruitment of adoptive parents or to the children they were placing. Many would not accept responsibility for finding suitable adopters for black children, only mentioning white children to potential white adoptive parents. Thus, unless adoptive parents themselves brought up the subject of black children, they were not placed.[88] This is the situation depicted in a poem by Jackie Kay, using the voice of a white adoptive mother. In the early 1960s, the agency tells her at first that "they had no babies", but when she chanced "it didn't matter what colour it was", they discovered that, after all, *"we have a baby for you"*.[89] The poem concludes,

to think she wasn't even thought of as a baby,
my baby, my baby.

The history of encounters between women and children in the welfare state follows no simple line. Although class and race are major themes, one effect of health discourse was to construct a division between the modern woman and all those who were seen as outside this, through their reliance on the advice of mothers or "old wives' tales", or refusal to listen to scientific expertise. Some providers as well as users of services were among those who were seen as falling outside definitions of the good home and the good mother. As workers in the welfare state women were also involved in offering very considerable support for other women and for children – delivering babies, distributing orange juice and milk, advising on feeding, teething and colic – as well as in prescription and scrutiny. Since both providers and users crossed so many lines of difference and providers in one role were users in another, the welfare state could be experienced as both supportive and oppressive, sometimes simultaneously. Buchi Emecheta records that when she went into hospital for the birth of her fifth child, a social worker found homes for her children, but despiteeeee her plea that all four should stay in one home, they were split between two. However, a nurse came to her aid in getting home to reunite her family. "She begged the ambulance man to drive me home and promised to see to it that they sent me a home nurse. . . . She was so young, yet she understood; but then we were both blacks and maybe, like me, she knew what the word 'family' ought to mean."[90]

Motherhood mandates

It is in the history of motherhood mandates that the raced construction of the good home is most apparent. It was generally defined by the presence of children, with childlessness in married couples assumed to be involuntary – a sad lack rather than a choice – reflecting a view of motherhood as a woman's ultimate completion and fulfilment. Motherhood was mandatory for most married women in constructions of white femininity and seen as a sign of psychological maturity. After 1945, there was increased emphasis on making medical help available to infertile married couples, and donor insemination, as well as hormone treatments for threatened miscarriages, began to be developed. But the motherhood mandate was not universal, with a variety of white women excluded, mainly because of their sexuality or marital status. Black women, however, were excluded regardless of these.

Jephcott's account of large families in Notting Hill as the "survival of byegone patterns" suggests some of the shifts in views of motherhood between 1945 and 1964 as well as the way in which black women were beginning to be seen as over-fecund by the mid-1960s. Pronatalist prescriptions in the late 1940s had judged women with small families to be deficient in their duty to the nation, although this was usually combined, even by the most ardent pronatalists, with an advocacy of "voluntary parenthood" through the use of birth control. During the 1950s the limitation of family size came to be seen as desirable although abortion remained illegal. The family with an "only child" – Margaret Jackson's "solitary ewe lamb" – was still commonly stigmatized, but the most common ideal of family size in the 1950s was the "pigeon pair" – one boy and one girl, preferably in that order.

The view of motherhood as a sign of psychological maturity was particular evident in constructions of white female sexuality. Despite more emphasis in ideals of companionate marriage on women's "sex fulfilment" and "sex happiness", and the democratization of sexual pleasure between husband and wife, the notion that pleasure was to be equally shared stressed a male sex drive in contrast to women's fulfilment through bearing children. As David Mace, one of the founders of the National Marriage Guidance Council, argued, ". . . it's only the unnatural masculine woman who can be satisfied for very long with sex alone".[91] Sex in such accounts always meant heterosexual intercourse. The British Medical Association argued in 1964 that:

> To have a baby is the instinctive wish of many girls. . . The psychological reactions of women to sex are much deeper and more complex than those of men. This is partly because, for women, sex is predominantly the route to motherhood and a family, and partly because of the age-long social and religious attitude towards womankind. For the woman, complete sexual satisfaction almost always demands an emotional relationship with her partner.[92]

Thus female sexuality was seen as part of an emotional commitment to relationships and a prelude to the joys of family life. In contrast the BMA argued that for men "sexual intercourse may be no more than a transient physical experience" which might "satisfy their desire without the development of any personal relationship".

Women who were usually regarded as over-active sexually – as unmarried mothers, adulteresses and prostitutes – were among those to whom the motherhood mandate did not extend. Lesbians, seen as overactive "addicts", but at the same time as frigid in relation to the requirement of heterosexuality, were also excluded. Spinsters who were commonly seen as under-active sexually became a focus of anxieties in a 1960 government report which argued that "in no circumstances should a single woman be artificially inseminated", and which also recommended that widows and married women living apart from their husbands should be excluded from donor insemination.[93] Nor did the mandate run among all married women. Mothers in "problem families" were seen as over-fecund, with the presence of "over-numerous children" one of the ways in which they were defined. The maternity of white women who were married to black men was seen as problematic rather than desirable.

Black women were excluded from the motherhood mandate regardless of their sexuality and marital status. In the 1950s this exclusion took the form of a construction of black femininity where it was not associated with motherhood or potential motherhood. Although achieving some limited visibility in the 1950s in cultural representations of "immigrants" as a figure who would tame and domesticate black men, the focus on "miscegenation" meant that it was white women's motherhood of children fathered by black men that was highlighted in race discourse, not black women's own motherhood. No images of black motherhood were produced in Britain which were comparable to the earth mother image in some Caribbean literature.[94]

The "mammy" image, common in America, also had little currency in Britain, although it was consumed by audiences of Hollywood films like Gone with the wind. The mammy, as one way in which black female bodies were defined in America, represented a nurturing, desexualized and motherly figure – usually large. Although constructing the black woman as without family – in an association with motherhood and children which was through her connections with white family life – the mammy image provided a notion of relationship between black and white women, where the former served the latter and her children in a spirit of devotion and contentment.[95] Its use in advertisements for a range of foods meant that black femininity in America was also associated with domesticity.

Where in America black women were employed as nannies in white families in the mammy tradition, the employment of black or Asian women in this role was rare in Britain. In a colonial context, Indian women had commonly been employed as ayahs to care for white children in memsahibs' households, but there was a clear division between what was seen as appropriate in a colonial context and in a metropolitan one. Rosina Visram has shown the way in which ayahs were employed to care for children as travelling nannies on voyages back from India to Britain, forming "the most valuable adjunct to the whole life style of the Raj between Britain and India". But they were usually discharged on arrival, with no provision for a return passage.[96] There are occasional hints of the mammy image in the way in which black nurses were seen in Britain after the war, but they also encountered white fear of intimate contact between black and white bodies. "I went to a hospital in Fulham as an auxiliary", one woman records, ". . . they [patients] don't want you to come near, they don't want you to touch them".[97] "Many of the patients were really horrible although they were ill", Lucille Newman records, "they don't want you even to touch them".[98]

Black women were not wanted as nannies in Britain. Mrs B, who came to Britain in 1955, had worked looking after children in Jamaica, but in Britain she worked making car parts in a factory. "At that time you wouldn't get that sort of job here," she records, "because they didn't even want to rent you a room, much less to say, well you could look after their kids".[99] As a student at Hull University, Amanda Murphy had a summer job working as a nanny, but her employers were a white American family.[100] The ways in which black women's bodies were seen as the opposite of nurturing and comforting in relation to their own babies is apparent in Beryl Gilroy's autobiographical account:

> One day I took my son to the Welfare Clinic, and was forced by the delay in seeing the doctor to feed him there. My brown breast with the darker circle around the nipple was a major attraction to the woman who sat beside me. "Look at it!" she appealed to all the other mothers, "that blackness round 'er tits! D'you reckon that's good for the baby?"[101]

In the early 1960s race discourse shifted attention away from miscegenation towards black women's reproduction. There was a preoccupation with numbers, with an array of figures produced in the context of discussion of the need to control numbers entering. Statistics were used to show that black and Asian women were taking up beds in maternity hospitals, and that it was "virtually impossible for English women to be admitted to hospital for first confinements because the beds were full of immigrants".[102] It was in the context of their increased visibility, focusing on their motherhood, that, in 1966, the Family Planning Association decided to extend advice on contraception to unmarried women. The decision was influenced by the view that "many respectable women who followed the West Indian men, who had been recruited to work London's trains and buses, had not actually married them. . . The decision to help the unwed came with the West Indians."[103] When black femininity was associated with motherhood it was in the context of concerns to limit black women's reproduction.

The exclusion of black women from motherhood mandates had implications for their position in relation to the provisions of the expanded post-war welfare state. In constructing indigenous women as primarily wives and mothers, the state gave them support, so long as they were seen as good mothers creating good homes. Provisions for women generally came through motherhood and were particularly for children, but they flowed in the direction of motherhood mandates.

The child-centredness of state policy is apparent in the wide range of support available to mothers and their children. Family allowances acknowledged for the first time a need for economic provision for women with more than one child. The Welfare Foods Service, begun in 1940 with the National Milk Scheme, provided a range of benefits for pregnant women and young children, including subsidized or free milk and cod liver oil. Welfare orange juice, available until the late 1950s, features strongly in accounts by women whose childhoods belonged to that period. The School Meals Service was expanded "with the aim of securing high standards of physique and general health".[104] The National Health Service meant free antenatal care for pregnant women and free childbirth and post-natal care at home or in hospital. Th 1944 Education Act raised the school leaving age and expanded the provision of special education for disabled children.

There were often very considerable gains for girls growing up in the 1950s as the welfare state secured for them standards of nutrition, medical care and educational provision to an extent unknown in their mothers' generation, and provided the route from grammar school to university which is such a common theme in their autobiographical accounts. As Carolyn Steedman records:

> The 1950s was a time when state intervention in children's lives was highly visible, and experienced, by me at least, as entirely beneficent. . . Within that period of time more children were provided with the goods of the earth than had any generation been before. What my mother lacked, I was given.[105]

As Steedman suggests, benefits for the women who were the mothers of the post-war generation were not necessarily commensurate with those of their children, and their gains through the range of provisions for their pregnancies, childbirth and children's welfare were mainly through motherhood. Those who were dedicated to familial goals frequently welcomed the chance to give their children better opportunities through health and educational services than they themselves had experienced. At the same time facilitating this provision often involved considerable work. State provision was predicated on the assumption that mothers would act as mediators, taking their children to clinics, hospitals, doctors' surgeries and schools. As the Central Office of Information reported in 1959:

> The practical concern of parents that their children should receive full advantage from the services available is shown by the fact that three out of four mothers take the trouble to attend welfare centres with their babies, by the success of the campaign for the voluntary immunisation of young children against diptheria, and by the growth of parent-teacher associations and other associations of parents.[106]

Mediating state provision also involved domestic work. While education and the National Health Service were free, children needed clothes, shoes and equipment to take advantage of provisions, and these had to be bought or made and maintained, involving shopping, sewing, mending, washing and tidying. Paid work was also undertaken by women so that children could take advantage of educational opportunities.

Housing recurs in many women's accounts as a provision which was highly valued, as the state subsidized not only houses in the public rented sector but also owner-occupation through tax relief on mortgages. Hierarchies of benefit are particularly apparent in the list provided by one writer on homelessness in the 1950s of those whose difficulties in securing the tenancy of a house could be almost insuperable. They were women who were unmarried, widowed or legally separated from or deserted by, husbands.[107] Housing also recurs in accounts from women in these groups as a main difficulty and, in the case of mothers, one which could mean parting from their children or a need to stay in unwanted marriages to avoid such partings. Unmarried mothers avoided separation from their babies through a variety of strategies, but many were affected by the increased emphasis on the desirability of adoption for their children in the period. Provision went to the woman who walked out of a mother-and-baby home with the baby – the adoptive mother – and not to the woman who emerged without. Others who experienced separation from their children included adulterous women and lesbians, who were among those least likely to be awarded custody of children in divorce cases.

Excluded from the list provided by the writer on homelessness, many migrants would have regarded his or her focus on "the tenancy of a house" as a high ambition, since they usually had very considerable difficulty in securing the tenancy of a room, a difficulty which while it applied to almost all migrants was much worse for those who had children with them. Concentrated in a sharply declining private rented sector on arrival, they were generally excluded from the benefits of state provision. As mothers, black migrants in particular were excluded from other benefits through separation from their children through the process of migration. The costs of caring for and educating children who were left back home were not borne by the British state, and earnings in Britain were often used by black women to send money back home for their support.[108]

Migrant women were also among those who gained least from employment in the welfare state. As women were increasingly recruited into health, education and social services, as nurses, midwives, cleaners in schools and hospitals, health visitors, caterers, teachers, organizers of school meals and social workers, migrant women were concentrated in the lower grades of services. This was particularly the case with black migrant women who in nursing were generally employed as State Enrolled rather than State Registered nurses. Irish women, with a long history of nursing in Britain, had more opportunity to train as SRNs.[109] Some of the migrant women who were recruited had trained before arrival in Britain so that the costs of this training were not borne by the British state.

Accounts of the patriarchal welfare state focus attention on the way in which it reinforces gender divisions: denying women full citizenship, assuming that much welfare provision is the task of women working unpaid in the home, particularly as carers, reinforcing women's economic dependence on men. In the history of this period these themes emerge particularly in the difficulties of mothers in getting housing or subsistence outside marriage, the separations from children this could involve, the difficulties of leaving unwanted marriages, including violent marriages, without housing or an income of their own, and the various ways in which women's reproduction was controlled.[110]

Such an analysis, however, does not encompass the ways in which women were differently positioned in relation to the welfare state and to the socially approved motherhood which it supported. In looking at indigenous women, sexuality and marital status are main themes in tracing the history of who benefitted, although generation is also important. In looking at migrant women, and particularly black migrants, these themes are generally irrelevant. Recruited into the welfare state as workers, black women were not constructed as economic dependants of men, they were not assigned roles as unpaid carers in the home, and denial of full citizenship was applicable as much to black men as to black women. Excluded from the motherhood mandate through constructions of race and regardless of any other aspect of their lives or identities, black women's main role in the post-war welfare state was to subsidize it through their labour. Their own motherhood was nevertheless seen in the 1960s as a burden on the welfare state, through taking up beds in maternity hospitals and over-fecundity.

The image of the over-fecund black mother suggests how far the good home was significant to a raced national identity which went beyond the opposition between the decency and respectability of English life in a quiet street and the domestic barbarism of "blacks next door". As the discourse of good homes shifted towards a greater emphasis on the good mother's natural and instinctive capacity for intimacy and relationship, black women were seen as close to nature in a quite different sense – mired in a primordial time far removed from the advent of child psychology. As mother-love came to be seen as a basis of national health and stability, it was particularly in the areas of intimacy, emotional well-being and psychological health that black life was pathologized. The representation of black people as incapable of personal relationship and familial life was particularly associated with black men in the 1950s – as rootless, transient and untamed. But it can also be seen in the ways in which black motherhood was constructed. A major symbol of psychological maturity and fulfilment, of intimacy and relationship – mother-love – was not attributed to black women.

127

Chapter Six

ﾞﾞ

Home and work

The 1950s produced the beginnings of a revolution in married women's participation in the labour market. In 1931 only 16 per cent of married women were in the labour force, but by 1951 the proportion had risen dramatically to 40 per cent, and by 1961 to 52 per cent.[1] Married women's employment had been underestimated in official figures for previous periods because of its seasonal, casual, part-time or home-based nature, but before the war. as Miriam Glucksmann argues, "married women worked in a hostile climate", and were often blamed for taking jobs away from single women.[2] After the war this climate changed and many major trends that were consolidated in the 1960s and 1970s became apparent. The marriage bar, suspended during the war, was generally dismantled after 1945. This meant that the birth of a first child rather than marriage was increasingly the moment when women broke their attachment to the labour market. However, as the 1961 census showed, this break was not decisive, because of the emergence of a bi-modal pattern of participation, first discernible in 1951, where women returned to the labour market when their children were older, often to part-time work.[3] The expansion of part-time work for married women and the consolidation of the distinction between part-time and full-time work were other notable developments in the period. There was also a reduction in regional differences in married women's participation rates.[4]

The debates which surrounded these changes defined women's employment in relation to their responsibility for home. Employed married women were generally referred to as "working wives" rather than as workers, a hybrid which signalled the way in which their employment was tacked on to their familial identity, and subordinated to it. Those who championed the cause of married women's employment envisaged this hybrid operating smoothly as women took on a dual role, where they combined home and work.

Those who censured their employment were anxious about its effects on their families, and especially their children, since "working wife" usually signified "mother". In the 1950s there were a range of anxieties about the ways in which the "working wife" deprived children of a "good home", and she was blamed for a wide variety of social ills. By the early 1960s, however, she became an increasingly acceptable figure, so long as she gave priority to familial goals and subordinated her employment to the needs of her family. Part-time work was often seen as the key to this, and provided assurance that women would not compete with men for jobs.

While there was substantial discontinuity with the inter-war period in the pattern of women's participation in the labour market, there was continuity in the trends in occupational distribution. Traditional sexual divisions of labour had been unsettled between the wars with the restructuring of industry and the feminization of a number of areas of employment, especially assembly-line work in the new consumer industries. Women who worked in these industries had generally been single before the war, but the movement was consolidated after 1945 incorporating many married women. A movement into clerical and retail, also apparent before the war, became particularly marked, and could represent upward mobility in employment away from manual occupations.[5]

Migrant women workers met part of the demand for labour in low-paid and feminized areas of employment, facilitating both the production of indigenous women as primarily wives and mothers and their upward mobility into clerical and retail. Migrant female labour was characteristically recruited at the bottom end of the occupational hierarchy. Black women in particular were excluded from the movement into shop and office work. The 1961 census showed nearly 40 per cent of all economically active women in these occupations in 1961: 25.9 per cent in clerical and 12.7 per cent in sales. But of economically active women born in the Caribbean only 7.6 per cent were in these occupations: 6.6 per cent in clerical and only 1 per cent in sales.[6] A survey by Political and Economic Planning in 1966 commented that "the retail and distributive trades are the sectors most resistant to the employment of coloured people, in all types of jobs but particularly in those which involve contact with the public".[7]

Women assigned different meanings to home and to work in

negotiating the relationship between them, producing a range of different priorities. Professional women, including many feminists, emphasized their own need for a life that was "more than family", resisting an exclusively relational identity as wives and mothers. Albeit trailing the family behind them, and acknowledging its claim upon their time, attention, energy and commitment, they envisaged themselves with an individual identity centred on their professional work, outside the way in which their family role and work defined them in relation to others. Indigenous women who were recruited into low-paid and low-status work, however, often used employment for familial rather than individualistic goals. Although the need to earn money for family survival declined, many used their earnings to facilitate family life, including improvements in housing and furnishings and better equipment, clothes and opportunities for children.[8] Migrant women often used employment as one strategy for family survival. Caribbean women in particular – seen in terms of an incapacity for familial life, especially through constructions of black motherhood – used their employment for familial goals, reversing the way in which their construction as workers denied them a domestic or familial identity. Their earnings contributed to family survival in a range of ways, including the support of family in the Caribbean, bringing their children over to join them, and paying for accommodation to secure the basis of familial and domestic life in Britain.

Work and identity

Between the wars, marriage bars usually meant that, for women, weddings brought a decisive break with employment, a situation where marriage was a call away from employment, the identity of full-time housewife was conceived as "a job", and home was defined in opposition to paid work. Accounts from women convey common ways in which their experiences and expectations of marriage were structured. A woman who had worked in the civil service before marriage records that "getting married was taking on a job – it was up to you to do the best of your ability, in return you got a nice home and what you needed . . . so all these tasks [housework] had to have priority".[9] A working-class woman in Liverpool offers a very similar account of marriage as a job and what this entailed: "I married on the understanding that it was the wife's job to be the careful thrifty housewife and to stay at home to manage the house to the best of my ability."[10] After the war the various calls to employment addressed to married women meant that employment was increasingly defined in relation to home rather than in opposition to it, opening up possibilities for the construction of different versions of the roles of wife, mother and housewife. Since women generally gave up employment on the birth of a first child rather than on marriage, it was motherhood that involved becoming a full-time housewife. Taking on the running of a home as a full-time "job" was part of becoming a mother, not a wife.

Calls to married women to take up employment came from a number of different places. The relationship between home and work was a major concern of feminists after the war, in an advocacy of dual roles for women spearheaded by Alva Myrdal and Viola Klein. Their text, subtitled "Home and work", addressed professional women in particular, arguing that they could and should combine family work with paid work outside the home.[11] Calls to employment from employers generally addressed rather different groups of women, fuelled by the need to recruit cheap labour in occupations which had been feminized before the war. The government, which had seen married women's employment as a temporary expedient in the late 1940s, was also involved in a number of recruitment initiatives. Shortages of teachers, for example, led in the 1950s and early 1960s to a series of attempts by the Ministry of Education to encourage married women to return. The government also facilitated married women's recruitment through the Factories (Evening Employment) Order of 1950, which instigated early evening "twilight shifts". The notion of a "twilight shift" exemplified both the characteristic view that employment was peripheral to a woman's main activities and the development of patterns of feminized work which ensured that employment could be fitted in around the needs of families.

Between the wars feminists had highlighted the needs of working-class women as wives and mothers in campaigns for birth control and family endowment. Myrdal's and Klein's text – *Women's two roles* – was part of a shift of attention to the professional woman and employment. Its origin was an invitation to Myrdal from the

International Federation of University Women to survey the needs of those who wanted to combine professional and family life, and their first proposal for a title was "Professional women and their opportunities for family life".[12] The book focused attention "quite deliberately" on women who had been trained for a profession.[13] Judith Hubback's study of *Wives who went to college* in 1957 also focused on educated and professional women.[14] This call to employment was taken up by many professional women who did not identify as feminists, and the advocacy of dual roles made by feminists and non-feminists alike. When Margaret Thatcher discussed "prejudice against this dual role" in 1952, and advocated "women combining marriage and a career", the question with which she was mainly concerned was: "Why have so few women in recent years risen to the top of the professions?"[15]

Thatcher was unusual in recommending that women carried on working when their families arrived, taking only a short leave of absence, as she herself had done. This was a course from which British feminism dissociated itself in the 1950s. *The feminine point of view*, the report of a conference of women including many feminists, shared Thatcher's concern about professional women combining a career with marriage and motherhood. However, they argued that:

> It is generally agreed that little children under five should spend most of their short day with their mothers (though in rare cases a woman may feel it better to depute the mothering of her small children to someone else). This means that women in professions or other more or less full-time careers will often have to interrupt their public work for a period of perhaps six to ten years.[16]

" 'Children first' is the motto writ large over all discussion of the merits and demerits of married women's employment," Myrdal and Klein acknowledged.[17]

Myrdal and Klein, however, redefined motherhood as a stage in a woman's life rather than the whole of it. Suggesting variously that full-time supervision by mothers might be necessary until the youngest child started school, or reached the age of 9 or 15, their argument that women should be able to return to the labour market when their children were older was a major way in which women's dual roles were envisaged.[18] Sylvia Pearson's view was characteristic. "If there is a strong case for Mother to regard the rearing of her children, and the making of her home, as a full-time job in the early life of the children," she argued, "there is an equally strong case for it to be not necessarily so regarded when the children grow older."[19] There was some recognition of the downward mobility middle-aged women might encounter in re-entering the labour market after interruptions. The British Federation of University Women reported that while their members found it possible to combine work outside the home with marriage and family, they had nearly all failed to achieve a career.[20] Richard Titmuss, arguing that women had completed "the cycle of motherhood" with practically half their life-expectancy still to run, recognized that both their date of birth and their motherhood might pose difficulties in finding constructive and satisfying work. None the less, he stressed the need for women with older children to "accept the need for adjustment and seek other interests".[21]

In redefining motherhood, dual-role advocates also reworked notions of women's relational identity. They claimed both that skills developed within their family roles made them better teachers and social workers, and that their employment made them better companionate wives and mothers. In middle-aged women, they argued, an exclusively relational identity was bad for family life, and especially for children. According to Richard Titmuss, women who clung to their roles as mothers were "over-possessive, frustrated and dissatisfied".[22] Sylvia Pearson argued that when mothers "gave up all" for them, children resented the "too-close emotional tie and the accompanying sense of obligation".[23] Myrdal and Klein said that "Modern mothers who make no plans outside the family for their future will not only play havoc with their own lives but will make nervous wrecks of their over-protected children and their husbands."[24]

Resistance to an exclusively relational identity is also suggested by the way dual-role advocates envisaged themselves oscillating between their professional work and motherhood. While this suggested how subordinate and fragile their occupational identity could be, it did acknowledge its importance. "The problem" as defined by Hubback was: "how great a contribution to society a highly-educated and married woman can make". Her answer was partly prescriptive, for she argued that "the educated woman should have enough sense of public responsibility to try to devote at least part of her energy and ability to socially valuable work". But she also defined this contribution as part of women's own need to use their abilities to the full.[25] Thus an identity as an individual who had an existence and role outside the family was claimed.

With the demise of residential service after the war, "housewife" was increasingly an identity which was assigned on the basis of gender rather than class. Those who advocated dual roles were particularly concerned to differentiate themselves from housewives, and in doing so they often assigned a primarily domestic identity to other women. Myrdal argued in 1945 that women on low wages, typified by the charwoman, should not be encouraged to combine motherhood and employment, but that the case was quite different for those who had the ability to pay for domestic work and who had a strong personal desire for a job.[26] Myrdal and Klein argued that those with higher education who had known the satisfactions of responsibility or skilled work would feel more frustration if they gave up careers for domestic routine than women in semi-skilled or routine work, including shorthand typists and shop assistants.[27] In Hubback's formulation it was "for the highly-educated woman" that "an entirely domestic existence is too limited" and "the family is not enough".[28] Despite these views, an increasing uneasiness about the identity of full-time housewife was not confined to professional women. Many women who adopted dual roles valued full-time motherhood highly when children were young, but were much more ambivalent about being full-time housewives.

Dual-role advocates grappled with the relationship between becoming a mother and being a housewife. Although most acknowledged the claims of family on their time when children were young, they took an altogether different view of the claims of housework. If done efficiently, they argued, this was a straightforward task which should not be regarded as a full-time occupation. "Domesticity," Hubback argued, "is essential in family life, but as it is not the be-all and end-all, it is something to be done as quickly and sensibly as possible in order to leave time and energy for other things."[29] Myrdal and Klein similarly adopted a brisk approach to the evidence they quoted from a 1951 Mass Observation survey, which showed that suburban working-class housewives in London spent an average of 71 hours a week on domestic work. The problem of "household drudgery" was, they argued, largely psychological; the housewife unconsciously expanded her tasks in order to allay feelings of frustration, and provide evidence that she was fully occupied and indispensable. If efficiently organized, housework could be discharged in much less time than this.[30]

This prising apart of the identities of housewife and mother was not confined to professional women. Viola Klein reported on changing attitudes in 1960:

> It is no longer thought virtuous but, on the contrary, to be a sign of lack of organising ability to spend your whole day doing housework. . . I think this is a change of attitude – they [married women] feel it is "lazy" to stay at home. I have heard it said in so many words that if she has no small children a woman is wasting her time if she does not do a job.[31]

Hannah Gavron's study, based on interviews with women in the same year, reported that while women in both her working-class and middle-class samples were aware of conflict between their roles as mother and worker, neither group saw any great conflict between roles as wife and worker, and that most wished to return to work when their children were older.[32]

In constructing different versions of the roles of wife, mother and housewife, advocates of dual roles championed a combination of home and employment, although with many provisos about women's continuing commitment to their families. Increases in married women's participation in the labour market were seen differently by those who argued that employment led to neglect of home, and who represented this as a threat to family and national life. Eleanor French focused on the damage it did to the young girl who would never know a home in the true sense, and would therefore, when her turn came, be "heavily handicapped in making a successful home of her own".[33] Basil Henriques argued that "the strength of the nation is built up on the strength of the home life of the citizens who comprise the nation", and saw mothers as central to this. "The centre and heart of a home has always been the mother," he claimed, "round 'Mum' everything has revolved." He proposed legislation to regulate the working hours of mothers of school-age children, arguing that "the trouble today is that the nation is not roused to realize the havoc that is being wrought on children".[34]

By the early 1960s the working wife was becoming an increasingly acceptable figure. Although T. R. Fyvel still saw working mothers as one cause of juvenile delinquency, they were increasingly incorporated into the notion of good homes.[35] A report commissioned by the Church of England argued that it would be difficult to dispense with their services in industry and the professions, especially teaching, nursing and social work. It stressed that they put home and children first, seldom going out to work when children were under school age, and usually returning to part-time work so that they were at home when older children returned from school. Ronald Fletcher in his study of *The family and marriage* produced the same arguments. "It is certain," he said, "that the full expansion of our economy now positively necessitates the employment of women." He dismissed fears of child neglect, since working mothers usually fitted their hours of work around family responsibilities. The Church of England recommended that "we should perhaps accept the situation as it is, and apply ourselves to the task of meeting the special needs of the married woman at work and particularly of her family and family life". This approach was shared by Fletcher, who recommended part-time work for women and public provision for child care.[36]

Work and family

Referring to the varied strategies adopted by married working-class women living on the poverty line before 1945, including paid employment, Regenia Gagnier calls their characteristic concern with family rather than individual survival "non-individualism".[37] After the war many women continued to use employment for familial goals, but their strategies were less likely to be about basic survival than improvements in domestic and familial life. However, family survival continued to be important to a range of indigenous women, and was often very important to migrants.

A general confidence after the war that full employment and improvements in men's wages had brought an end to family poverty was shared by Myrdal and Klein, who recorded their "disinclination" to subscribe to the traditional view that married women went out to work through "economic necessity".[38] Their assumption of a sexual divison of labour in which adequate financial provision for families was made by men, together with their emphasis on professional married women, meant that they had little to say about women whose earnings from employment were crucial for their children's support. Among indigenous women, these included single mothers, those whose husbands kept back a large share of their "family wage", and women with low-waged or unemployed husbands.

Single mothers, whether widowed, divorced, separated or unmarried, were often in positions of great financial hardship. Audrey Best, who served in the WAAF during the war, was widowed in 1950, when she had two sons, aged 3 and 13 months. She records:

> I received a death allowance of thirty pounds. I remember a health visitor asking me what I needed most. I asked for clothes for the children to come out of hospital with, and I heard nothing more. I took in sewing to pay off the rest of the funeral money owing. . . It was a great struggle providing for my children. Living in a mining area where miners used to have their coals delivered at the door, I was allowed to put these coals, by barrow loads, into their coal houses, several yards away. For this I would receive three barrow loads for myself to keep us warm and heat the water in the winter. I also took in sewing and washing and cleaned houses.[39]

Maria Woods, who was separated from her husband, experienced similar difficulties. After emigration to America as a GI bride, her vision of a better life faded almost immediately on arrival and she eventually returned to England to escape her husband's violence, living on National Assistance initially, until her children were of school age, when she took a variety of low-paid jobs:

> I suffered incredible hardship bringing up the children, it was hard going and at times I never thought I'd make it. Sometimes I didn't always have a lot of patience with my children, simply because I was working two jobs, and I had to earn money to keep them, and I felt guilty about that. I wanted to give them more in life. You wanted your children to be the same as everybody else's children, you didn't want a stigma attached to them. "Oh, she's on her own", which is a thing that people say. I used to do two cleaning jobs, one in the morning and another in the afternoon, and then I'd have to be back by 4 o'clock. I had to be there for them. I used to have a job as a dinner lady, so that when they were at home in the summer I was home as well. You had to keep on rearranging your life all the time, to cope

with problems. It was mentally tiring as well as physically tiring, because you always had some problem you had to conquer – whether it was finding money for shoes, or being home.[40]

Dual-role advocates also ignored the distribution of resources in many households whereby men frequently kept a substantial proportion of their earnings for themselves, and where the common habit of expecting a wife to buy contraceptives out of her housekeeping money was bitterly resented by many women.[41] Despite increased male wages and their own earnings, tight budgets remained a common feature of many married women's lives. Gladys Petty's husband kept back part of his wages as pocket money, and she records of her own earnings, "You'd just got to have them to manage. Anything I earned always . . . had got to go for managing the house. He never gave me a lot." As soon as her elder son went to school, she took cleaning jobs where her younger son could accompany her, and when both sons were at school she worked as a school cleaner, doing two shifts, which enabled her to be at home to get the children dinner as well as when they came home from school. For six months she combined these two shifts with a third "twilight shift" in a factory, doing machining work, while her husband looked after the children on his arrival home.[42]

Redefinitions of family needs also meant that, even if women's earnings were no longer so necessary to basic survival, they were often required to resist a range of social exclusions – particularly for children. When child-centredness was combined with post-war consumerism there was frequently an emphasis on providing a wider range of goods and opportunities for children. Maria Woods's account of what her earnings as a single mother could not provide for her children reflects this:

> They would get Christmas presents and birthday presents, but perhaps it wouldn't be a brand new bike, it might be a second-hand one. School clothes were a terrible struggle, school uniforms. Probably I would have to get a second-hand blazer, or hand the eldest boy's blazer down to the next boy. I always had these feelings of not coming up to scratch. I wanted so much to give them, and I couldn't. No matter how hard I worked there was never enough money to be able to do everything I wanted for them.[43]

Paid work was also undertaken so that children could take advantage of educational opportunities. Win Kewley, for example, did overtime in addition to her part-time job to finance equipment for her daughters at grammar school:

> I didn't want them not to have what the other girls at high school had – if they wanted a new tennis racquet, for instance. By then I was working part-time, but sometimes I had the opportunity of going back to the restaurant at night. I would opt for that.[44]

Child-centredness meant that children were increasingly free from any obligation to contribute to the family budget. In her own pre-war adolescence, from leaving school at 14 in 1935 through to her marriage in 1940, Kewley had "tipped up" her earnings to her mother, receiving pocket money. Although in some working-class families children still tipped up to their mothers in the 1960s, this was a declining practice. The raising of the school leaving age made children dependent on parents for longer, especially if they went on to further education as Kewley's daughters did. Thus women who had tipped up to their mothers in adolescence were less likely to have contributions from their own adolescent children when they became mothers, and might, in middle age, provide support for their families once again through their earnings – this time for their children.

New school uniforms and brand new bikes required money, but women also made other clothes at home. Kewley's account is of a variety of jugglings of paid and domestic work at different stages of her children's lives. Committed to staying at home when her children were young, she earned money by giving dinners to other children whose mothers worked. When her youngest child was of school age, she took part-time work in a restaurant, so that she could always be at home when they returned from school. Her account also stresses the importance of domestic work in provision for children:

> I usually had the most kids in the street. But I didn't want to be one of those people where others say, "her with all them kids". So mine had to be well-dressed. I might be prepared to stop up all night to sew them a dress or knit them a cardigan. . . One of the proudest things was the eldest girl. She was always top of the class, and I took a great pride in that. I once went up on parents' evening and the teacher said to me, "she's always so

beautifully dressed, but of course, she's an only child". I swelled. I said, "she is not an only child, I've got a big family". But the fact that she looked as if she was nicely enough dressed to be an only child, that did wonders for me. No longer was I "her with all them kids".

I had this thing about, how with hand-knitted clothes they looked more cared for. I had this thing about being a good mum somehow, and if they had a hand-knitted thing on people said, "Have you knitted that?", or "where did you get that cardigan from?" And my daughter would say, "my mum knitted it". So that you didn't seem to be poor. You weren't acting poor. A kind of pride I suppose it is, that you didn't want to admit that you were having a struggle, that you weren't very well off.[45]

While employment in advocacies of dual roles was about resisting exclusion from individuality, Kewley's account suggests the way in which dual roles were also used for familial goals, resisting a wide range of other forms of social exclusion.

Employment as a strategy for family survival, while declining among indigenous women, was frequently important to migrant women, and especially to black migrants. Few of the themes articulated by advocates of dual roles fitted their experience. Their employment was often a precondition of any sort of family life and frequently involved full-time rather than part-time work. The requirement to earn through employment was sometimes particularly acute when children were young. One theme which was generally neglected by dual-role advocates was particularly pertinent to black women: the difficulties of combining full-time work with motherhood in the absence of much public provision of child care.

Employment was frequently crucial for financial support of families, and since black women's families usually included members back home as well as in Britain, there were often a range of calls on their earnings, from sending food, money and parcels back home to providing for children in Britain, whether brought over or born after migration. Migrant women from the Caribbean often used their earnings to bring children over. Since black men's wages were commonly lower than white men's, this range of family needs was unlikely to be provided through male breadwinners, even when they used their earnings to meet them. As Constance Nembhard records: "Once we came here we had to work. Because there was no way you could get anything with just one person working. You couldn't live in one room for ever. To get out of it you had to go out to work."[46] In common with white women, black women might have other reasons for supporting families – as single mothers, whether widowed, divorced, separated or unmarried.

Many of these themes are apparent in Vi Chambers's account of her life as a mother and worker in the 1950s and early 1960s. Migrating from Jamaica in 1956 to join her husband, she left two daughters behind with her mother. Her third daughter was born in 1957, but by then her marriage had ended:

> It was an absolute nightmare. The worry, you just live . . . you don't know how you are going to manage. You are on your own, my husband went off to Canada, he didn't care, he never supported our daughter, never sent anything for us – not a penny. . . I was surprised my baby was so healthy as I wasn't eating well, but I had vitamin tablets from the hospital. . . I worked in a sewing factory until I was seven months pregnant. The boss was Irish and he was really great to me. I had a lot of time off when my daughter was ill and he paid me. I stayed there for twelve years until he closed the business. I worked all along, and whilst working I sent for my children. I borrowed some money to send for them and paid back the money over a period of time, a monthly payment. It was important to me to go on working as I had to make a life for my children.[47]

Mrs H's account traces similar themes. She also migrated from Jamaica to join her husband, leaving one daughter with her mother, her marriage ending soon after her arrival. Her earnings went on parcels to her mother, and later to bring her daughter over and to support her in Britain:

> Sometimes we would eat less or buy the cheapest thing to send for them home. . . We had a hard time over here making it, but I determined that since I'm here already. . . I make a parcel, and post it. That's why they [family] believe we are so rich over here, because we would deny ourselves to always care for them there. . . I sent for my big daughter, and when she came she was alright because she had me to come to and she was well catered for. She went to a good school. I sent her to a

church school. I do overtime at the children's hospital. I go in
early at five o'clock. I start work at six, cleaning... And
when I finish at three o'clock, I might run home, jump on a bus
and run, and get something for my daughter coming from
school, and leave it covered for her. And go back to the hospital
and start work from six to eight or nine.[48]

Full-time work, often on shifts, meant not only finding day-care
for young children, but also someone who would look after them
outside school hours, when they were older. Through migration
women were usually separated from their mothers, who might
otherwise have provided care. Nembhard who came to London
from Jamaica in 1956 to join her husband, worked in the finance
department of the London County Council, and had three children
by the early 1960s. Her mother came to Britain to look after them
while she went to teacher training college between 1961 and 1964,
but this was not an option available to most black women.[49] Some
found places for their children in public day nurseries, where
priority was given to mothers who had no financial support from
men, but the general shortage of public provision meant that most
had to look for child-minders in the private sector.

Finding a place was not always the solution, since day care could
pose further problems. Mary, who came to Britain from Grenada in
1961, had her first child in 1963 and found a child-minder. She
records:

> You just bring your child there and they didn't look after the
> children at all. It was terrible. You used to go back and the child
> would be soaked, wet, hungry. A lot of children were
> maltreated. It was just the same as everything else. You
> couldn't have any place. Nursery wasn't available, like homes.
> You couldn't get places to stay.[50]

In Buchi Emecheta's *Second class citizen*, the difficulty of finding
day care for young children is a major theme. Adah works full-time
as a librarian to support her student husband who, although he
rarely studies, is unwilling to take responsibility for them. The child-
minder leaves her son and daughter to play with rubbish from the bin
and water leaking from the toilet, in her back yard. It is only when
Adah's son contracts viral meningitis that she is offered a place for
her children in a public nursery.[51]

Shifting identities

When Margaret Thatcher advocated dual roles for professional women in 1952, she issued a bracing call to others to follow her example: "wake up women!" One of the questions with which she was concerned was "why not a woman Chancellor – or Foreign Secretary?"[52] Her insertion of women into narratives of individualism where they carved out their own destiny, unfettered by the claims of family, was particularly explicit. Other professional women were generally more tentative about these possibilities. But most advocates of dual roles chipped away at the notion that, for educated women, a relational identity was all-encompassing. They identified employment as a route to greater autonomy, asserting an identity which, through its associations with professional status and career, differentiated them from other women.

Few women who adopted dual roles in the period, however, were answering calls to employment which were to do with the production of individuality. To be a working wife for the majority of women meant employment rather than career, and did not provide much scope for a sense of worth or status. Occupational identity could be valued for a range of reasons, including continuity of employment in a particular occupation, the scope provided for the exercise of skills, the rewards and satisfactions offered, or association with upward mobility. But women's concentration in low-paid and low-status work meant that their attachment to an occupational identity was usually quite tenuous. Moreover, if they entered and returned to the labour market on the terms required of them, subordinating employment to the needs of families, they acquired a fragmented and discontinuous employment history: working until the birth of a first child, surrendering an identity as working wife in favour of full-time motherhood, reassuming it once again when children were older. The shifting meanings of wife, mother and housewife meant shifting identities for women in various combinations of these roles, together with full-time or part-time work outside the home, at different stages of their lives. As their employment was often denigrated – "little jobs" which earned some "pin-money", the "twilight shift" dubbed in some areas the "granny shift" – the "working wife", like the full-time housewife, was distinguished not by her individuality but by her ordinariness.[53]

Norma Steele's account of her arrival in England from Jamaica in 1962 to join her parents traces the way in which low-paid and low-status work produced commonalities not only between black and white female migrants, but also between migrants and indigenous women, through sexual divisions of labour in the workplace and the home:

> When I arrived in the great metropolis . . . my mother was still forced to go out to work, but even worse, she wound up doing night shift work – working as a nurse in a hospital. We had to share the house with other people, other Black and white people. The women, including the white women (some of whom were from different countries), were working as cleaners, nurses – doing low paid dirty jobs in the service industries. . . And this [housework] was really hard as the house was damp and cold and no matter how much cleaning and polishing you did, it still looked grubby and smelt dank. The women also had to cook and clean for their men and for the single men too, as this was easier than having to clean up after them as they weren't used to housework.[54]

Despite these commonalities, there were a range of ways in which indigenous women's employment was associated with upward mobility in this period. "Bettering myself", a theme in many narratives, refers to a number of areas that women's earnings could facilitate, including better housing and home ownership. It also commonly refers to provisions for children, including daughters – clothes, toys, educational opportunities – reflecting the extent to which "bettering *myself*" can refer to familial rather than individualistic goals. "Bettering myself" can also refer to upward occupational mobility, especially in the movement into office and shop work. At the same time, women who made this move before childbirth could experience downward mobility when they returned to employment in middle age, often to lower-status jobs.

Black women were generally excluded from upward mobility in employment, and arrival in Britain for those with an occupational identity in professional or clerical work was more likely to involve a shifting identity which was to do with downward mobility. The experience of being shifted into a unitary black category meant a collapse of distinctions within this category, which could be experienced particularly through refusals of employment in professional, office or shop work. Attachment to an occupational identity as teacher is a main theme of Beryl Gilroy's autobiography, which also recounts many refusals of teaching jobs in the 1950s. Vi Chambers records refusals of clerical jobs:

> I'd done a commercial course back home. I went for quite a few jobs for which I was qualified, and I didn't get them because they were office jobs. Most of the places just didn't want black people. They wouldn't talk to you at all.[55]

Cecilia Wade's account concerns attitudes to black women both as teachers and as clerical workers on her arrival in London in 1956:

> The first week when I arrived my brother said I had to sign on on Monday at the labour exchange. The first Monday I took my references from home saying I was a teacher. This woman at the counter said, "Oh, you were a teacher back home were you? Well you won't get teaching here!" I said, "Well, what have you got to offer?" "Nothing at the moment. Come back next week." The following Monday I went and she looked me up and down again and said, "All I have to offer you is 'Lyon's Tea Shops', or there is a job going at a hospital in Clacton. Which would you prefer?" I said, "I don't know much about 'Lyon's Tea Shop' because, as I said, I was a teacher and I'm looking for clerical work." "Oh! You won't get clerical work here." She was positive.[56]

As these accounts suggest, calls to employment addressed migrant and indigenous women in different terms. Migrant women were not envisaged as suitable applicants to fill the shortages of teachers in the 1950s. Black women were not part of the movement into office work, and those who were recruited into nursing were concentrated in the lower grades and in the lower-status branches – geriatric and mental health. Black women were in any case generally seen as of low status, regardless of their own occupation.

It was, however, particularly in relation to the way in which employment was defined in relation to home that migrant and indigenous women were addressed in different terms. Migrant women were not assigned the primarily relational identity embodied in the notion of a "working wife". Wanted as workers, they were not wanted as people who would establish family life in Britain, with all the complex notions that suggested: settlement, housing, education and other provision from the expanded post-war welfare state.

Black women especially, although wanted as nurses and cleaners in the National Health Service, including its maternity services, were not wanted as mothers. Wanted to provide goods and services for indigenous people, migrant women were not seen as needing provision for themselves. Defined as workers, not as "working wives", there was no expectation that they would subordinate their employment to the needs of family.

Chapter Seven

Domestic identities

By the early 1960s a generation of educated women, born during or immediately after the war, began to define home as an oppressive, over-private and stultifying place for women. The first generation to be born into a servantless world and one where marriage bars had generally been dismantled, they experienced the transition from an educated and career-oriented identity to the role of full-time and servantless housewife on the birth of their first child. In a literature on the "housebound mother" they articulated this as an experience of loss of identity, self-esteem and self-confidence. In 1960 Maureen Nicol identified exile with being at home. She wrote to the *Manchester Guardian*, "Since having my first baby I have been constantly surprised how women seem to go into voluntary exile in the home once they leave their outside work."[1] Her letter prompted a response from readers, which led to the formation of the Housebound Wives Register in London, and subsequently to the National Housewives Register.

This idea of home foreshadowed the view of the family and domestic labour as a main site of women's oppression which was prominent within the writings of the Women's Liberation movement in the late 1960s, when both housework and family relations became a central concern of feminist politics. However, it was a view which did not acknowledge the very wide and often contradictory range of meanings and values that women assigned to home and the ways in which these were shaped by class and race. For indigenous women, class and race influenced meanings in a variety of ways as they responded to developments in the period which made the home significant as a marker of white privilege and status, but much less reliable as a marker of class status. For black women, however, race was the dominant factor in shaping the meanings of home, as they experienced serious difficulties in securing any sort of domestic comfort or familial life, regardless of class. Black women were particularly unlikely to experience home as a private and stultifying place. The racism of the housing market in all sectors meant that they were concentrated in a declining private rented sector on arrival in Britain in overcrowded, multi-occupied houses where they had to share facilities, and were constantly refused access even to this accommodation.

The demise of residential domestic service after the war meant that housework was a task assigned on the basis of gender rather than class. This was perhaps the most notable way in which the home became less reliable as a symbol of class status for indigenous women, but other developments contributed to this. Owner-occupation could no longer be regarded as marking middle-class status: a development already apparent between the wars when it had extended to some working-class families, but one which accelerated after 1945. Fixed baths in bathrooms, a sign of middle-class status in the early twentieth century, and more common in working-class homes between the wars, became a feature of the majority of homes in the 1950s.[2] Spacious living, declining between the wars, was more or less over by 1945, while the building of new estates for public rental and owner-occupation, with modern facilities, led to an increasing democratization not only of indigenous women's roles within the home but of the setting in which they did housework. For many women this became some version of the "little house" which Mass Observation recorded as the object of a "wistful longing" among women in 1943.[3]

Although indigenous women's relationship to domesticity became more common across class, this did not produce a common meaning of home. The demise of service was portrayed in a genre of autobiography by former domestic servants as liberation for working-class women in a transformation of the world of domesticity and of class relationships between women. It produced rather different reactions among former employers of servants. The identity of "ordinary housewife" was ambivalent for those who had previously employed one maid-of-all-work – the dominant pattern of servant-keeping between the wars – and who could no longer allocate the most menial of tasks, such as cleaning floors and lavatories, to working-class women. It was even more problematic for women who had employed several servants before the war and could no longer rely on spacious living and elaborate housekeeping as markers of their status. Those who found themselves newly responsible for all the housework included women who as colonizers had employed servants and who, if they returned to Britain, found themselves servantless. This condition may have influenced the view that colonial life was more English than the life to which they returned, and the continued availability of servants contributed to a movement of British-born emigrants to Rhodesia and South Africa after 1945.[4]

It was in this context that the literature on "housebound mothers" was produced. Maureen Nicol's view of the home as a place of exile for women was in strong contrast to that of black women who arrived in Britain in the period and for whom a sense of exile was produced particularly through their experiences of refusals of places to live, ranging from "no coloureds" signs to slammed doors to notification that rooms had just been let to someone else. It was on arrival, often within hours, that they discovered that although their labour was required in Britain and gave them access to places defined as public, there were no places for them to live. Accounts by white migrants tell of similar experiences as the sign "no coloureds, no Irish" was joined in some areas by advertisements for accommodation which announced "no Poles or East Europeans".[5] Black and white women were generally very differently positioned in relation to housing and domesticity, but there was a close correspondence between the position of white and black migrants, a position which was also shared by white indigenous women who were married to black men. The strategies developed by black and white migrants to resist the racism of the housing market and get out of the private rented sector were also similar, particularly in purchasing houses and financing mortgage payments through letting off rooms, often to other migrants.

Those who found themselves newly servantless in post-war Britain included some black and Asian women whose arrival in Britain from colonies and former colonies involved the loss of servants they had employed before migration. Racism generally produced a common meaning of home to black women – the sense of exile embodied in the yearning for "back home". However, this could have particular meanings for those whose status before arrival had been shaped by their education, occupational identity, family background, servant-keeping or place within a "pigmentocracy", but who found on arrival that they were shifted into a unitary black category. Although employment was sometimes a way in which the collapse of distinctions within this category were experienced, it was particularly the refusal of places to live that exemplified the construction of black as a unitary and undifferentiated category which did not belong in Britain.

Class and race were thus very important to the multiple, complex and often contradictory meanings that women assigned to home. As it became a less reliable marker of class differentiation but one of the most significant markers of racial divisions, women responded in a variety of ways. At the same time the meanings of home could shift for individual women not only over the course of a life-time, but in different contexts during the course of a year, or even of a day.

The democratization of housework

Alison Ravetz has suggested that 1950 might be taken as a watershed in the history of women's relation to domesticity. "By then," she writes, "two things of profound significance for women had occurred: the middle-class wife had finally and irrevocably lost her servants and the working-class wife had gained, or was in the process of gaining, a whole house to look after."[6]

The decline of residential domestic service is dated by some historians to the inter-war period, with the increased figures for 1931, when 23 per cent of employed women were engaged in service, seen as a localized response to economic depression.[7] It was the late 1940s, however, which was widely perceived as the period when this process was complete, and the long history of working-class women employed as residential servants at an end. This was the perception of former domestic servants, who in a developing genre of servants' autobiography wrote of their occupation as "dead and gone" only after 1945.[8] It was a perception shared by those who were formerly servant-keepers. Violet Markham was the daughter in a Victorian household with seven servants, and had employed maids in her own household before the war, parting from them to live on alone in London when bombing began.[9] In 1945 she reported to the government that the war "has not so much solved as dissolved the whole structure of domestic service".[10] In Mollie Panter-Downes's novel One fine day the inter-war period is a time when "in the

kitchen, caps and aprons shrieked with sudden merriment". But by
the end of the war Ethel and Violet have departed and there is only
Mrs Prout, coming in daily "to circulate the dust a little".[11] In 1947,
94 per cent of women were without help of any sort in the house.[12]
As addressed by Kay Smallshaw in her manual *How to run your
home without help*, they were "both mistress and maid".[13]

The demise of service was celebrated by working-class women as
an end to the psychic as well as economic misery that their work
involved. In tracing the story of their employment between the wars,
they delineate a world in which they were denied any individuality,
for the most part invisible in their station "below stairs", and when
noticed treated as sub-human.[14] Writing about her life in 1968,
Margaret Powell recorded:

> It may seem as if I was very embittered with my life in domestic
> service. Bitterness does come to the fore because it was the
> strong feeling I had, and the experiences are the ones that stay
> in my mind now. I know it's all dead and gone. Things like that
> don't happen now. But I think it's worth not forgetting that
> they did happen.[15]

Powell had left domestic service on her marriage before the war,
although she returned as a "daily" during and after the war. Like
much working-class autobiography, her account can be read as a
narrative of social progress, allowing the reader a sense that the
difficulties and struggles portrayed are "dead and gone". What she
relegates to the past, however, is not so much poverty and hunger as
the servant-keeping way of life, and the class relationships between
women that this had involved.

In Jean Rennie's autobiography, published in 1955, this way of
life has vanished so completely by the end of the war that it is
scarcely possible to believe it once existed, although there are some
ghostly reminders:

> I had the experience, a few years ago, of working for one of the
> Ministries in a house close to Eaton Square near the one in
> which I had worked twenty years before, and identical in every
> way. I cannot describe the feeling, a kind of ghostly shiver as I
> walked in the front door and up to my office, which had once
> been a drawing-room. . . It was a physical pain in my heart –
> *not*, I must hasten to add a nostalgic pain – to go down to the
> basement where we kept rows and rows of files. . . This dark

> dungeon, with the long dresser and this great ugly stove . . .
> had been the kitchen where I, and others like me, had quite
> literally sweated away an existence that was accepted as "that
> station in life". If any of the girls came down to look for a file, I
> tried to say, "Look, people used to work down here – this was
> the kitchen; look, this was the scullery," they used to look at
> me as though I had two heads and one eye, then say with a
> shiver, "God! What a dump! There's ghosts here, or some-
> thing." They just didn't believe me.[16]

Rennie here, speaking about the late 1940s, uses the incredulity of
her fellow workers to denote the extent to which her own life before
the war is now part of a vanished world, although one which can
continue to haunt her. "Yes, there are ghosts," she writes, "and I
was one of them."

These accounts of domestic service suggest a confidence that the
vanished world portrayed will be of interest to an audience who, if
they do not respond with incredulity, are likely to share a sense of
outrage at the pain and misery one class of women caused another.
Although sometimes rendered as comic, the purpose of the story, as
Powell affirms, is to offer testimony about the past to a world where
"things like that don't happen now". In that sense, the story is about
celebrating chances as well as detailing the shocking nature of what
went before, and it is a celebration not so much of individual
progress, in the release from domestic service, but of collective
progress for working-class women in a transformation of the world
of domesticity, where service is a bygone misery, a "station in life"
and an experience of exploitation which they no longer have to
endure or resist.

The individual movement away from domestic service could also
give "my own home" particular meanings. Margaret Powell records
that when she left domestic service on marrying:

> I didn't want to go out to work. The time never hung on my
> hands at all, I was only too glad to have nothing to do for a
> while. Although I was feminist and stuck up for the rights of
> women, it didn't go that far. I asserted an independence as
> regards the running of the home, I wasn't subservient in any
> way to my husband. . . So much of my time had been spent
> thinking about getting out of service that it was a long while
> before I felt that home life wasn't enough, and by then I had

collected a family of three children, so that any aspirations I had had to go by the board for the time being. Looking after three children is a fulltime job to me at any rate, because I was a mother in the full sense of the word, I think.[17]

Here the role of housewife is associated with the independence and autonomy involved in running her own home rather than someone else's, and particularly with a strong commitment to full-time motherhood.

The meaning of servant-keeping had been very different for those who employed servants, with the "servant problem" receiving a good deal of attention between the wars. A popular genre was the account of middle-class domestic life serialized in newspapers. As told by Jan Struther in *The Times*, this is a celebration of domestic pleasures and comfort, where Mrs Miniver is a confident and calm mistress of a resident nanny, parlourmaid and cook and where domestic crises, such as they are, barely ruffle the surface of her ordered world.[18] As told by Mary Wylde in the *Evening Standard*, it is a story which is constantly fractured by domestic crises, as servants intrude on her privacy, invite their relations to stay in her house unannounced, litter her kitchen with newspapers, wake her up at night coming in late, and disturb her during the day by slamming doors. Their "delinquencies" and "grandiose disregard for cleanliness" mean that she has to be constantly alert to limit the damage which they would otherwise cause, and to be constantly intervening herself in work which should be their responsibility. Housekeeping, in this account, becomes a nightmare – a continual and unceasing campaign against disintegration and decay, which is for the most part attributed to the slovenly habits and stupidity of servants.[19]

These two accounts suggest something of the different meanings attached to homemaking when it involved servant-keeping. Struther rarely represents servants, but it is their work behind the scenes which allows Mrs Miniver her contented and peaceful existence, relatively unrestricted by the constraints of motherhood and domestic work. When her relations with servants are portrayed they are those of a competent and sensible manager, serving as a sign of her maturity, and these qualities are mirrored by the servants in their different "station in life" with even Mrs Burchett, the charwoman, character- ized as a "large, neat cheerful woman".[20] This is a world without many conflicts, one where, whatever their station, women know what is appropriate to it and behave more or less impeccably.

In contrast, Wylde presents herself as the victim of servants. When they leave, and she has to clean the gas stove, she purges herself afterwards by throwing away the dress she wore when doing so. Dusting and polishing can be "lady-like jobs", but she feels degraded by the rough work of cleaning, and is particularly anxious about the effects on her hands, and how this may betray her menial role. At each domestic crisis she debates the merits of a service flat or modern, labour-saving house, but struggles on. This is in part because of her commitment to spacious living and the status of elaborate housekeeping, where the maintenance of champagne glasses, silver coffee pots, damask tablecloths and linen sheets are a major preoccupation. It is this detailed attention to the minutiae of housekeeping rather than family life which is identified in her account with home as she presents herself as one of the remaining upholders of old standards which others are abandoning, lamenting "the decay of home life".[21]

After the war, concerns about "the decay of home life" focused on a "servant problem" which was not about the difficulties of hiring suitable servants, but the impossibility of hiring them at all. Violet Markham reported to the government in 1945 that with the decline of domestic service "the future of the home, that cornerstone of the national life is at stake", arguing that "family life among the middle and upper classes in this country has for generations rested largely on the assumption of domestic help of some kind being available".[22] In 1953 she was concerned about "how far in the future people will be able to live in large individual homes", a question she suggested "lies in the lap of the gods".[23]

Markham's particular concerns about the decline of spacious living were not necessarily shared by those who had adopted the common form of servant-keeping between the wars, employing one maid-of-all work or "general". However, unless a "daily" was employed, the loss of a "general" meant doing housework which had previously been regarded as "the rough".

In household manuals of the 1950s addressed to the middle classes the timetable for a housewife with a full-time resident maid allots the maid responsibility for doing "the rough", while the housewife dusts, makes beds and helps with washing if necessary. The scheme for a housewife with part-time help is divided along similar lines, although here on certain days the housewife has to sweep and clean floors herself. For the "single handed housewife", however, what had conventionally been regarded as menial tasks join dusting and polishing as part of her regular daily round.[24]

The decline of domestic service had different meanings for those who came from servant-keeping families but growing to adulthood during and after the war, did not employ servants themselves. In Elizabeth Arthur's account parting from servant-keeping coincides with leaving home, and she details various ways in which this influenced her work as a VAD in the war, and her own experience as a housewife on her marriage in the early 1960s:

> When I was nursing I'd never cleaned a lavatory, and I remember the sister saying to me "Have you cleaned the lavatories?" She said, "you put the rubber gloves on, get down on your knees", and I had to put my hand in the lavatory and scrub all round it by hand. Another thing I hadn't done was to cut bread, and I remember that was difficult. We'd had a cook, a housemaid, a tweeny – whatever that was – and a charwoman. Neither the cook nor the parlour-maid did any really rough work. My sister reminded me recently that when we'd been out at night, the maids were meant to stay up to clear up after us. I always wondered why I found it hard to do housework in my own house later. But as a child home meant to me sitting down and being waited on.[25]

A report commissioned by Ernest Bevin from Violet Markham and Florence Hancock represented one response to lack of servants, outlining a number of ways in which to promote the recruitment of more servants. Like similar schemes at the end of the First World War, it advocated reforms both of the conditions and image of service to make it more attractive, deplored the contempt and ridicule with which servants were regarded, and made recommendations about wages, hours, uniforms and accommodation. The emphasis on training, embodied in proposals for a National Institute of Houseworkers to undertake the certification of domestic workers, also echoed concerns expressed in 1916.[26]

A further response was a call for the rationalization of housework. Markham's and Hancock's proposals for training emphasized the skilled nature of domestic work, but dual-role advocates saw it as a task which need not take up too much time and energy. In many ways, their prescriptions echoed advice to the servantless between the wars, which had also offered bracing ideas for the rationalization of housework, advising the housewife to study her work along scientific management lines, dedicate herself to efficiency, put away her ornaments and silver, dispense with her basement and adopt labour-saving ideas and appliances.[27] But while advice between the wars had rarely specified what a housewife would do with the time saved, beyond a rather vague notion that she would have more leisure, advocates of dual roles for women were more specific about its purpose.

The focus of the professional middle-class woman's identity was increasingly seen as her employment. Servant-keeping allowed Mrs Miniver considerable scope for leisure activities, while for Mary Wylde it made possible the elaboration of domestic life that was a main purpose of her housekeeping. Within advocacies of dual roles, however, those who maintained the hope that domestic servants could be recruited envisaged them not as helping middle-class women to run their homes, but rather as enabling professional women to contribute to national life through the pursuit of their careers. The British Federation of University Women urged the government to take action on shortages of servants if they were serious about encouraging more married women to go back to work as teachers, doctors and social workers, and, surveying a sample of their members who managed to combine career and motherhood in 1964, found that as many as 84 out of 90 employed some domestic help, including residential maids and mother's helps, au pairs and charwomen.[28] At the same time a recognition that society was newly servantless led to encouragement to women to get through house-work in the shortest possible time, rather than spending time on elaborate arrangements which displayed their status.

Those who advocated schemes to recruit more servants never proposed the recruitment of black women. The "Aunt Jemima" image, like the mammy image of which it was part, had no currency in Britain. Black and Asian people – both men and women – had commonly been employed as domestic servants in the colonies, and this employment continued in the post-war period. By the twentieth century, however, black people were no longer employed as servants in the metropolis. White migrants were an important source of domestic servants between the wars, when Irish women in particular were recruited. In the context of the sharp decline of service after the war, such recruitment continued. Black migrant women did not enter domestic service.

Although a role caring for and servicing white families, constructed as private as well as public in a colonial context, was not extended to the private sphere in the metropolis, black women were seen as particularly suitable for public domestic work, which was both menial and "dirty". They were recruited to clean hospitals, offices, hotels, and London Transport. This view of black women's domestic labour – as public rather than private – was part of the way in which they were excluded from associations with private domesticity, whether as housewives or domestic servants. At the same time constructions of black people as dirty meant a reluctance to employ black women as waitresses. Sheila Patterson found that fear of possible public reaction meant that firms in London, while employing black people on the food-processing side of the business, and some black women behind the scenes in kitchens, did not employ them in jobs which involved "contact with the public".[29] A survey by Political and Economic Planning in 1966 found a similar reluctance to employ black women in shops as counter or sales staff, especially in food shops. "They'd be all right, say, for tinned goods but not fresh food. People think they're a bit dirty." Again this led to a separation between public and private where they were employed only "behind the scenes".[30]

A servantless condition, although always seen as something which troubled white middle-class women, or for which they found bracing and rational solutions, extended to some black women in post-war Britain, whose migration involved the loss of servants they had employed back home. Vi Chambers records that in Jamaica:

When I got married we had a maid who came in the mornings, and she did all the cooking and cleaning and washing, because we didn't have washing machines. The clothes had to be washed by hand. I never learnt to cook until I came to this country. This was one of the problems I had with my husband. I soon picked it up, but I couldn't cook very well. I could boil an egg, fry an egg. But the basic things like roast a chicken – I'd never done that before in my life.[31]

While this suggests some commonalities with white women who found themselves servantless, and also had to learn how to cook, the loss of servants had particular meanings for black women. Through the construction of black as a unitary category, with no distinctions of class, they found themselves not only without servants, but also seen as particularly suited to the type of dirty and menial work that was associated with being a servant. This is a strong theme in Chambers's account of her resistance to that construction, and to any form of domestic labour, whether as a maid herself, or as a cleaner in the public sphere. She records:

> One of the things that I said when I came to this country is, "If I can't get a job, no way am I going to work in a toilet or do any sweeping or cleaning, no way." I wouldn't be a maid for anyone. I wouldn't work in anybody's house cleaning for them. If I'm going to clean toilets it'll be in my own country. If I wanted to clean toilets, I wouldn't spend all that money to come here. . . I would not take it as my job to clean for anyone. The thing is I'd never done it in my own country. But not only that, if the people in Jamaica knew that I was doing that here, I could never go back to Jamaica. They'd laugh me to scorn. My friends and family know that I was doing that – oh God they would laugh me to scorn.[32]

In Amanda Murphy's account, the experience of coming from a family who employed servants is also linked to resistance to the idea of scrubbing floors in Britain – a job which she did take for a short period:

> I resented it badly, very badly. . . In our house we had people who came in to do that kind of work for us, and they were like part of our family. They ate at the table with us, and it was just as if they were another member of the family, doing part of the jobs of the house. I did all the washing and ironing in our house. Three of us older girls did all the baking – our own breads. My mother did the shopping. The boys swept the yard. And this woman who was part of our family did all the housework. She lived with us all week, and went home to her own family on the weekend. I never told my father – my family never knew that I did menial jobs. That would have killed my Dad, because he's a very proud man. . . These people treated

you like muck. I sometimes want to cry really when I think about it. I don't really think about that bit of it.[33]

Housebound mothers

It was educated women who became adult towards the end of the 1945–64 period, and mothers of young children in the early 1960s, who produced a literature which highlighted the "housebound mother" and the alienation of her life, particularly in suburbia. In many ways their concerns were similar to those who had advocated dual roles in the 1950s, although they were generally of a different generation. They focused on the needs of educated and professional women and defined these as "more than family", resisting an exclusively relational identity. They rarely challenged women's economic dependence on men or sexual divisions of labour in the home or workplace. They attempted to prise apart the identities of mother and housewife. Their work is distinctive in its redefinition of home as an oppressive place for women – over-private, stultifying and isolated. Their focus on the "housebound mother" identifies this meaning of home as one associated with motherhood and they make the problems of maternity for women their main theme.

This group of women, born just before or during the war, could be seen as representing a number of post-war developments. They had generally taken the route from grammar school to university that the post-war welfare state had opened up to increasing numbers, although in 1963 women still comprised only 25 per cent of all university students.[34] They represented a generation for whom the home could no longer serve as a main mark of class differentiation. Hannah Gavron commented, "In fact what has probably happened is that the now servantless middle-class wives with young children are leading a life not dissimilar to that of many workers' wives."[35] Their dates of birth made them a generation who entered the labour market after the general dismantling of marriage bars, so surrendering their occupational identity on the birth of a first child rather than on marriage. Gavron said of the middle-class young mothers she interviewed between 1960 and 1961, "The impact of the birth of the first child . . . was tremendous, because it changed them from being a new kind of woman to being the traditional woman. It meant in

particular the loss of independence."[36] Many of Gavron's inter-
viewees in this group were recruited through the Housebound Wives
Register in London which had been formed in response to the
correspondence produced by Nicol's letter to the *Manchester
Guardian*.

Many women in this group associated a loss of identity and
submergence in domesticity with the birth of a first child. Suzanne
Gail, a graduate whose first child was born in the mid-1960s,
records:

> It was never a burden to me to be a woman before I had Carl.
> Feminists had seemed to me to be tilting at windmills; women
> who allowed men to rule them did so from their own free
> choice. . . But afterwards I quite lost my sense of identity; for
> weeks it was an effort to speak. . . Yet it never occurs to
> anybody that young educated mothers are a social problem,
> and could be given some help in readjusting.[37]

Ambivalence about the identity of mother is often a submerged
theme in this writing, but the main problem identified is the slippage
from mother into housewife. Gail writes that "Carl and housework
are so closely interwoven that I cannot mention one without the
other", but also describes her son as "quite the best thing that has
ever happened to me", and staying at home as a housewife, even
part-time, as a possibility that she would never have considered
without a child to humanize the work.[38] In Margaret Drabble's first
novel, *A summer bird-cage*, ambivalence is expressed through the
conflict between two graduate sisters, discussing the fate of a
graduate friend who has embarked on motherhood. "It's the worst
catastrophe I've ever seen," Louise asserts. In order to convey how
terrible, she describes domestic detail – "a horrid little terrace
house", wet nappies, a litter of plastic toys, a door blocked by a
pram, the friend now so submerged in domesticity that "she never
took her apron off the whole time I was there". Louise's verdict on
this encounter is: "I will never have children." Her sister, Sarah,
reacts to this statement with horror.[39]

The theme of graduate woman's relationship to motherhood is
further developed in Drabble's third novel, *The millstone*. Sarah's
verdict is explored through its central character, Rosamund, who
not only has a child, but highly values her identity as mother, in a
novel which offers a powerful celebration of motherhood. The

problem Louise had identified about this identity in *A summer bird-cage* – the threat of submergence in domesticity – is generally resolved through a contrast between Rosamund and working-class women. Rosamund is mother but not housewife, never wears an apron, and is able to maintain her career despite childbirth. Working-class women are mother/housewife. As Rosamund's experience of pregnancy and childbirth allows her to glimpse their world through ante-natal appointments and childbirth within the National Health Service, she finds this sight profoundly distasteful and depressing. Although the novel expresses anxieties about the possibility of slippage from mother to housewife even for graduate women, these are resolved by making Rosamund unmarried, with a need for a career to support her baby and without a husband to service.

Working-class mothers are sometimes invoked in *The millstone* as comic figures, their submergence in domesticity a sign of class, excluding them from individuality. Across her NHS bed Rosamund hears them debate the merits of soapflakes and detergents, hand-washing versus launderettes, which child likes kippers and which prefers cheese on toast. They are named "Woman A", "Woman B" and "Woman C". More generally, working-class women are seen as oppressed, hopeless and passive, especially through attention to their bodies, coarsened and immobilized by pregnancy and its aftermath. In contrast to the muscles of Rosamund's own belly which snap back into place without a mark, the working-class women on her ward "looked as big as they had looked before" and she is haunted by the memory of "the way they walked, large and tied into shapeless dressing gowns, padding softly and stiffly". It is after an encounter at an ante-natal clinic with a woman who represents this oppressed condition – described as Italian or half-Italian – that Rosamund begins to think seriously about employing a child-minder so that she can continue with her work.[40] While working-class motherhood is seen as an awful fate, almost beyond endurance, this is a fate which Rosamund has no intention of sharing. After Octavia's birth she finishes her dissertation, and gets an academic post.

The millstone, in prising apart the identity of mother and housewife, offers an example of the way in which educated women distanced themselves from the latter identity by associating it with

163

working-class women. In the history of the Housebound Wives Register, later called the National Housewives Register (NHR), this theme is also apparent. Recruitment literature was aimed at "housebound wives with liberal interests and a desire to remain individual", and Nicol explained in 1960 that many existing members were graduates and ex-professional women, although no educational qualifications were required to join. Defining themselves in their title as housewives, many NHR groups nevertheless banned discussions of domestic subjects.[41]

As Alison Light has noted, "It is interesting, if somewhat disquieting, that it is not until the 1950s, when the servant class is finally a disappearing species, that the next generation of women begin to write of privacy itself as a form of oppression."[42] What is particularly apparent in the writings of groups who distanced themselves from the identity of housewife is an attachment to an educational or occupational identity which was not centred on the home. In the NHR's determination to maintain wide culture and interests, they not only identified those who were submerged in domesticity as working-class women, but also differentiated themselves from all women whose lives centred on the home and family. Those preoccupied with "domestic trivia" – the "cake-icers" as they were labelled by one member – were seen as over-domestic and lacking individuality.[43] The dismantling of the marriage bar and the increased participation of women in further and higher education contributed to this, but it could also be seen as a move to reinstate markers of female class identity which were no longer readily available through domesticity and home life.

In this early 1960s literature some of the preoccupations of the Women's Liberation Movement of the late 1960s are already apparent. Leonore Davidoff has speculated:

> It is possible that some of the impetus for the modern Women's Movement was fuelled by the servantless young middle-class housewife of the late 1960s and early 1970s confronted with taking on not just the increase in physical tasks of food preparation, washing dishes and clothes and round-the-clock care of small children, but the additional unrelenting dependence of all family members on her for emotional attendance, to the detriment of her own interests and identity.[44]

It is possible. Ann Oakley, who published her devastating analysis of the housewife's role in 1974, had made a list around 1968 of all the things she most wanted in the world. Alongside a mincer, a Hotpoint automatic washing machine, two more children and some huge meals in posh places she listed "a cleaning lady".[45]

A home of my own

"My home", the title of a women's magazine founded between the wars, is a phrase that recurs in women's oral testimony, both between the wars and in the post-war period. Often used interchangeably with "my own place", "our first place" and "our own home", it suggests the extent to which "a home of my own" was a place which women strongly desired. Its acquisition had begun to emerge as a real possibility for many women between the wars with the expansion of house-building for rent and for purchase, cheap credit, and the growth of building societies.[46] Substantial house-building programmes in the 1950s and 1960s made it a goal that was more easily realizable after the war, and led to a revolution in tenure. Home ownership inceased dramatically; 47 per cent of all houses in England and Wales were in owner-occupation by 1966 compared to only 26 per cent in 1945. There was a similar increase in the proportion of houses rented from local authorities or new town corporations, which doubled from 12 per cent in 1947 to 25 per cent in 1961.[47] By 1964 one family in four was living in accommodation that had been built since the war. The facilities that homes offered were also transformed. In 1947, 54 per cent of households were without their own bathroom and 59 per cent without a handbasin. By 1960 these figures had fallen to 20 per cent and 33 per cent.[48]

Religious and fairy-tale imagery were frequently used by those who made the movement into the expanding public rental or owner-occupied sector in the 1950s. Getting a house – especially a new house – was seen as miraculous, and the house itself often named a "palace" in comparison with what had gone before. One woman who had lived in a Nissen hut after the war described her move to a home in Harlow new town as "from purgatory to heaven".[49] While this partly reflects the acute housing shortages of the late 1940s, when many lived with in-laws or parents and some squatted in ex-army camps, it also suggests the extent to which improvements in housing were invested with emotional significance and value.

"My own" and "our own", often used as interchangeable terms by women, indicate not only the association of home with marriage, but also the ways in which marriage could produce material, social and psychological benefits in providing access to a home and what it might offer – a desired privacy, a sense of autonomy in not being subject to the authority, restrictions or interventions of others, a sense of worth and status. This meaning is apparent between the wars, when conforming to the ideals set out for them could offer women a way of avoiding a sense of subordination within marriage. To assert their authority and expertise within their own sphere offered scope for some measure of self-esteem within a model of family life which gave them little sense of having needs of their own or individualistic goals, in a period when marriage bars generally meant that weddings brought the end of any contact with working life outside the home. Although the meaning of marriage shifted after the war with the dismantling of marriage bars, it continued to be the main route to home for most indigenous women, and the associations of home with automony remained strong.

Some of the meanings of "a home of my own", and the ways in which it could be associated with privacy and autonomy, are highlighted by the experiences of single women. Elizabeth Arthur lived in rented accommodation in London as a single woman in the 1950s, sometimes sharing flats with friends. She records: "It never entered my head to buy a house. I wanted a home of my own. I'd lived in rented places. I associated marriage with a home of my own. That was terribly important – your own home, your own place."[50]

Chris, who also lived as a single woman in London in the 1950s, records:

> Even if I'd had the thought – oh, lovely to own my own home – where would the money have come from? I had no savings, and nobody would have given me a mortgage, so it never crossed my mind. . . I suppose I could have rented some rather dreary little bedsit, and had a little landlady keeping an eye on what was going on in the house, but I never went in for that until much later in my life.[51]

As Chris's account indicates, owner-occupation was particularly unlikely for single women since house purchase was associated with marriage and families, building societies did not favour loans to them, and their earnings were often too low to finance deposits and mortgage payments. Hostels were the solution that Chris found, and during the 1950s she lived in a series of London hostels which made provision for single women. Her account emphasizes the advantages of these, in providing a sense of security and safety, as well as companionship and support from other women. It also shows the ways in which those who lived in hostels were subject to a variety of rules and restrictions, and often had little privacy:

I was living in London when my father came home from the war, in a girls' hostel in Baker Street. I was sleeping in a dormitory, but I was used to that from boarding school, and from being in the WRNS. You were safe. In the circumstances it was an excellent place. You had to be in by 10 o'clock, and you did not have your own front door key unless you were going to be in late on a Saturday night, and even then you had to be in by 11 o'clock, but that was good considering what a lot of ropy people there were about in London. A YWCA I lived in near Victoria Station was approached through Wilton Road, which was crowded with prostitutes in shop doorways.

In the circumstances it was not an over-repressive set-up provided you were used to a communal life. When I moved to another hostel, I remember being seen by the superintendent or housekeeper. She was pretty good at summing people up, whether they were going to be honest and clean, and she accepted me. So I moved in there with my few belongings. We girls supported each other, as people do, women do. So I feel I was quite fortunate. The meals were not terribly exciting, but they were quite wholesome and adequate – some rationing was still in force. In one hostel I lived in you just had a small wardrobe, chest-of-drawers and bed, and that was it. You were partitioned off from your neighbour. The first hostel I lived in after the war was just like a hospital ward, with curtains you could draw if you wanted to dress. You didn't have much privacy in those places.[52]

Chris had a variety of jobs in this period, mainly in clerical and secretarial work. Other single women's route to accommodation

167

was through their employment. A range of occupations provided residential accommodation – from domestic service, through nursing, to teachers' training or Oxbridge colleges. The accommodation therefore varied, from the suite of rooms inhabited by a Cambridge don to the attic room in which some domestic servants still found themselves.

Many working-class single women in the 1950s lived with family. Michael Young and Peter Willmott's study of the East End of London showed that as many as 13 per cent of married daughters in the survey lived with parents, but the figure for those who were unmarried – both women and men – was over 50 per cent, and of the remainder more than half lived with siblings or other relatives. The notion that daughters would need a home of their own on marriage was reflected in a pattern whereby mothers helped to get houses for them by putting in a word for them with rent collectors, and occasionally bribing agents.[53] Single women would sometimes inherit housing on their parents' death, whether tenancies or owner-occupancy, but this was less likely when there were several children in the family. Mary Webster's foundation of the National Council for the Single Woman and her Dependants in 1965 drew attention to the numbers who, far from living an independent life, had caring as well as financial responsibilities for older parents, and little or no income of their own.[54]

A wedding-ring, while no guarantee of housing, usually helped very considerably. In her survey of marriage Rachel Pierce found that respondents' definitions of a "place of their own" varied, ranging from a furnished room or two to nothing less than an entire owner-occupied house. Only 25 per cent of her respondents had started marriages with an entire house or a self-contained unfurnished flat, but as many as 65.1 per cent had a home of their own on marriage when the definition was extended to include a furnished self-contained house or flat.[55]

Marriage influenced indigenous women's access to home in a variety of ways. It was not only single women who faced difficulties, but also those whose marriages ended. In these situations it became apparent that home was not literally "my own", for conveyancing was usually in the sole name of the husband, and in the rented sector most tenancies were held in the husband's name only. This caused considerable problems for those who were widowed, divorced or separated, especially if they had children, and many women who might otherwise have considered divorce stayed in marriages because they had nowhere to go, and no money of their own to find alternative accommodation. The route back to "home" for divorced or separated women was often through remarriage.[56]

The desire for "my home" as a place of autonomy is apparent in a hierarchy of desirability, which also reflected the ways in which home was valued by women as a place which could facilitate the production of domestic and familial life without the drudgery they often associated with their mothers' lives. There was a general blurring of class disinctions in housing – in the facilities that women used to do housework, the type of house they did it in, the tenure of that house, and how far they could allocate housework to other women through servant-keeping. But the hierarchy of desirability also reflected status. It was generally the modern owner-occupied detached house or bungalow that came at the top, although there were many ways in which the hierarchy was disrupted by distinctions of age and district. Georgian and Recency terraces in "good" or fashionable districts, for example, were regarded very differently from back-to-backs. Age could confer status, especially when it had historical associations, but was increasingly seen as inconvenient, especially in spacious housing. As Violet Markham commented, "The single-handed care of an old-fashioned house with stone passages, coal fires and an antiquated range has proved a heavy task during the war for a mistress bereft of maids."[57] Household manuals addressed to the middle classes warned that the large Victorian house needed to be in really good structural condition and repair to warrant serious consideration in a more or less servantless age.[58]

A preference for houses over flats partly reflected the low status of flat dwelling, although this did not apply in the same way in Scotland. Englishness was not associated with flat dwelling, and in *Brief encounter* the comfortable, spacious and chintzy interior of Laura's home is in marked contrast to the flat, which is given sordid associations as a place from which Laura flees to escape the possibility of extra-marital sexuality. Flats were also disliked because they did not guarantee privacy since, as one interviewee in Mass Observation's enquiry into people's homes in 1943 put it, "you're at the mercy of anyone who moves in above".[59] The same enquiry, where nearly 90 per cent of those interviewed were women, noted that "flats . . . are unpopular among the vast majority of people, particularly those with small children".[60] Hannah Gavron's interviews with women in London in the early 1960s recorded similar reservations about flats, highlighting the difficulties they presented for the mothers of young children.[61]

Within the preference for houses over flats, there was a further hierarchy, where detached houses or bungalows were often at the top, while semi-detached were usually preferred to terraces. A strong desire for privacy and autonomy also runs through these preferences. There were often objections to sharing facilities like front doors, lavatories and wash-houses, as well as accommodation itself. Being overlooked by neighbours was also disliked – whether this was in gardens, on balconies or inside houses.[62] Private tenancies were sometimes disliked because of the interventions of landlords or landladies. One interviewee reported to Mass Observation, "you're always having landladies poking about minding your business", while another had found owner-occupation a solution to this – "you're entirely on your own, no miserable landladies saying what you shall do".[63] Restrictions and rules imposed by public rental could also be resented – no pets, no lodgers.[64] In Harlow tenants put up net curtains and shrouded windows with pelmets in contravention of the architects' intention that houses should be light, airy and open-plan. They could thus subvert the rules, and at the same time facilitate privacy.[65] However desired, privacy could also be experienced as a miserable isolation. Accounts of the post-war movement to new towns converge on the theme of homesickness, misery and depression, often referred to as the "new town blues".[66]

Joyce Storey records a tiny pang of disappointment when "our first home" turned out to be one of a block of four with an alleyway between. "I would have preferred one of a pair," she writes, "they seem to me to be superior."[67] While types of house were associated with particular kinds of status, these were also disrupted by distinctions of tenure. Though by no means a universal aspiration, with rental sometimes preferred because it involved less financial commitment and less responsibility for property, the status of owner-occupation was high, as Jean Grant records:

My fiance lived in a council house, but one of the new council houses built after the war. They were semis with gardens front and back, central heating, new bathrooms. And we lived in a privately owned house. And my mother and father felt they were superior to his family because they owned theirs. We'd no bathroom, no central heating, no garden, just a backyard, and my mother and father felt superior to my fiance's family, just because his was a council-owned.[68]

The values associated with home within this hierarchy are apparent in Joyce Storey's account of her life after the war, where home in various contexts meant a desired privacy, a sense of worth and status, and the promise of a relief from drudgery through modern facilities. At the same time her account also shows the extent to which home was experienced by women as a place of economic dependence and subordination to men. The different, complex and often contradictory meanings of home in her account, and of her role within it, also suggest something of the way in which such meanings could shift and change for women in different contexts.

Storey describes the arrival of a letter from the council in 1947 allocating her a house as a "miracle" and her account of "our first home" to which it gives access seems to promise not only escape from drudgery, particularly through modern facilities, but also the sense of worth involved in being someone who owns a bathroom:

I wandered upstairs to view the bedrooms and to stand at the door to look around and imagine all of them carpeted and furnished in different colour schemes. When I came to the bathroom, this to me was the ultimate in luxury. Never in my whole life had I lived in a house with a bathroom. . . No more having to drag it [the tin bath] down every week and boil up saucepans of hot water to have a bath. I closed my eyes in sheer ecstacy. Just thinking about it brought a feeling of pride at the thought of owning a bathroom. There was more. There was a toilet upstairs next to the bathroom and another in the garden along with a coalhouse and a shed. No more chamber pots under the bed and the drudgery of having to toil up and down the stairs with slop pails to empty the wretched things.[69]

The context here is complex, going back to Storey's dream of fitted carpets and red velvet curtains as a girl which were associated with a desire to refuse her mother's life. It is also more immediate in her experiences of a succession of overcrowded, damp and dreary billets during the war and her post-war life with her two children in one room in a house owned by relatives. But there is a further meaning produced by her husband's opposition to moving away from this one room because they cannot afford the rent for the new house. As Storey asserts her determination to move even if she has to go out to work to pay the rent, and John forbids her, arguing that "your place is at home looking after my children and me", home becomes "just like a prison sentence".[70]

The dream of fitted carpets and red velvet curtains comes back to mock Storey in the new house, as the meaning of home becomes "the never-ending struggle to make ends meet out of a meagre weekly housekeeping allowance" and "lino [ends] at the foot of the stairs, and after that it was just bare boards".[71] But Storey makes her acquisition of a prefab in 1949 the ending of one volume of her autobiography as "my dream come true". Prefabs had been, in any case, "the desire and love of my life", a meaning which is associated particularly with the facilities they offer, in their "ultra-modern design".[72] The context here is also complex. The dream is partly of "a cottage with roses round the door", a recurrent image in her narrative which draws on representations of home in the English pastoral tradition. It is also, as home and children, the "happy ending to all the books and films we had ever read or seen". But, she records, "a tiny doubt like a dark cloud on the horizon kept nagging me". Storey hears her mother's voice – "don't think your life will be any different to mine". The image here is not of the open door of a new home, nor of the closed door of safety and privacy, nor of the fitted carpets through which she might refuse her mother's life, but the "loud slamming of the door" after marriage, and this produces a different meaning of home as confinement – "there is nothing else outside the narrow creativity of home and family".

"My beloved prefab" acquires another meaning in the context of John's desire for a son which Storey initially refuses: "Don't you understand? I really do not want any more children!" After her son is born, "life assumed a monotonous domestic pattern, an endless round of washing, cooking and cleaning which I believed would never end". This birth also means that she has to leave "the safe and secure haven of labour saving luxury in the little prefab", because it only has two bedrooms.[73] What she calls "the golden days of my beloved prefab" are over.

Storey's movement into owner-occupation in the 1960s, through the purchase of a council house, produces further meanings of home. A workmate tells her "if you buy your council house you won't be working-class any more", reminding her of her mother's warning about her dream of fitted carpets – "don't get ideas above your station".[74] Storey resists this meaning, and when John tells her he has bought the house she describes these as "magic words". Telling him of her desire for central heating, he promises her that if she pays for it through her earnings her name will go on the deeds. In the context of this desire, home has one meaning when the heating is installed – "a thrill of pride for the dream that my efforts had brought to fruition". In the context of John's response it has another. "Your name will never go on the deeds to this house," he tells her. "I pay the mortgage and it belongs to me. It will always be *mine*."[75] Through all the range of shifting meanings – avoiding the life of her mother, domestic drudgery, a safe and secure haven, happy home life, modernity, the pastoral – subordination to her husband becomes the dominant meaning of home. *Joyce's dream* opens with John's death and moves to his will, where "instead of being left the house as his next of kin, I had inherited only a fifth share".[76]

Race and home

The values embodied in the hierarchy of desirability for ideal homes were ones from which black people, at the bottom of this hierarchy, were excluded. Racism throughout all sectors of the housing market meant that modern houses, whether in new towns, on council estates or in the owner-occupied sector, were generally accessible only to white people. Black people were noticeable by their absence in new towns and from provision in the public sector.[77] As Sheila Patterson noted, "the public housing sector is locally based and locally oriented towards 'our own people' ".[78] When buying houses, black people were often denied access to what were seen as "better areas" by estate agents, building societies and other agencies allocating mortgages.[79]

Most accounts by black migrants focus on experiences of racism in the private rented sector. This was the sector where racism was at its most overt. The Milner Holland report on housing in London found that only 11 per cent of such property which was advertised did not specifically exclude black people, through "no coloureds" specifications.[80] Local authorities also sometimes boasted about racist policies. The Mayor of Lambeth, for example, denied charges that the borough favoured black applicants by claiming that "only six West Indian families have been rehoused in the worst type of requisitioned property – because no one else would take it".[81]

However, racism by local authorities was often more discreetly practised. In selecting areas for slum clearance or redevelopment, and the consequent duty to rehouse those whose properties were demolished, they could avoid designating areas where black people lived, and so the obligation to rehouse them.[82] They could enforce residential qualifications before an application could get on the register or start to be effective.[83] They could ask for information about country of origin on applications, or more discreetly mark forms in pencil. As one of the informants in the 1966 Political and Economic Planning survey reported, "We do make a note of the coloured applicants both on the list and on the interview sheets during a redevelopment scheme. I am not sure that we would like this to be known or that the committee would approve. . . . Usually we make a pencil mark on the form which can be rubbed out if necessary."[84] According to the 1961 10 per cent Census report *Commonwealth immigrants in the conurbations*, which included migrants from Cyprus and Malta as well as Africa, the Caribbean, and South Asia, only 4.5 per cent of Commonwealth households in six conurbations were council tenants compared with 23 per cent of all households. These statistics were widely regarded as defective because of their inclusion of large numbers of former colonizers returning to Britain, especially after Indian independence.[85] The 1966 Political and Economic Planning survey found "the proportion of coloured people in council housing is negligible: less than 1 per cent".[86]

White migrants as well as black were generally concentrated in the private rented sector on arrival in Britain – a sector which declined sharply in the period, halving between 1947 and 1961, although it declined much less sharply in large cities, particularly London. Where movement into new towns or new homes in the public rented or owner-occupied sector was one main marker of improved status for many indigenous women in the period, housing served as an important symbol of migrants' inferior status. The private rented sector had the worst conditions in terms of facilities like bathrooms, washbasins, sinks or hot water. While in 1960 only about 20 per cent of all households were without fixed baths, for example, the figure was nearly 50 per cent for privately rented households.[87] Moreover most migrants were concentrated in the furnished rather than the unfurnished part of this sector, which had the worst facilities.[88] In Bedford in the mid-1950s, anti-Italian feeling centred on multi-occupied housing, and the *Bedfordshire Times* depicted Italians as "ear-shattering neighbours", complaining of "the din caused by these voluble and highly excitable people".[89] Black migrants were constructed as dirty and primitive through reference to the over-crowded conditions which racism produced.

The low status of their housing could be experienced particularly sharply by those who had enjoyed higher status back home, as on arrival in Britain all distinctions of status were collapsed. Neither the "no coloureds, no Irish" sign in the private rented sector nor the ways in which council housing was allocated on a racial basis made any distinctions of class. As the 1966 Political and Economic Planning survey noted: "Colour prejudice and the discrimination that follows from it operates in a blanket, indiscriminating way and there is no attempt to distinguish between coloured people."[90]

Students could sometimes circumvent this barrier through student halls of residence, but many were left to the mercies of the private sector. Leena Dhingra, the daughter of Indian parents who were refugees in Paris following partition, first came to England in the mid-1950s to a Quaker boarding school. But she records that when she left "the protected precincts of my boarding school" for London:

"Are you coloured?" said the voice on the 'phone.
"I beg your pardon?" was my reply.
"Where have you come from?" said the voice.
"From Paris," said I.
"Are you French?" said the voice again.
"No, no no. I'm Indian," came my reply.
"Sorry dear, but we can't take no coloureds here."
Surprise ceded to shock, followed by indignation. A stink

bomb had been thrown open and without realising it at the time I had absorbed its smell, as for my next call, I said:

"Excuse me, but, I am an Indian student calling about the room you advertised."[91]

In Buchi Emecheta's novel *Second class citizen* Adah finds herself living with Nigerians with whom she would not have associated back home. They encourage her to conform to British ideas of blackness and work in a factory, but what is most demeaning about this advice is that it comes from people with whom she has to share accommodation. Her priorities are not only finding a job as a librarian, but also, with great difficulty, seeking alternative accommodation.

Adah's conditions – "cramped together in one half-room" – with her children and husband, also suggest something of the way in which black women were excluded from privacy.[92] Mrs B records:

I just didn't like it, especially the living conditions were bad. When we came we had just a bed, and three of us into the one room. In Jamaica we live as a family, but when we came we had to live amongst strangers to get a room. . . At least I thought I could have a room of my own, the privacy which we didn't get. . . When I first came all my intention was to go back home. I sit in the room and cried. . . But we couldn't walk it home, walk it back to Jamaica, so you had to cope.[93]

Vi Chambers records:

I was expecting so much. I was so shocked to come and live in one room, sharing kitchen and bathroom with three other people and there was no space, whereas at home we had acres of land to roam. It was completely different. If I'd had the money and could have afforded it, I'd have gone straight back home.

A main theme in narratives by many migrants – "you couldn't get places to stay" – usually refers to acute difficulty in securing any sort of familial life. "No children", although it did not usually appear on signs, was a restriction that was common in the private sector, making the search for accommodation – difficult enough for most migrants without children – much worse for those who had children with them. It is a theme in accounts by Irish and Polish migrants.[94] Una Cooper arrived in London from Dublin in 1954 to join her husband, and they lived at first in a flat in the private rented sector, staying for some two years before they were evicted and she began a search for accommodation:

"No Coloured or Irish need apply". It was Houses to let, Flats to let, Rooms to let, but every one of them "No Irish or Coloured need apply". So I thought, I'll present myself at their doors. But when they'd hear my accent some of them would say, "It's gone." Of course, I had no bus fare or anything. I would have to walk. I would go anyway but no way would they take children.[95]

"No way would they take children" is also a recurrent theme in accounts by black migrants. Constance Nembhard records that ". . . if you had children, nobody wanted to rent to you, not even your own people. When they bought their own house they didn't want anybody with children."[96] Urena Phillips came to London from Jamaica in 1959 to join an aunt and worked in a factory making television cables, leaving her three children in Jamaica with her mother. When she had a child in Britain, she records, it was very difficult to find rented rooms: "Very hard, very, very. Because they didn't want any children, and if you knock on an English house they would say no, no coloureds, and black people didn't have any places much at that time. So it was very hard."[97]

Landlords – both black and white – who did let to women with children usually made it clear that they were there on sufferance and often used intimidation to get them out. Urena Phillips records that "I have to move every three months. Because the children would play, and they would complain and they would give you notice you've got to go somewhere else and you keep moving and moving about. I could count some places."[98] Elsie George, who was recruited into nursing from Nigeria in 1950, lived initially in a nurses' home. Her problems over accommodation came when she married and had children:

On a sunny day I tried to sit with them outside in the garden. And the landlady said, "Oh no, I'm sorry you can't take these children and put them outside while the neighbours passing by, they don't want to see the black children." So when I had the third one, she said we had to leave the flat, she didn't know we were going to have a big family. We looked around again for a long long while . . . the notice nearly expired and we were more worried that we'd be evicted.[99]

In her autobiography Emecheta records that her first black landlord and landlady complained that her baby cried a lot and tore

the wallpaper, and that her toddler wet the couch so that it stank –
"in short they wanted us out". In *Second class citizen* Adah's
children are "hushed and bullied into silence so that the black
landlord and his wife are not disturbed", and to remove them the
landlord advertises for a foster-mother.[100]

The difficulties involved in domestic arrangements are also a
strong theme in accounts by migrant women. Rented rooms in the
private sector were often in houses which lacked bathrooms.
Constance Nembhard records:

> In those days it took nearly three days by 'plane. I left Kingston
> on Sunday afternoon and I arrived in the building about half
> past seven on Tuesday morning. And the first thing I asked for
> was the bathroom, to be told there was none. . . The places we
> had to live in were damp and awful. You lived in them because
> there was nowheree else to go. . . I lived in this country for over
> two years without getting a proper bath. I'm not ashamed to
> say it, because I refused to go to a public bath, because I just felt
> I was going to catch something. My husband used to go off
> every Sunday morning to this bath with his towel. I wouldn't
> go – I said, "I'm not bathing there". And I didn't have a child
> then, but I bought one of those baby's baths, and I put it in
> front of the fire, and that's where I had my wash every night. I
> didn't have a full bath for about two years, because the houses
> didn't have any baths in them.[101]

The combination of inadequate facilities, cramped conditions and
sharing with others made domestic arrangements difficult, arduous
and unsatisfactory, and the attainment of any sort of domestic
comfort almost out of the question. Mrs Wilson, who migrated from
Trinidad in 1957, records:

> Life was a bit rough because we only lived in one room. You
> had to have a lamp in it to keep you warm. . . When you wash
> your clothes you have to hang it around because there's
> nowhere outside to hang anything.[102]

Nembhard also lived in one room on arrival in 1956 with a stove in
one corner:

> There were certain things you couldn't eat – because if you fried
> bacon or anything, all your clothes just stank. That was the first
> place. We left there after a while and went somewhere else
> which wasn't quite so bad in that the cooker was on the

landing. But there was no form of heating, so we had to resort to paraffin which stank your clothes out.[103]

One strategy that black women used to get accommodation was the use of a variety of subterfuges to conceal their identity. Amanda Murphy, as a student at Hull University, spent her first three months in halls of residence, but then had to look for a room when she could no longer afford halls:

The lad who was a doctor who was my friend and his girlfriend got the flat below me. And they . . . concocted a surname for me. They called me Craig! What a name. But he said that was a good Hull name. He said they like short names, they don't go for long names, don't get something like Prendergast. . . And I had got references, and they never saw me. It was just all done through the university letting services. . . They never saw me at all.[104]

Emecheta represents Adah in *Second-class citizen* disguising her voice when she telephones to make enquiries about an advertisement for a vacant room. Despite the fact that there is no "no coloureds" sign on it, she remains cautious:

She knew that any white would recognise the voice of an African woman on the phone. So to eradicate that, she pressed her wide tunnel-like nostrils together as if to keep out a nasty smell. She practised and practised her voice in the loo, and was satisfied with the result. The landlady would definitely not mistake her for a woman from Birmingham or London, yet she could be Irish, Scots or an English-speaking Italian. At least, all these people were white.[105]

White women married to black men also sometimes adopted a version of this strategy. Sometimes the wife would wait until the tenancy was signed and the house occupied before revealing her husband's identity.[106]

Mrs Wilson records, "You had to be thankful to the Poles and Hungarians that were here, because as foreigners as well, they help us along by renting us a room." Gloria Lewis, who came to Leamington Spa in 1960 from Jamaica, found that "it was mostly Indians who'd rent you a house. A lot of white people wouldn't rent to you, just the Indians." In Vi Chambers's experience, "I found somewhere by word of mouth. You see I could never get a place. For instance, if a white person had a place they wouldn't let it to you.

It was always a black person who had a room you could get."[107]
As this evidence suggests, one common strategy used by many
migrants to get out of the private rented sector was to move into the
owner-occupied sector and finance mortgage payments by letting
off rooms, often to other migrants. One Polish family who had no
furniture or money after buying their own house took in lodgers
two to a room, while the seven family members all slept in one
room.[108]

When Genowefa Dziewanda and her husband bought a house in
Oldham in 1949 they adopted this system, pooling resources with
another Polish couple, and letting off a bedroom to two Polish
women who wanted to move into private lodgings, away from the
hostel where they were accommodated. Two years later they bought
a larger, three-bedroom house and again let off rooms as private
lodgings to a variety of single people who wanted to move out of
hostels – Polish and Irish – as well as families. Dziewanda's account
suggests the way in which this form of housing could also serve to
foster networks of support and friendship, forging a Polish
community in Britain which was also promoted by Polish clubs:

> When we moved to the three-bedroom house there were three
> families of us. We were all friends. When Christmas came we
> always got together – pay so much and we make one meal and
> sit together. Men sometimes playing cards, and we women in
> the front bedroom sitting doing a bit of sewing, have a
> chat.[109]

The "sou sou" or "pardner" system of pooling resources to
provide deposits for house purchase was used by Caribbean people
in Britain, and women played an important part in initiating and
organizing "pardners" which were also used to support families in
the Caribbean.[110] Better housing could also be used to foster black
community, by offering a place for religious worship and community life in the context of racism in white churches. Valentina
Alexander argues that "what was obvious from the start was that if
you were to survive at all you would have to be anchored in a strong
network of support, and it was precisely this kind of life-line that
many women discovered in the Black-led Church."[111] Services were
often held at first in front rooms of houses.[112] Mrs H., a Pentecostal
preacher, bought her own house through a "pardner", and used her
front room as a "Revival Centre" to hold Sunday services.[113]

Home was thus very important in black women's resistance to the range of meanings of "you couldn't get places to stay" – that there was no place for black people in Britain, that they were rootless and transient, that black women were required as workers but had no domestic or familial identity or life. Acquiring better housing, when this could be achieved, did not usually bring with it a sense of belonging in Britain, and for many the meaning of home remained back home. But it could provide a sense that there was some area of life in Britain which was "my own". "In this country," one black woman records, "the women came and they decided they couldn't live in these terrible conditions, and so this saving to go home in two years had to go, because they needed houses to live in."[114] Vi Chambers, who lived in a series of rooms over 13 years, finally got a council house in 1969. She records:

This was like heaven, this was my first real home. I'm the only person that has lived in here. I moved in when it was new. . . Actually it was amazing that they gave me this. I was so shocked when I came to see this place. It was so beautiful. There was no furniture in, so it looked massive, and I was so pleased because I didn't expect that they would have given me a new place. I was expecting a dump. That's what they always did to black people then. . . This is my first home, I love it here.[115]

Constance Nembhard records:

That was the greatest thing that happened to me, getting my own house. . . We decided we had to save to buy somewhere to live after my first child was born. We came in 1956 and we managed to get our own place in 1959. We hadn't heard about council places, we didn't know anything about things like that at all, and the few friends we met all decided we would help each other to get our own places. There were about four of us, and we did. And from then on it wasn't too bad. We bought these houses and we had to rent to people to be able to pay for the mortgage. That also created a problem for me because I hadn't lived with people before, other than just my family. . . And after that, I'd had enough. I said, "my children are growing up, and I don't want them to grow up with all these different types of people around". And then we bought this, it was just us, and it felt more like home. . . We grew up, just my father and mother and brothers and sisters in one house.

Nobody else. And I felt at last I was able to give my children what I got . . . at least they didn't have to go through what we had to go through when we came here first.[116]

Una Cooper finally got a house only after several years of homelessness in London. Her experience of the private rented sector involved both eviction by a private landlord and, as an Irish woman with children, constant rejections in her search for alternatives. Homelessness meant reliance on what the council offered – in her case a hostel for homeless people where only mothers and their children were allowed, so separating her from her husband. The solution offered by the council was return to Dublin:

I said, "No, I'm not going back now. Everything has gone. My home has gone. I've nothing left. I'm going to make a life for myself here, I'm not going back." And that really made me angry, to think that he could get me a Corporation house in Dublin to walk into, and they'd pay my fare, after going through all this.[117]

She was transferred to short-stay homeless accommodation until a doctor intervened, writing and eventually phoning Camden council to insist on the urgency of her needs and her children's:

And, do you know, within twenty-four hours I was offered a house. And when we went up to see it I couldn't believe it, you know, I just couldn't believe we'd got it.[118]

Epilogue

Enoch Powell's notorious "rivers of blood" speech in 1968 lies outside the period covered here. By that date British rule over an empire which in 1945 had still encompassed India was virtually at an end. This did not always mean the end of white rule. UDI in Zimbabwe was declared in 1965. In 1967 Britain made its second bid to join the EEC. This was one step in a turn to Europe which, as Catherine Hall argues, was one response to the loss of imperial power.[1] There was a further Immigration Act in 1968 which, along with those of 1962 and 1965, could be seen as a further response.

Powell's speech is remarkable in its complete absence of references to empire. Steeped in Britain's imperial history, Powell said in 1991, "When I resigned my chair in Australia in 1939 in order to come home to enlist, had I been asked, 'What is the State whose uniform you wish to wear and in whose service you expect to perish?' I would have said, 'The British Empire'."[2] In 1947 he argued that the result of socialism in imperial affairs "threatened the eclipse of the whole Empire, which is the structure on which we are dependent for our very existence".[3] But by the end of the 1950s, faced with the fact of the end of colonial rule, Powell began to forget the history of the British empire.[4]

By the time of his 1968 speech, imperial national identity, so strongly claimed by Powell during and immediately after the war, is completely forgotten. In his account of "immigration" the countries that Britain had colonized become simply "immigrants' countries of origin" – places to which, in his proposals for repatriation, they should return. It is the final chapters of imperial history that come back to haunt the speech through this forgetting – in Catherine Hall's terms – a "blind eye . . . turned to the past" – what he both knows and does not know. It is what he does not mention, the end of empire, that makes "immigration" the focus of his concerns about national decline.

Powell's speech draws on themes that began to be developed in 1948 in the letter from MPs to Attlee. The concern to control national borders which they had articulated in response to the arrival of the *Empire Windrush*, "by legislation if necessary", is reiterated. Like them Powell constructs the "colour problem" as something which belongs to other countries – he specifies America – and which is being introduced as an alien element in British cultural life through "immigration". He represents "immigration" as a "national danger" to which the answer is "stopping . . . further inflow and . . . promoting the maximum outflow".[5]

The speech also draws extensively on cultural representations of race developed in the 1950s and early 1960s, with their construction of differences between white and black in terms of home and family. Powell is concerned particularly with numbers – "numbers are of the essence". This is not simply about compiling arrays of statistics on numbers entering, but includes themes which had been developed in the early 1960s about black reproduction. He is concerned about the "immigrant" birth rate. He is also concerned that the "existing population" find "their wives [are] unable to obtain hospital beds in childbirth".

Powell also produces a vision of "ordinary English people" threatened in their homes by "immigrants". "Home" is an important term in the speech. Through the alleged letter from a constituent that he quotes, he symbolizes "ordinary English people" through the figure of a white woman – described as an old age pensioner who had lost her husband and sons in the war. Home as housing is the white woman's livelihood as she earns money by letting accommodation to white tenants after the loss of her husband and sons. As neighbourhood, it is her "quiet street" which is turned into "a place of noise and confusion" when "the immigrants moved in". As a private sphere it is subject to constant threat on the boundaries between public and private. Here the speech focuses on these boundaries – the chain on the door which affords some protection from attack, the windows which are broken, the letter-box through which excreta are pushed. The small-scale and familiar – home, neighbourhood, locality – are made into symbols of a nation under siege. "Immigrants", denoted implicitly as black male, collapse the boundaries between public and private through their invasion of her home and "quiet street".

The story of nation in imperial national identity had been a story of white masculinity signifying power, conquest, action and discovery in vast territory and Britain's supremacy in the world. Powell's "rivers of blood" speech reverses this imagery. The story of nation he tells is about powerlessness and vulnerability in an English street, and it has at its centre the figure of a white woman.

Notes

Introduction

1. Leonore Davidoff & Catherine Hall, *Family fortunes: men and women of the English middle class 1780–1850* (London: Hutchinson, 1987); Leonore Davidoff, *Worlds between: historical perspectives on gender and class* (Cambridge: Polity, 1995).
2. Some feminist work has revalued the private sphere as a site where women could create networks of female power and routes to political influence. For a critical discussion of this literature see Alice Kessler-Harris, "Gender ideology in historical reconstruction: a case study from the 1930s", *Gender and History* 1, Spring 1989.
3. Recent work includes "The question of 'home'," *New Formations* 17, Summer 1992; George Robertson, Melinda Mash, Lisa Tickner, Jon Bird, Barry Curtis, Tim Putnam (eds), *Travellers' tales: narratives of home and displacement* (London: Routledge, 1994); Rosemary Marangoly George, *The politics of home: postcolonial relocations and twentieth-century fiction* (Cambridge: Cambridge University Press, 1996).
4. See, for example, bell hooks, *Feminist theory: from margin to center* (Boston, Mass: South End Books, 1984); Patricia Hill Collins, *Black feminist thought: knowledge, consciousness and the politics of empowerment* (London: Routledge, 1991); bell hooks, *Yearning: race, gender and cultural politics* (London: Turnaround, 1991); Carol Boyce Davies, *Black women, writing and identity: migrations of the subject* (London: Routledge, 1994).
5. Martin Pugh, "Domesticity and the decline of feminism", in *British feminism in the twentieth century*, Harold Smith (ed.) (Aldershot: Edward Elgar, 1990), p. 162; Lynn Segal, "A feminist looks at the family", in *Understanding the family*, John Muncie, Margaret Wetherell, Rudi Dallos, Allan Cochrane (eds) (London: Sage, 1995), p. 298; Lynn Segal, 'Look back in anger: men in the fifties", in *Male order: unwrapping masculinity*, Rowena Chapman & Jonathan Rutherford (eds) (London: Lawrence & Wishart, 1988), p. 77; Lynn Segal, *Straight sex: the politics of pleasure* (London: Virago, 1994), pp. 2–4. For a critical discussion of the 1950s as a nadir for women, see Alison Light, *Forever England: femininity, literature and conservatism between the wars* (London: Routledge, 1991), pp. 217–21.

6. Shabnam Grewal, Jackie Kay, Liliane Landor, Gail Lewis, Pratibha Parma (eds), *Charting the journey: writings by black and third world women* (London: Sheba, 1988), pp. 10–11.
7. Delia Jarrett-Macauley argues that "Black women in Britain . . . are still under-produced, under-explored, under-researched. We are a long way from the dynamic cultural and literary activities of African-Americans and in any event, our specific histories are quite different, as are the political practices and ideologies that have developed out of these." Delia Jarrett-Macauley (ed.), *Reconstructing womanhood, reconstructing feminism: writings on black women* (London: Routledge, 1996), p. xii. Other literature which is specific to the British context includes Amrit Wilson, *Finding a voice: Asian women in Britain* (London, Virago, 1978). Hazel Carby, "White women listen! Black feminism and the boundaries of sisterhood", in *The empire strikes back*, Centre for Contemporary Cultural Studies (London: Hutchinson, 1982); Pratibha Parmar, "Gender, race and class: Asian women in resistance", in *ibid.*; Valerie Amos, Gail Lewis, Amina Mama, Pratibha Parmar (eds) "Many voices, one chant", *Feminist Review* 17, Autumn 1984; Beverley Bryan, Stella Dadzie, Suzanne Scafe, *The heart of the race: black women's lives in Britain* (London: Virago, 1985); Kum-Kum Bhavnani & Margaret Coulson, "Transforming socialist feminism: the challenge of racism", *Feminist Review* 23, June 1986; Lauretta Ngcobo (ed.), *Let it be told: black women writers in Britain* (London: Virago, 1987); Ziggi Alexander, "Let it lie upon the table: the status of black women's biography in the UK", *Gender and History* 2, Spring 1990; Pratibha Parmar, "Black feminism: the politics of articulation", in *Identity, community, culture, difference*, Jonathan Rutherford (ed.) (London: Lawrence & Wishart, 1990); Razia Aziz, "Feminism and the challenge of racism: deviance or difference?" in *Knowing women: feminism and knowledge*, Helen Crowley & Susan Himmelweit (eds) (Cambridge: Polity, 1992); Avtar Brah, "Women of South Asian origin in Britain: issues and concerns", in *Racism and antiracism: inequalities, opportunities and policies*, Peter Braham, Ali Rattansi, Richard Skellington (eds) (London: Sage, 1992); Amina Mama, "Black women and the British state: race, class and gender analysis for the 1990s", in *ibid.*; Gail Lewis, "Black women's employment and the British economy", in *Inside Babylon: the Caribbean diaspora in Britain*, Winston James & Clive Harris (eds) (London: Verso, 1993); Claudette Williams, "We are a natural part of many different struggles: black women organising", in *ibid.*; Amina Mama, *Beyond the masks: race, gender and subjectivity* (London: Routledge, 1995); Lola Young, *Fear of the dark: "race", gender and sexuality in the cinema* (London: Routledge, 1996). Carole Boyle Davies argues that the family is sometimes represented as a site of oppression in black women's autobiographical literature. Boyce Davies, *Black women, writing and identity*, p. 21.
8. A major historical work on white women and racism in a British

context is Vron Ware, *Beyond the pale: white women, racism and history* (London: Verso, 1992).

9. Andrew Nocon, "A reluctant welcome?: Poles in Britain in the 1940s", *Oral history*, Spring 1986, p. 82.

10. Kathleen Paul, "The politics of citizenship in post-war Britain", *Contemporary Record* **6**, 1992; Kathleen Paul, "British subjects and British stock: Labour's postwar imperialism", *Journal of British Studies* **34**, 1995.

11. Carby, "White woman listen!", pp. 218–19.

12. Bill Schwarz argues that "the conventional historiography of decolonisation . . . presents a stunning lack of curiosity about the impact of decolonisation within the metropolitan formation, or, more particularly, within the heartland of England itself". See Bill Schwarz, "The only white man in there: the re-racialisation of England, 1956–1968", *Race and Class* **38**, 1996, p. 65.

13. Sheila Patterson used "dark strangers" as the title of her study of West Indian migrants in Brixton. See Sheila Patterson, *Dark strangers: a sociological study of the absorption of a recent West Indian migrant group in Brixton, South London* (London: Tavistock, 1963).

14. For constructions of Britishness and Englishness, see Tom Nairn, *The break-up of Britain: crisis and neo-nationalism* (London: New Left Books, 1981); Eric Hobsbawn & Terence Ranger (eds), *The invention of tradition* (Cambridge: Cambridge University Press, 1983); Patrick Wright, *On living in an old country: the national past in contemporary Britain* (London: Verso, 1985); Robert Colls & Philip Dodd (eds), *Englishness: politics and culture, 1880–1920* (London: Croom Helm, 1986); Paul Gilroy, *"There ain't no black in the union jack": the cultural politics of race and nation* (London: Hutchinson, 1987); Raphael Samuel (ed.), *Patriotism: the making and unmaking of British national identity* (3 vols.] (London: Routledge, 1989); Bernard Crick (ed.), *National identities: the constitution of the United Kingdom* (Oxford: Blackwell, 1991); Light, *Forever England*; Roy Porter (ed.), *Myths of the English* (Cambridge: Polity, 1992); Floya Anthias, Nira Yuval-Davis, Harriet Cain, *Racialised boundaries: race, nation, gender, colour and class and the anti-racist struggle* (London: Routledge, 1992); Robin Cohen, *Frontiers of identity: the British and the others* (London: Longman, 1994); Judy Giles & Tim Middleton (eds), *Writing Englishness, 1900–1950: an introductory source book on national identity* (London: Routledge, 1995).

15. For the feminization and domestication of Englishness between the wars, see Light, *Forever England*; Raphael Samuel, "Exciting to be English", in *Patriotism*, vol. 1, pp. xxii–xxv.

16. George Orwell, "England your England", in *Inside the whale and other essays* (Harmondsworth: Penguin, 1971, first published 1941), p. 89; Charles Curran, "The new estate in Great Britain", *Spectator*, 20 January 1956; Charles Curran, "The politics of the new estate", *Spectator*, 17 February 1956.

17. For a review of the literature on the "problem family", see A. F. Philp & N. Timms, *The problem of the "problem family": a critical review of the literature concerning the "problem family" and its treatment* (London: Family Service Units, 1957).

18. Betty Jerman, *The lively-minded women: the first twenty years of the National Housewives Register* (London: Heinemann, 1981), pp. 1–2, 5, 11; Betty Friedan, *The feminine mystique* (London: Gollancz, 1963); Hannah Gavron, *The captive wife: conflicts of housebound mothers* (London: Routledge & Kegan Paul, 1966).

19. Richard Broad & Suzie Fleming (eds), *Nella Last's war: a mother's diary 1939–45* (Bristol: Falling Wall Press, 1981), p. 296.

20. Maureen Lawrence, *A telling and a keeping: a writer's autobiography* (London: Women's Press, 1989), p. 11.

21. Nocon, "A reluctant welcome?", pp. 79–80; Bogusia Temple, "Telling tales: accounts and selves in the journeys of British Poles", *Oral history*, Autumn 1995, pp. 60–64.

22. See especially Tariq Modood, " 'Black', racial equality and Asian identity", *New Community* 14, 1988. For a discussion of these debates, see Avtar Brah, "Difference, diversity and differentiation", in *"Race", culture and difference*, James Donald & Ali Rattansi (eds) (London: Sage, 1992), pp. 127–31.

23. Buzz Johnson, *"I think of my mother": notes on the life and times of Claudia Jones* (London: Karia Press, 1985), pp. 79–90.

24. W. W. Daniel, *Racial discrimination in England, based on the PEP Report* (Harmondsworth: Penguin, 1968), p. 40; Clifford Hill, *How colour prejudiced is Britain?* (London: Gollancz, 1965), pp. 14, 75.

25. Winston James, "Migration, racism and identity formation", in James & Harris (eds), *Inside Babylon*, p. 234.

26. A number of historians have made comparisons between American and British history in relation to the treatment of immigration and racism. Tony Kushner and Kenneth Lunn comment that "unlike America, the study of immigration, minority groups and racism has not concerned the 'mainstream' of historians in Britain". Panikos Panayi argues that

     It would be impossible to write a history of the USA without reference to the central issues of slavery and immigration. However, in Britain histories of the country constantly appear without reference, for instance, to Irish and Jewish immigration during the nineteenth century. . . The situation in Britain is aggravated not only by a reluctance to accept the role of immigrants in the country's history, but also by the national myth, which revolves around the concept of Britain as a tolerant state.

     See Tony Kushner & Kenneth Lunn, *The politics of marginality: race, the radical right and minorities in twentieth century Britain* (London: Frank Cass, 1990), p. vii; Panikos Panayi, "The historiography of immigrants and ethnic minorities: Britain compared with the USA", *Ethnic and Racial Studies* 19, 1996, pp. 834–5.

27. Stuart Hall comments that the term "immigrant" "places one equivocally as *really* belonging *somewhere else*. 'And when are you going back home?' " Quoted in Boyce Davies, *Black women, writing and identity*, p. 114.

28. Bernard Crick argues that "After 1950, the end of empire obviously caused greater psychological problems for the English than for the others. An exaggerated sense of power continued amid visible symptoms of decline." Bernard Crick, "The English and the British", in *National identities*, p. 99.

29. Elizabeth Roberts has recently provided a very substantial extension of oral history work on this period in *Women and families: an oral history, 1940–1970* (Oxford: Blackwell, 1995). Other main works on women's history in the period are Elizabeth Wilson, *Only halfway to paradise: women in post-war Britain 1945–1968* (London: Tavistock, 1980); Denise Riley, *War in the nursery: theories of the child and the mother* (London: Virago, 1983); Jane Lewis, *Women in Britain since 1945* (Oxford: Blackwell, 1992); Martin Pugh, *Women and the women's movement in Britain 1914–1959* (Basingstoke: Macmillan, 1992). None of these have any particular focus on race. General historiographies of the post-war period, while sometimes including brief references to race, generally exclude reference to gender. See, for example, Peter Catterall, "The state of literature on post-war British history", in *Post-war Britain, 1945–1964: themes and perspectives*, Anthony Gorst, Lewis Johnman, W. Scott Lucas (eds), (London: Pinter Publishers, 1989).

30. Donald Hinds, *Journey to an illusion: the West Indian in Britain* (London: Heinemann, 1966); Elyse Dodgson, *Motherland: West Indian women to Britain in the 1950s* (London: Heinemann, 1984); Bryan et al., *The heart of the race*; Lambeth Council & the Voice, *Forty winters on: memories of Britain's post-war Caribbean immigrants* (London: South London Press, 1988); Ben Bousquet & Colin Douglas, *West Indian women at war: British racism in world war II* (London: Lawrence & Wishart, 1991); Chapeltown Black Women's Writers Group, *When our ship comes in: black women talk* (Castleford: Yorkshire Art Circus, 1992). *"Sorry, no vacancies": life stories of senior citizens from the Caribbean* (London: Notting Dale Urban Studies Centre, 1992); Ethnic Communities Oral History Project, *The motherland calls: African Caribbean experiences* (London: Ethnic Communities Oral History Project, 1989); Roots Oral History, *Rude awakening: African/Caribbean settlers in Manchester* (Roots Oral History Project, 1992). Recent histories of black and Asian people in Britain before 1945 include Peter Fryer, *Staying power: the history of black people in Britain* (London: Pluto, 1984); Ron Ramdin, *The making of the black working class in Britain* (Aldershot: Gower Publishing, 1987); Rosina Visram, *Ayahs, lascars and princes: Indians in Britain 1700–1947* (London: Pluto Press, 1986).

31. Liz Heron (ed.), *Truth, dare or promise: girls growing up in the 50s*

(London: Virago, 1985); Carolyn Steedman, *Landscape for a good woman: a story of two lives* (London: Virago, 1991).

32. Terry Lovell, "Landscapes and stories in 1960s British realism", *Screen* **31** (4) Winter 1990, p. 375.

33. Laura Marcus, " 'Enough about you, let's talk about me' ": recent autobiographical writing, *New Formations* **1**, Spring 1987, p. 83.

34. Carolyn Heilbrun, *Writing a woman's life* (London: Women's Press, 1989).

35. Passivity is a theme in daughters' sense of self in Lawrence, *A telling and a keeping*; Mary Evans, *A good school: life at a girls' grammar school in the 1950s* (London: Women's Press, 1991).

36. Ros Coward, *Our treacherous hearts: why women let men get their way* (London: Faber & Faber, 1993), pp. 91–2.

37. Margaret Forster, *Hidden lives: a family memoir* (London: Viking, 1995), p. 296.

38. *Ibid.*, pp. 306–7.

39. See for example Personal Narratives Group (ed.), *Interpreting women's lives: feminist theory and personal narratives* (Bloomington: Indiana University Press, 1989); Rosalind Edwards, "Connecting method and epistemology: a white woman interviewing black women", *Women's Studies International Forum* **13**, 1990; Sherna Gluck & Daphne Patai (eds), *Women's words: the feminist practice of oral history* (London: Routledge, 1991); Susan Geiger, "What's so feminist about doing women's oral history?", in Cheryl Johnson-Odim & Margaret Strobel (eds), *Expanding the boundaries of women's history: essays on women in the third world* (Bloomington: Indiana University Press, 1992); Jennifer Scanlon, "Challenging the imbalances of power in feminist oral history: developing a take-and-give methodology", *Women's Studies International Forum* **16**, 1993; Bogusia Temple, "Constructing Polishness, researching Polish women's lives: feminist auto/biographical accounts", *Women's Studies International Forum* **17**, 1994; Tamara Jack, "Countering voices: an approach to Asian and feminist studies in the 1990s", *Women's Studies International Forum* **17**, 1994; Mary Stuart, "You're a big girl now: subjectivities, feminism and oral history", *Oral History*, Autumn 1994; Lynn Echevarria-Howe, "Reflections from the participants: the process and product of life history work", *Oral History*, Autumn 1995; Diane Reay, "Insider perspectives on stealing the words out of women's mouths: interpretation in the research process", *Feminist Review* **53**, 1996.

40. Daphne Patai, "Is ethical research possible?", in *Women's words*, Gluck & Patai (eds) p. 139.

41. Anne McClintock, *Imperial leather: race, gender and sexuality in the colonial contest* (London: Routledge, 1995), p. 311.

42. Patai, "Is ethical research possible?", p. 150.

43. Audre Lorde, *The cancer journals* (London: Sheba, 1985), p. 15.

44. Hazel Carby, *Reconstructing womanhood: the emergence of the Afro-*

American woman novelist (Oxford: Oxford University Press, 1987), pp. 9–10.

45. Catherine Hall, "The ruinous ghost of empire past", *The Times Higher Educational Supplement*, 8 March 1996.

46. Susan Friedman, "Beyond white and other: relationality and narratives of feminist discourse", *Signs: Journal of Women in Culture and Society* 21, Autumn 1995, p. 5.

47. Hall, "The ruinous ghost".

48. John Mackenzie, *Propaganda and empire: the manipulation of British public opinion 1880–1960* (Manchester: Manchester University Press, 1984), p. 92.

49. Stuart Hall comments,

> the development of an indigenous British racism in the post-war period begins with the profound historical forgetfulness – what I want to call the loss of historical memory, a kind of historical amnesia, a decisive mental repression – which has overtaken the British people about race and Empire since the 1950s. Paradoxically . . . the native, home-grown variety of racism begins with this attempt to wipe out and efface every trace of the colonial and imperial past.

(Stuart Hall, "Racism and reaction", in *Five views of multi-racial Britain*, Commission for Racial Equality, 1978.) In the 1980s Thatcherism produced a wave of nostalgia for empire. For discussion of the history of imperial nostalgia, including the resurrection of empire in the 1980s, see Annie Greet, Syd Harrex, Susan Hosking (eds) *Raj nostalgia: some literary and critical implications* (Adelaide: CRNLE, 1992).

Chapter 1

1. J. B. Priestley, *English journey* (London: William Heinemann, 1934), p. 133.

2. Quoted in Angela Holdsworth, *Out of the doll's house: the story of women in the twentieth century* (London: BBC Publications, 1988), p. 73.

3. Pilgrim Trust, *Men without work: a report made to the Pilgrim Trust* (London: Cambridge University Press, 1938), pp. 232, 240.

4. Quoted in Barry Turner & Tony Rennell, *When daddy came home: how family life changed forever in 1945* (London: Hutchinson, 1995), p. 117.

5. "How to welcome a soldier home", *Picture Post*, 21 April 1945.

6. J. B. Priestley, *Postscripts* (London: William Heinemann, 1940) pp. 34–8; William Temple, *The hope of a new world* (London: Student Christian Movement, 1940).

7. Priestley, *Postscripts*, p. 36.

8. Peter Hennessy, *Never again: Britain 1945–51* (London: Jonathan Cape, 1992), p. 2.

9. Lord Horder, "Introduction", in *Rebuilding family life in the post-war world*, James Marchant (ed.) (London: Odhams, 1945), p. 5.
10. Turner & Rennell, *When daddy came home*, p. 172.
11. Rex Pope, "British demobilisation after the second world war", *Journal of Contemporary History* 30 (1995) p. 69.
12. *Ibid.*, p. 67.
13. "Betty Summers", (pseudonym) Oral testimony, 1991.
14. Maureen Lawrence, *A telling and a keeping: a writer's autobiography* (London: Women's Press, 1989), pp. 26–7.
15. Raynes Minns, *Bombers and mash: the domestic front 1939–1945* (London: Virago, 1980), pp. 194–6.
16. Quoted in *ibid.*
17. Quoted in *ibid.*, pp. 190–91.
18. Quoted in *ibid.*, p. 195.
19. "Phyllis Dewsbury" (pseudonymn), Oral testimony, 1991.
20. "Betty Summers" (pseudonym), Oral testimony, 1991.
21. Central Office of Information, Social Survey Division, *The British household by P. G. Gray based on an inquiry carried out in April, 1947* (London, 1950), p. 10.
22. "Eva Holt" (pseudonym), Oral testimony, 1991.
23. Quoted in Jane Lewis, David Clark, David Morgan (eds) *"Whom God hath joined together": the work of marriage guidance* (London: Routledge, 1992) p. 37.
24. Alice Woodward, oral testimony in television programme: *Presumed guilty: a women's history of divorce, 1945–1969*, BBC, 1993.
25. Sheila Ferguson & Hilde Fitzgerald, *Studies in the social services* (London: HMSO & Longman, 1954), p. 133.
26. *Ibid.*, pp. 100, 124–5.
27. Quoted in Arthur McNalty, "Influence of war on family life", in Marchant (ed.), *Rebuilding family life*, p. 133.
28. Ferguson & Fitzgerald, *Studies in the social services*, p. 98.
29. "Vera", (pseudonym) Oral testimony, 1993.
30. *Ibid.*
31. Ferguson & Fitzgerald, *Studies in the social services*, p. 99.
32. *Ibid.*
33. "How to welcome a soldier home", *Picture Post*, 21 April 1945.
34. Margaret Hadley-Jackson, "A medical service for the treatment of involuntary sterility", *Eugenics Review* 36, January 1945.
35. Mark Abrams, *The population of Great Britain* (London: Allen & Unwin, 1945); Fabian Society, *Population and the people* (London: Allen & Unwin, 1945); Eva Hubback, *Population facts and policies* (London: Allen & Unwin, 1945); Grace Leybourne & Kenneth White, *Children for Britain* (London: Target Series, Pilot Press, 1945). G. F. McCleary, *The menace of British depopulation* (London: Allen & Unwin, 1945); G. F. McCleary, *Race suicide* (London: Allen & Unwin, 1945); Marchant, *Rebuilding family life*; Mass Observation, *Britain and her birth-rate* (London: John Murray, 1945).

36. Margaret Hadley-Jackson, "Causes and significance of the dwindling family", in Marchant, *Rebuilding family life*, p. 89.

37. Diana Hopkinson, *Family inheritance: a life of Eva Hubback* (London: Staples Press, 1954), p. 175.

38. Denise Riley, *War in the nursery: theories of the child and mother* (London: Virago, 1983), pp. 167–8.

39. Eliot Slater & Moya Woodside, *Patterns of marriage: a study of marriage relationships in the urban working classes* (London: Cassell, 1951), pp. 189–90.

40. Care of Children Committee, *Report* (London: HMSO, 1946, Cmd. 6922), p. 148.

41. *Ibid.*, pp. 163, 159.

42. See, for example, Susan Isaacs (ed.), *The Cambridge evacuation survey: a wartime study in social welfare and education* (London: Methuen, 1941).

43. Women's Hygiene Committee of the Women's Group on Public Welfare, *Our towns: a close-up* (Oxford: Oxford University Press, 1943).

44. John Bowlby, *Maternal care and mental health: a report prepared on behalf of the World Health Organization* (Geneva, 1952).

45. For a critical view of this argument, see Denise Riley, *War in the nursery*.

46. Mass Observation, *Britain and her birth-rate*, p. 24.

47. Richard Titmuss, "The statistics of parenthood", in Marchant, *Rebuilding family life*, p. 23.

48. *Ibid.*, p. 22; Royal Commission on Population, *Report* Cmd. 7695 (London: HMSO, 1949), p. 128; Graeme Dunstall, "The social pattern", in Geoffrey Rice (ed.), *The Oxford History of New Zealand* (Oxford: Oxford University Press, 1995), p. 453.

49. Royal Commission on Population, *Report*, pp. 125–30, 226.

50. West Indian Royal Commission, *Report* (London: HMSO, 1945), p. 12.

51. Quoted in Clive Harris, "Images of blacks in Britain 1930–1960", in *Race and social policy*, Sheila Allen & Marie Macey (eds), (London: ESRC, 1988), p. 37.

52. Learie Constantine, *Colour bar* (London: Stanley Paul, 1954), p. 100.

53. St Clair Drake, "The 'colour problem' in Britain: a study of social definition", *Sociological Review* 3, December 1955, p. 207; Mary Ellison, *The adopted child* (London: Victor Gollancz, 1958), p. 116; Harris, "Images of blacks in Britain", pp. 36–7.

54. Quoted in Harris, "Images of blacks in Britain", p. 38.

55. Elizabeth Wilson, *Only halfway to paradise: women in postwar Britain 1945–1968* (London: Tavistock, 1980), p. 44.

56. Paul Addison, *Now the war is over: a social history of Britain 1945–51* (London: BBC & Jonathan Cape, 1985), p. 187.

57. L. H. C. Tippett, *A portrait of the Lancashire textile industry* (Oxford: Oxford University Press, 1969).

58. "Bridget Poulton" (pseudonym), Oral testimony, 1994.
59. Diana Kay & Robert Miles, *Refugees or migrant workers?: European Volunteer Workers in Britain 1946–1951* (London: Routledge, 1992), p. 74.
60. Riley, *War in the nursery*, pp. 190–91; Denise Riley, "The free mothers: pronatalism and working women in industry at the end of the last war in Britain", *History Workshop* **11**, 1981. See also Penny Summerfield's comments on the usefulness of this question in "Approaches to women and social change in the second world war", in *What difference did the war make?* Brian Brivati & Harriet Jones (eds) (Leicester: Leicester University Press, 1993), p. 72.
61. For accounts of the British Housewives League see Bea Campbell, *The iron ladies: why do women vote Tory?* (London: Virago, 1987), pp. 76–82; James Hinton, "Militant housewives: the British Housewives League and the Attlee government", *History Workshop* **38**, 1994.
62. Alison Ravetz, "Housing the people", in Jim Fyrth (ed.), *Labour's promised land?: culture and society in Labour Britain 1945–51* (London: Lawrence & Wishart, 1995), p. 159.
63. Central Office of Information, *The British household* p. 27.
64. Mrs Price, Letter to author, 31 July 1994.
65. Campbell, *The iron ladies*, pp. 76–7.
66. Madeleine Henrey, "The new feminism", *Spectator*, 4 May 1951.
67. U. Henriques, "The new feminism", *Spectator*, 11 May 1951.
68. Tony Kushner, *The holocaust and the liberal imagination* (Oxford: Basil Blackwell, 1994), pp. 96–100; Tony Kushner, "Politics and race, gender and class: refugees, fascists and domestic service in Britain 1933–1940", *The politics of marginality: race, the radical right and minorities in twentieth century Britain*, in Tony Kushner & Kenneth Lunn (eds), (London: Frank Cass, 1990).
69. J. A. Tannahill, *European Volunteer Workers in Britain* (Manchester: Manchester University Press, 1958), p. 43.
70. Help for housewives, *Listener* **35**, 11 April 1946.
71. Sylvia Walby, *Patriarchy at work: patriarchal and capitalist relations in employment* (Cambridge: Polity, 1986), p. 202–4.
72. Ferdynand Zweig, *Productivity and trade unions* (Oxford: Blackwell, 1951) pp. 157–8; Kay & Miles, *Refugees or migrant workers*, p. 73.
73. Quoted in Riley, *War in the nursery*, p. 134.
74. "Help for housewives", p. 465; Ferdynand Zweig, *Women's life and labour* (London: Gollancz, 1952) p. 35.
75. Riley, *War in the nursery*, pp. 109–49.

Chapter 2

1. Claudette Williams, We are a natural part of many different struggles: black women organising", in *Inside Babylon: the Caribbean diaspora*

in Britain, Winston James & Clive Harris (eds), (London: Verso 1993), p. 154.

2. Quoted in Clive Harris, "Post-war migration and the industrial reserve army", in *Inside Babylon*, James & Harris, pp. 24–5.

3. There has been much recent work challenging the view that Britain operated a policy of unrestricted entry for citizens of the empire and Commonwealth before the Immigration Act of 1962. See, for example, Bob Carter, Clive Harris, Shirley Joshi, "The 1951–55 Conservative government and the racialisation of black immigration", *Immigrants and Minorities* 6, 1987; Ian Spencer, "The open door: labour needs and British immigration policy, 1945–55", *Immigrants and Minorities* 15, 1996.

4. Quoted in Judy Giles & Tim Middleton (eds), *Writing Englishness 1900–1950: an introductory source book on national identity* (London: Routledge, 1995), p. 53.

5. Paul Rich, *Race and empire in British politics* (Cambridge: Cambridge University Press, 1900), p. 130. See also Laura Tabili, *"We ask for British justice": workers and racial difference in late imperial Britain* (Ithaca NY: Cornell University Press, 1994); Laura Tabili, "The construction of racial difference in twentieth-century Britain: the Special Restriction (Coloured Alien Seamen) Order, 1925", *Journal of British Studies* 33, 1994; Diane Frost, "West Africans, Black Scousers and the colour problem in inter-war Liverpool", *North West Labour History* 20, 1995/6.

6. Quoted in Barbara Brookes, *Abortion in England 1900–1967* (London: Croom Helm, 1988), p. 134.

7. Quoted in Kathleen Paul, " 'British subjects' and 'British stock': Labour's postwar imperialism", *Journal of British Studies* 34, April 1995, p. 267.

8. Quoted in Elizabeth Wilson, *Women and the welfare state* (London: Tavistock, 1977), p. 152.

9. Eva Hubback, *The population of Britain* (Harmondsworth: Penguin, 1947), pp. 114–15.

10. Anna Davin, "Imperialism and motherhood" in *Patriotism: the making and unmaking of British national identity*, Raphael Samuel (ed.), Vol. 1 (London: Routledge, 1989).

11. Hubback, *The population of Britain*, pp. 121, 271.

12. Margaret Humphreys, *Empty cradles* (London: Doubleday, 1994), p. 56.

13. Quoted in *ibid.*, pp. 233–4.

14. Quoted in *ibid.*, p. 261.

15. *Ibid.*

16. *Ibid.*, p. 56, Paul, " 'British subjects' and 'British stock' ", p. 259.

17. Paul, " 'British subjects' and 'British stock' ", pp. 257, 259.

18. *Ibid.*, pp. 256–9; R. T. Appleyard, *British emigration to Australia* (London: Weidenfeld & Nicolson, 1964), p. 36.

19. Quoted in Appleyard, *British emigration to Australia*, p. 34.

20. Paul, " 'British subjects' and 'British stock' ", p. 252.
21. Quoted in *ibid*.
22. J. A. Tannahill, *European Volunteer Workers in Britain* (Manchester: Manchester University Press, 1958), p. 42.
23. Royal Commission on Population, *Report* Cmd. 7695 (London: HMSO, 1949), p. 130.
24. Quoted in Harris, "Post-war migration and the industrial reserve army", p. 24.
25. The notion of "suitable immigrants" was a particularly late-1940s idea, and gave some visibility to white migrants to Britain. By the mid-1950s the "immigrant" was rarely seen as white. White migrants have also been less visible than black in histories of post-war migration, and most work on white migrants has focused on the late 1940s, with little information available on their experiences in the 1950s and 1960s. I am heavily indebted to this work for the account that follows, especially to Terri Colpi, *The Italian factor: the Italian community in Britain* (Edinburgh: Mainstream, 1991); Kathleen Paul, "The politics of citizenship in post-war Britain", *Contemporary Record* 6, 1992; Diana Kay & Robert Miles, *Refugees or migrant workers?: European volunteer workers in Britain 1946–1951* (London: Routledge, 1992).
26. Paul, "The politics of citizenship", p. 467.
27. Quoted in *ibid*., p. 464.
28. Royal Commission on Population, p. 124.
29. Colpi, *The Italian factor*, p. 146.
30. Sheila Patterson, "The Poles: an exile community in Britain", in *Between two cultures: migrants and minorities in Britain*, James Watson (ed.) (Oxford: Blackwell, 1977), p. 224; Andrew Nocon, "A reluctant welcome?: Poles in Britain in the 1940s", *Oral History*, Spring 1996, p. 81.
31. Royal Commission on Population, p. 125.
32. Harris, "Post-war migration and the industrial reserve army", p. 34.
33. *Ibid*., p. 14; Sylvia Walby, *Patriarchy at work: patriarchal and capitalist relations in employment* (Cambridge: Polity, 1986), pp. 232–4.
34. Tannahill, *European volunteer workers in Britain*, p. 22.
35. Kay & Miles, *Refugees or migrant workers?*, p. 68; Colpi, *The Italian factor*, p. 145.
36. Antonietta Zelenczuk, Oral testimony, 1996.
37. Quoted in Paul, "The politics of citizenship", p. 460.
38. *Ibid*.
39. Sheila Patterson, *Immigrants in industry* (London: Oxford University Press, 1968), p. 20.
40. Lesley Doyal, Geoff Hunt, Jenny Mellor, "Your life in their hands: migrant workers in the National Health Service", *Critical Social Policy* 1, 1981, p. 55.
41. Ann Dummett & Andrew Nicol, *Subjects, citizens, aliens and others:*

nationality and immigration law (London: Weidenfeld & Nicolson, 1990), p. 178.

42. Tannahill, *European Volunteer Workers*, p. 45.
43. *Ibid.*
44. Kay & Miles, *Refugees or migrant workers?*, p. 58.
45. Tannahill, *European Volunteer Workers*, p. 46.
46. R. B. Davison, *West Indian migrants: social and economic facts of migration from the West Indies* (London: Oxford University Press, 1962), pp. 70, 74.
47. Tannahill, *European Volunteer Workers*, pp. 41, 44, 47.
48. Kay & Miles, *Refugees or migrant workers?*, p. 60.
49. Coralie Younger, *Anglo-Indians, neglected children of the Raj* (Delhi: BR Publishing, 1987), p. 63.
50. Keith Sword records that a factory at Radcliffe, near Bury, was opened and adapted for disabled Polish people in 1949. Keith Sword, *The formation of the Polish community in Great Britain 1939–1950* (London: University of London, 1989), p. 285.
51. Mary Chamberlain has emphasised the importance of family support for Barbadian migration to Britain, as well as the ways in which migration assisted in the maintenance of the family back home. Her work identifies family models as a primary locus of migration motivation which, she argues, has been obscured in metropolitan based studies. See Mary Chamberlain, "Family and identity: Barbadian migrants to Britain", in Rina Benmayor & Andor Skotnes (eds), *Migration and Identity: International yearbook of oral history and life stories* Vol. 3, (Oxford, Oxford University Press, 1994).
52. Gail Lewis, "Black women's employment and the British economy", in *Inside Babylon*, James & Harris, p. 82.
53. Margaret Prescod-Roberts & Norma Steele (eds), *Black women: bringing it all back home* (Bristol: Falling Wall Press, 1980), pp. 19, 25.
54. Sword, *The formation of the Polish community*, p. 273.
55. Mary Lennon, Marie McAdam, Joanne O'Brien, *Across the water: Irish women's lives in Britain* (London: Virago, 1988), p. 25.
56. Kay & Miles, Refugees or migrant workers?, p. 74.
57. Sword, *The formation of the Polish community*, pp. 271–2.
58. Genowefa Dziewanda, Oral testimony, 1996.
59. Kay & Miles, *Refugees or migrant workers?*, p. 170
60. Walby, *Patriarchy at work*, p. 207.
61. Colin Holmes, "Historians and immigration", *Migrants, emigrants and immigrants: a social history* in Colin Pooley & Ian Whyte (eds), (London: Routledge, 1991), p. 193.
62. Tony Kushner, *The holocaust and the liberal imagination: a social and cultural history* (Oxford: Blackwell, 1994), p. 235.
63. *Ibid.*, p. 232.
64. Quoted in *ibid.*, p. 237.
65. Tony Kushner, *The persistence of prejudice: antisemitism in British*

society *during the second world war* (Manchester: Manchester University Press, 1989), p. 133.

66. *Ibid.*, p. 199. Bill Williamson, "Memories, vision and hope: themes in an historical sociology of Britain since the second world war", *Journal of Historical Sociology* 1, 1988, p. 173.
67. Nocon, A reluctant welcome?, pp. 80–82.
68. Sarah Thompson, Oral testimony, in Lambeth Council & the Voice, *Forty winters on: memories of Britain's post-war Caribbean immigrants* (London: South London Press, 1988).
69. "Mary" (Pseudonym), Oral testimony, 1995.
70. "Mrs B", Oral testimony, 1995.
71. "Vi Chambers" (pseudonym), Oral testimony, 1995.
72. Quoted in Elyse Dodgson, *Motherland: West Indian women to Britain in the 1950s* (London: Heinemann, 1984), p. 10.
73. Beryl Gilroy, *Black teacher* (London: Bogle-l'Ouverture Press, 1994), p. 34.
74. Winston James, "Migration, racism and identity formation: the Caribbean experience in Britain", *Inside Babylon*, in James & Harris, pp. 240–44.
75. "Vi Chambers" (pseudonym), Oral testimony, 1995.
76. Mrs H, Oral testimony, 1995.
77. Constance Nembhard, Oral testimony, 1995.
78. Buchi Emecheta, *Head above water* (London: Fontana, 1986), pp. 26–29.
79. Mrs C, Oral testimony, 1995. The reference is to Queen Victoria's birthday, the date on which Empire Day was celebrated.

Chapter 3

1. Elspeth Huxley, *Back street new worlds: a look at immigrants in Britain* (London: Chatto & Windus, 1964), pp. 43–4.
2. Quoted in Lord Elton, *The unarmed invasion: a survey of Afro-Asian immigration* (London: Geoffrey Bles, 1965), p. 51.
3. *Ibid.*, pp. 26–32.
4. Elspeth Huxley, *White man's country: Lord Delamere and the making of Kenya* [2 vols] (London: Chatto & Windus, 1956, first published 1935), vol. 1, p. viii.
5. Elspeth Huxley, *Race and politics in Kenya: a correspondence between Elspeth Huxley and Margery Perham* (London: Faber & Faber, 1944); Elspeth Huxley, *A new earth: an experiment in colonialism* (London: Chatto & Windus, 1960); Robert Edgerton, *Mau Mau: an African crucible* (London: I. B. Tauris, 1990), p. 147.
6. Huxley, *Race and politics in Kenya*, p. 24.
7. Church of England Moral Welfare Council, *Moral crisis: the Church in action* (London: Church Information Board, 1950), p. 23.

8. Anthony Storr, *Sexual deviation* (Harmondsworth: Penguin, 1968), pp. 12–13.
9. Quoted in Michael Banton, *The coloured quarter* (London: Jonathan Cape, 1955), p. 152.
10. Trevor Philpott, "Would you let your daughter marry a negro?", *Picture Post*, 30 October 1954; Colin MacInnes, "A short guide for jumbles (to the life of their coloured brethren in England)", in *England, half English* (London: MacGibbon & Kee, 1961, first published 1956), p. 25.
11. Edith Kirton, Oral testimony, 1995.
12. Colin MacInnes, *City of spades* (London: Allison & Busby, 1993, first published 1957).
13. Barbara Pym, *Jane and Prudence* (London, Jonathan Cape, 1979, first published 1953), p. 70.
14. Roots Oral History, *Rude awakening: African/Caribbean settlers in Manchester* (Roots Oral History Project, 1992), p. 36.
15. Dorothy Prosper, Oral testimony, 1994.
16. Clifford Hill, *How colour prejudiced is Britain?* (London: Gollancz, 1965), p. 229.
17. Banton, *The coloured quarter*, p. 153.
18. Carol Smart, "Law and the control of women's sexuality: the case of the 1950s", in *Controlling women: the normal and the deviant*, Bridget Hutter & Gillian Williams (eds) (London: Croom Helm, 1981), p. 50; Elton, *The unarmed invasion*, p. 76.
19. For a summary of the literature which linked venereal disease to black male immigrants, especially West Indians, see Elton, *The unarmed invasion*, pp. 75–6.
20. Quoted in Marika Sherwood, *Many struggles: West Indian workers and service personnel in Britain* (London: Karia Press, 1985), pp. 127–8.
21. Sydney Collins, "The social position of white and 'half-caste' women in colored groupings in Britain", *American Sociological Review* **16**, December 1951, p. 796.
22. Barbara Tizard & Ann Phoenix, *Black, white or mixed race?: Race and racism in the lives of young people of mixed parentage* (London: Routledge, 1993), p. 23.
23. Quoted in John Solomos & Les Back, *Race, politics and social change* (London: Routledge, 1995), p. 48.
24. Quoted in *ibid.*
25. A major work on race and gender in film in a British context is Lola Young, *Fear of the dark: "race", gender and sexuality in the cinema* (London: Routledge, 1996) which includes discussion of *Flame in the streets*.
26. David Maughan-Brown comments that " 'Mau Mau' is . . . the term which, perhaps more than any other, still signifies for many whites the 'atavism' and 'primitivism' of 'darkest Africa'." See David Maughan-

Brown, *Land, freedom and fiction: history and ideology in Kenya* (London: Zed Books, 1985), p. 1.

27. Richard Dyer, "White", *Screen* **29**, Autumn 1988, p. 51.
28. Beryl Gilroy, "I write because", in *Caribbean women writers: essays from the first international conference*, Selwyn Cudjoe (ed.) (Wellesley, Mass: Calaxous Publications, 1990), p. 200.
29. Amanda Murphy, Oral testimony, 1995.
30. Manual Alvarado, Robin Gutch, Tena Wollen, *Learning the media: an introduction to media teaching* (Basingstoke: Macmillan, 1987), p. 215.
31. G. L. C. Bertram, *West Indian immigration* (London: Eugenics Society, 1958), p. 16.
32. Keith Waterhouse, "Introducing to you the boys from Jamaica", *Daily Mirror*, 8 September 1958.
33. Sydney Collins, *Coloured minorities in Britain* (London: Lutterworth Press, 1957), pp. 253, 137.
34. Amanda Murphy, Oral testimony, 1995.
35. Sheila Patterson, *Dark strangers: a sociological study of the absorption of a recent West Indian migrant group in Brixton, South London* (London: Tavistock, 1963), pp. 283–4; Collins, *Coloured minorities*, p. 25.
36. Peter Keating (ed.), *Into unknown England 1866–1913: selections from the social explorers* (London: Fontana, 1976), p. 145.
37. *Ibid.*, p. 150.
38. *Ibid.*, pp. 65–6.
39. *Ibid.*, pp. 66–8.
40. *Ibid.*, p. 137.
41. Judy Giles, *Women, identity and private life in Britain, 1900–50* (Basingstoke: Macmillan, 1995), p. 102.
42. Patterson, *Dark strangers*.
43. Huxley, *Back street new worlds*, p. 46.
44. *Ibid.*, pp. 46–7.

Chapter 4

1. Charles Curran, "The politics of the new estate", *Spectator*, 17 February 1956.
2. Stuart Laing, *Representations of working-class life 1957–1964* (Basingstoke: Macmillan, 1986).
3. Charles Curran, "This new England: the passing of the tribunes", *Encounter*, 6 June 1956, p. 20; Mark Abrams, "The home-centred society", *Listener*, 26 November 1959; Ferdynand Zweig, *The worker in an affluent society: family life and industry* (London: Heinemann, 1961), pp. 208–10.
4. Richard Hoggart, *The uses of literacy: aspects of working-class life with*

special reference to publications and entertainments (Harmondsworth: Penguin, 1969, first published 1957), pp. 206, 24, 149–54.

5. See Alan Sinfield, *Literature, politics and culture in postwar Britain* (Oxford: Blackwell, 1989), pp. 60–85.

6. Quoted in *ibid.*, p. 156.

7. *Ibid.*, pp. 76–7; Lynn Segal, "Look back in anger: men in the fifties", in *Male order: unwrapping masculinity*, Rowena Chapman & Jonathan Rutherford (eds) (London: Lawrence & Wishart, 1988), pp. 84–5.

8. George Orwell, "England your England", in *Inside the whale and other essays* (Harmondsworth: Penguin, 1971, first published 1941), p. 89.

9. J. B. Priestley, *English journey* (London: Heinemann, 1934), p. 401.

10. T. R. Fyvel, "This new England: the stones of Harlow, reflections on Subtopia", *Encounter*, 6 June 1956, p. 15.

11. Wayland Young, "This new England: return to Wigan pier", *Encounter*, 6 June 1956, p. 5.

12. Alison Light, *Forever England: femininity, literature and conservatism between the wars* (London: Routledge, 1991), pp. 208–21.

13. Sally Alexander, "Becoming a woman in London in the 1920s and '30s", in *Becoming a woman, and other essays in 19th and 20th century feminist history* (London: Virago, 1994), p. 204.

14. Abrams, "The home-centred society".

15. *Ibid.*

16. Curran, "This new England", p. 20.

17. Janet Finch & Penny Summerfield, "Social reconstruction and the emergence of companionate marriage', in *Marriage: domestic life and social change*, David Clark (ed.) (London: Routledge, 1991), p. 7.

18. John and Elizabeth Newson, *Patterns of infant care in an urban community* (London: Allen & Unwin, 1963), p. 145.

19. Michael Young & Peter Willmott, *Family and kinship in East London* (London: Routledge & Kegan Paul, 1957), p. 10.

20. *Ibid.*, p. 119.

21. Zweig, *The worker in an affluent society*, p. 208.

22. *Ibid.*, p. 207.

23. Church of England Moral Welfare Council, *The family in contemporary society* (London: SPCK, 1959), p. 104.

24. Zweig, *The worker in an affluent society*, pp. 209–10.

25. Curran, "This new England", p. 20.

26. *Ibid.*; Abrams, "The home-centred society"; Zweig, *The worker in an affluent society*, p. 208.

27. Zweig, *The worker in an affluent society*, p. 208.

28. Abrams, "The home centred society".

29. Curran, "This new England", pp. 20–21.

30. Zweig, *The worker in an affluent society*, p. 208.

31. Hoggart, *The uses of literacy*, pp. 41–50.

32. *Ibid.*, p. 295.

33. Terry Lovell, "Landscapes and stories in 1960s British realism", *Screen* **31**, Winter 1990, pp. 360, 364. See also Carolyn Steedman, *Landscape for a good woman: a story of two lives* (London: Virago, 1991), pp. 6, 16–17, 100.
34. Hoggart, *The uses of literacy*, p. 50.
35. Young & Willmott, *Family and kinship*, p. 15.
36. Ronald Fletcher, *The family and marriage in Britain* (Harmondsworth: Penguin, 1968, first published 1962), pp. 131–2.
37. Abrams, "The home-centred society".
38. Alexander, "Becoming a woman in London", p. 220.
39. *Ibid.*, p. 205.
40. "Maria Woods" (pseudonym), Oral testimony, 1994.
41. Quoted in *Daily Telegraph*, 5 February 1975.
42. Win Kewley, Oral testimony, 1993.
43. John Hill, "Working-class realism and sexual reaction: some theses on the British 'new wave' ", in *British cinema history*, James Curran & Vincent Porter (eds) (London: Weidenfeld & Nicolson, 1983), pp. 304–5.
44. Lovell, "Landscapes and stories", p. 367.
45. John Osborne, *Look back in anger* (London: Faber & Faber, 1962, first published 1957), pp. 30, 42, 64.
46. Micheline Wandor, *Look back in gender: sexuality and the family in post-war British drama* (London: Methuen, 1987), pp. 8–14; John Hill, *Sex, class and realism: British cinema 1956–1963* (London: British Film Institute, 1986), p. 25.
47. Osborne, *Look back in anger*, pp. 37–8.
48. *Ibid.*, p. 95.
49. *Ibid.*, p. 92.
50. *Ibid.*, p. 17.
51. *Ibid.*, p. 68.

Chapter 5

1. Pearl Jephcott, *A troubled area: notes on Notting Hill, London* (London: Faber & Faber, 1964), p. 84.
2. A. F. Philp & N. Timms, *The problem of the "problem family": a critical review of the literature concerning the "problem family" and its treatment* (London: Family Service Units, 1957), p. 5.
3. D. Ford, in a 1955 study quoted in *ibid.*, p. 14.
4. Tess Cosslett, *Women writing childbirth: modern discourses of motherhood* (Manchester: Manchester University Press, 1994), pp. 9–46.
5. John Bowlby, *Child care and the growth of love* (Harmondsworth: Penguin, 1959, first published 1953), p. 173.
6. Cosslett, *Women writing childbirth*, p. 10.
7. *Biology and human affairs*, October 1950, p. 59.

8. Personal knowledge, St Albans Girls Grammar School, where sex education in the first form was called hygiene in 1958–9.
9. Sir William Arbuthnot Lane (ed.), *The hygiene of life and safer motherhood* (London: New Age Books, n.d.).
10. Bowlby, *Child care and the growth of love*, pp. 182, 181, 107.
11. C. P. Blacker, *Eugenics: Galton and after* (London: Duckworth, 1952), p. 311.
12. Quoted in Philp & Timms, *The problem of the "problem family"*, p. ix.
13. Theodore Tucker, *Children without homes: the problems of their care and protection* (London: Bodley Head, 1952), pp. 163–4.
14. D. W. Winnicott, *The child and the family: first relationships* (London: Tavistock, 1962), pp. 143–4.
15. National Society of Children's Nurseries, *Working wives: what of the children?* (London, 1960), p. 16.
16. Winnicott, *The child and the family*, pp. 20–21.
17. *Ibid.*, p. 4.
18. Gladys Petty, Oral testimony, 1994. Elizabeth Roberts shows through oral testimony that some women regarded doctors' advice as the *proper* thing, and favoured visits to the doctors over visits to clinics. Elizabeth Roberts, *Women and families: an oral history 1940–1970* (Oxford: Blackwell, 1995), pp. 146–7.
19. Wynn Nixson, Oral testimony, in television programme *Bringing up baby*, BBC, 1994.
20. Pam McKinlay, Oral testimony, in *ibid.*
21. Good Housekeeping, *Home encyclopaedia* (London, 1970, first published 1951), pp. 251–2.
22. Bowlby, *Child care and the growth of love*, p. 109.
23. Christine Cooper, *The illegitimate child* (National Council for the Unmarried Mother and her Child, 1955), p. 8.
24. Leontine Young, *Out of wedlock* (New York: McGraw Hill, 1954).
25. *Washing away the stain*, BBC, 1993.
26. Lettice Fisher, *Twenty-one years and after: the National Council for the Unmarried Mother and her Child 1918–1939* (n.d.), p. 14.
27. *Ibid.*, p. 12; Virginia Wimperis, *The unmarried mother and her child* (London: Allen & Unwin, 1960), pp. 237–8.
28. Cooper, *The illegitimate child*, pp. 6–8
29. Bowlby, *Child care and the growth of love*, pp. 111–18.
30. Martine Spensky, "Producers of legitimacy: homes for unmarried mothers in the 1950s", in *Regulating womenhood: historical essays on marriage, motherhood and sexuality*, Carol Smart (ed.) (London: Routledge, 1992), pp. 111–12; Wimperis, *The unmarried mother*, p. 238.
31. Spensky, "Producers of legitimacy", p. 108.
32. "Elizabeth Arthur" (pseudonym), Oral testimony, 1992.
33. Quoted in Sheila Jeffreys, *Anticlimax: a feminist perspective on the sexual revolution* (London: Women's Press, 1990), pp. 47, 24.
34. M. E. Landau, *Women of forty* (London: Faber & Faber, 1956), pp. 15–28.

35. *Ibid.*, pp. 33–5.
36. Joan Clarke, *Disabled citizens* (London: Allen & Unwin, 1951), pp. 33–4.
37. Bowlby, *Child care and the growth of love*, p. 89.
38. Beryl Gilroy, *Black teacher* (London: Bogle L'Ouverture Press, 1994), p. 63.
39. "Vi Chambers" (pseudonym), Oral testimony, 1995.
40. Gilroy, *Black teacher*, p. 52.
41. *Ibid.*, p. 24.
42. Elsie George, Oral testimony, 1995.
43. Colin MacInnes, *City of spades* (London: Allison & Busby, 1993, first published 1957), p. 66.
44. Mrs H, Oral testimony, 1995.
45. "Vi Chambers" (pseudonym), Oral testimony, 1995.
46. D. W. Winnicott, "Some thoughts on the meaning of the word democracy", in *The family and individual development* (London: Tavistock, 1965), pp. 169, 161–3.
47. British Medical Association, *Venereal disease and young people: a report by a committee of the British Medical Association on the problem of venereal disease particularly among young people* (London, 1964), p. 41.
48. Richard Hoggart, *The uses of literacy: aspects of working-class life with special reference to publications and entertainments* (Harmondsworth: Penguin, 1969, first published 1957), p. 100.
49. Mary Stott, *Forgetting's no excuse* (London: Virago, 1989), pp. 112–15, 199.
50. Pauline Crabbe, Oral testimony, 1994.
51. Evelyn Haythorne, *On earth to make the numbers up* (Castleford: Yorkshire Art Circus, 1991), p. 113.
52. Kath Davies, Julienne Dickey, Teresa Stratford (eds), *Out of focus: writings on women and the media* (London: Women's Press, 1987), p. 89; Keith Howes, *Broadcasting it: an encyclopaedia of homosexuality on film, radio and TV in the UK 1923–1993* (London: Cassell, 1993), p. 455; Niamh Baker, *Happily ever after?: Women's fiction in postwar Britain 1945–60* (Basingstoke: Macmillan, 1989), p. 78.
53. Dilys Rowe, "A quick look at the lesbians", *Twentieth Century* 171, 1962–3, p. 68.
54. Pat G. and Rachel Pinney in Suzanne Neild & Rosalind Pearson (eds), *Women like us* (London: Women's Press, 1992), pp. 71, 23.
55. Marie in *ibid.*, p. 157.
56. Diana Gittins, *Fair sex: family size and structure 1900–39* (London: Hutchinson, 1982).
57. "Winifred James" (pseudonym), Oral testimony, 1990.
58. Penny Summerfield & Nicole Crockett, "You weren't taught that with the welding: lessons in sexuality in the second world war", *Women's History Review*, 1992.

59. Women's Group on Public Welfare, *The education and training of girls* (London: National Council of Social Service, 1962), p. 68.
60. British Medical Association, *Venereal disease and young people*, p. 9.
61. Committee on Homosexual Offences and Prostitution, *Report* Cmnd. 247 (London: HMSO, 1957), p. 21.
62. Michael Schofield, *The sexual behaviour of young people* (London: Longman, 1965), pp. 101–2.
63. Mary Evans, *A good school: life at a girls' grammar school in the 1950s* (London: Women's Press, 1991), p. 62; Angela Holdsworth, *Out of the doll's house: the story of women in the twentieth century* (London: BBC Books, 1988), p. 149.
64. "Jean Grant" (pseudonym), Oral testimony, 1995.
65. *Ibid.*
66. Barbara Marsh in *Dutiful daughters*, Jean McCrindle & Sheila Rowbotham (eds) (Harmondsworth: Penguin, 1979), pp. 247–8. Elizabeth Roberts looks at the post-war generation's ignorance about sexuality in *Women and families*, pp. 60–62.
67. "Jean Grant" (pseudonym), Oral testimony, 1995.
68. Neild & Pearson, *Women like us*, p. 20.
69. Eliot Slater & Moya Woodside, *Patterns of marriage: a study of marriage relationships in the urban working classes* (London: Cassell, 1951), p. 107.
70. J. H. Robb, review of Slater & Woodside, *Social Work*, 9, April 1952, p. 687.
71. Philp & Timms, *The problem of the "problem family"*, pp. 15, 24, 48–55; Home Office, *Sixth report on the work of the Children's Department, May 1951* (London: HMSO, 1951), p. 41; Central Office of Information, *Children in Britain* (London: HMSO, 1959), pp. 35–6.
72. Care of Children Committee, *Report* Cmd. 6922 (London: HMSO, 1946), p. 146.
73. Home Office, *Sixth report on the work of the Children's Department*, p. 6; Home Office, *Eighth report on the work of the Children's Department 1961* (London: HMSO, 1961), p. 25.
74. Philp & Timms, *The problem of the "problem family"*, p. 15.
75. Cooper, *The illegitimate child*, p. 4.
76. C. P. Blacker (ed.), *Problem families: five inquiries* (London: Eugenics Society, 1952), p. 33.
77. Quoted in Eileen Younghusband, *Social work in Britain 1950–1975: a follow-up study* (London: Allen & Unwin, 1978), p. 219.
78. "Elizabeth Arthur" (pseudonym), Oral testimony, 1992.
79. Richard Titmuss, "The family as a social institution", in British National Conference on Social Work, *The family* (National Council of Social Service, 1953), p. 10.
80. Elizabeth Wilson, "Memoirs of an anti-heroine", in *Radical records: thirty years of lesbian and gay history 1957–1987* Bob Cant & Susan Hemmings (eds), (London: Routledge, 1988), p. 44.
81. Slater & Woodside, *Patterns of marriage*, pp. 246–8.

82. Gilroy, *Black teacher*, p. 75.
83. Pauline Crabbe, Oral testimony, 1994.
84. *Ibid.*
85. Gilroy, *Black teacher*, p. 52. Marina Warner records: "at my convent school in Berkshire, England, we were still 'adopting' Black Babies by making an offering, and following it up by regular prayers in order to earn, as sponsor, a photograph of the designated, newly baptised fosterchild". Marina Warner, "Between the colonist and the creole: family bonds, family boundaries", in *Unbecoming daughters of the empire* Shirley Chew & Anna Rutherford (eds), (Sydney: Dangaroo Press, 1993), p. 203.
86. Mary Ellison, *The adopted child* (London: Gollancz, 1958), p. 153; Jane Rowe, *Parents, children and adoption* (London: Routledge & Kegan Paul, 1966), p. 142.
87. Spensky, "Producers of illegitimacy", pp. 114, 115.
88. Diana Karah, *Adoption and the coloured child* (London: Epworth Press, 1970), pp. 30–31.
89. Jackie Kay, *The adoption papers* (Newcastle-upon-Tyne: Bloodaxe Books, 1991), p. 24.
90. Buchi Emecheta, *Head above water* (London: Fontana, 1986), p. 41.
91. Quoted in Jane Lewis, David Clark, David Morgan, *"Whom God hath joined together": the work of marriage guidance* (London: Routledge, 1992), p. 69.
92. British Medical Association, *Venereal disease and young people*, p. 37.
93. Departmental Committee on Human Artificial Insemination, *Report*, Cmnd. 1105 (London: HMSO, 1960), p. 34.
94. David Dabydeen & Nana Wilson Tagoe, *A reader's guide to West Indian and black British literature* (London: Hansib Publishing, 1988), p. 43.
95. For a discussion of the mammy image in America see Patricia Hill Collins, *Black feminist thought: knowledge, consciousness and the politics of empowerment* (London: Routledge, 1991). For a discussion of the absence of the mammy image in Europe see Jan Nederveen Pieterse, *White on black: images of Africa and blacks in western popular culture* (New Haven Conn.: Yale University Press, 1992).
96. Rosina Visram, *Ayahs, lascars and princes: Indians in Britain 1700–1947* (London: Pluto Press, 1986), pp. 9, 16–17, 29–30.
97. Quoted in Elyse Dodgson, *Motherland: West Indian women to Britain in the 1950s* (London: Heinemann, 1984), p. 34.
98. Lucille Newman in *To make ends meet: women over 60 write about their working lives* Jo Stanley (ed.), (London: Older Women's Project, n.d.), p. 71.
99. Mrs B, Oral testimony, 1995.
100. Amanda Murphy, Oral testimony, 1995.
101. Gilroy, *Black teacher*, p. 112.
102. Lord Elton, *The unarmed invasion: a survey of Afro-Asian*

immigration (London: Geoffrey Bles, 1965), pp. 30–31; Peter Griffiths, *A question of colour?* (London: Frewin, 1966), p. 149.

103. Nikki Knewstub, "Committed to the young people upstairs", *Guardian*, 15 December 1978; Elizabeth Wilson, *Only half way to paradise: women in post-war Britain 1945–1968* (London: Tavistock, 1980), p. 100.

104. Central Office of Information, *Children in Britain*, p. 22.

105. Carolyn Steedman, *Landscape for a good woman: a story of two lives* (London: Virago, 1991), pp. 121–2.

106. Central Office of Information, *Children in Britain*, pp. 6–7.

107. E.H., Homeless and fatherless families, *Case Conference*, July 1955, p. 16.

108. Fiona Williams, *Social policy: a critical introduction* (Cambridge: Polity, 1989), pp. 76–7.

109. Mary Lennon, Marie McAdam, Joanne O'Brien, *Across the water: Irish women's lives in Britain* (London: Virago, 1988), p. 26.

110. There is an extensive feminist literature on the welfare state representing a wide range of feminist perspectives. See especially Elizabeth Wilson, *Women and the welfare state* (London: Tavistock, 1977); Clare Ungerson (ed.), *Women and social policy: a reader* (Basingstoke: Macmillan, 1985); Jennifer Dale & Peggy Foster, *Feminists and state welfare* (London: Routledge & Kegan Paul, 1986); Clare Ungerson (ed.), *Gender and caring* (Hemel Hempstead: Harvester Wheatsheaf, 1990); Sylvia Walby, *Theorising patriarchy* (Oxford: Blackwell, 1990). Fiona Williams discusses the ways in which the welfare state is racially structured. See Fiona Williams, *Social policy: a critical introduction* (Cambridge: Polity, 1989); Fiona Williams, "The welfare state as part of a racially structured and patriarchal capitalism", in *The state or the market: politics and welfare in contemporary Britain* Martin Loney, Robert Bocock, John Clarke, Allan Cochrane, Peggotty Graham, Michael Wilson (eds), (London: Sage, 1993).

Chapter 6

1. Joanna Bourke, *Working-class cultures in Britain 1890–1960: gender, class and ethnicity* (London: Routledge, 1994), p. 100.

2. Miriam Glucksmann, "In a class of their own?: Women workers in the new industries in inter-war Britain", *Feminist Review* 24, 1986, p. 20.

3. Jane Lewis, *Women in Britain since 1945* (Oxford: Blackwell, 1992), p. 74.

4. Sylvia Walby, *Patriarchy at work: patriarchal and capitalist relations in employment* (Cambridge: Polity, 1986), pp. 202–7.

5. Sally Alexander, "Becoming a woman in London in the 1920s and '30s", in *Becoming a woman, and other essays in 19th and 20th century feminist history* (London: Virago, 1994); Glucksmann, "In a class of

their own?"; Miriam Glucksmann, *Women assemble: women workers in the new industries in inter-war Britain* (London: Routledge, 1990); Joanna Bourke, *Working-class cultures in Britain*, (London: Routledge, 1994), pp. 100–103.

6. Sheila Patterson, *Immigration and race relations in Britain 1960–1967* (London: Oxford University Press, 1969), p. 136.

7. W. W. Daniel, *Racial discrimination in England, based on the PEP Report* (Harmondsworth: Penguin, 1968), p. 109.

8. Elizabeth Roberts, *Women and families: an oral history 1940–1970* (Oxford: Blackwell, 1995), pp. 124–5.

9. Quoted in Kay Sanderson, "A pension to look forward to. . . ?: Women civil service clerks in London, 1925–1939", in *Our work, our lives, our words*, Leonore Davidoff & Belinda Westover (eds) (Basingstoke: Macmillan, 1986), p. 157.

10. Quoted in Pat Ayers & Jan Lambertz, "Marriage relations, money and domestic violence in working-class Liverpool, 1919–39", in *Labour and love: women's experience of home and family, 1850–1940*, Jane Lewis (ed.) (Oxford: Blackwell, 1986), p. 197.

11. Alva Myrdal & Viola Klein, *Women's two roles: home and work* (London: Routledge & Kegan Paul, 1956).

12. *Ibid.*, p. ix; Jane Lewis, "Myrdal, Klein, *Women's two roles* and postwar feminism 1945–1960", in Harold Smith (ed.), *British feminism in the twentieth century* (Aldershot: Edward Elgar, 1990), p. 177.

13. Myrdal & Klein, *Women's two roles*, p. 151.

14. Judith Hubback, *Wives who went to college* (London: Heinemann, 1957).

15. Margaret Thatcher, "Wake up women", *Sunday Graphic*, 17 February 1952.

16. Olwen Campbell, *The report of a conference on the feminine point of view* (London: Williams & Norgate, 1952), p. 47.

17. Myrdal & Klein, *Women's two roles*, p. 116.

18. *Ibid.*, p. 24.

19. Sylvia Pearson, *Mothers at work* (London: Epworth Press, 1964), p. 8.

20. British Federation of University Women, *The occupational outlook for graduate women: interim report on one-day conference* (London, 1964), p. 21.

21. Richard Titmuss, "The family as a social institution", in British National Conference on Social Work, *The family* (London: National Council of Social Service, 1953), p. 13.

22. *Ibid.*

23. Pearson, *Mothers at work*, p. 8.

24. Myrdal & Klein, *Women's two roles*, p. 24.

25. Hubback, *Wives who went to college*, pp. 2, 6, 1.

26. Denise Riley, *War in the nursery: theories of the child and mother* (London: Virago, 1983), p. 186.

27. Myrdal & Klein, *Women's two roles*, pp. 9–10.

28. Hubback, *Wives who went to college*, pp. 11, 6.

29. *Ibid.*, p. 12.
30. Myrdal & Klein, *Women's two roles*, p. 38.
31. Viola Klein, "Working wives", in National Society of Children's Nurseries, *Working wives: what of the children?* (London, 1960), p. 37.
32. Hannah Gavron, *The captive wife: conflicts of housebound mothers* (Harmondsworth: Penguin, 1968, first published 1966), p. 143.
33. Eleanor French, "The young mother at work", *Biology and human affairs* 17, January 1952, p. 135.
34. Basil Henriques, *The home-menders: the prevention of unhappiness in children* (London: Harrap, 1955), pp. 33–4.
35. T. R. Fyvel, *The insecure offenders: rebellious youth in the welfare state* (London: Chatto & Windus, 1961), p. 216.
36. Church of England Moral Welfare Council, *The family in contemporary society* (London: SPCK, 1959), pp. 103–5; Ronald Fletcher, *The family and marriage in Britain* (Harmondsworth: Penguin, 1968, first published 1962), pp. 151–3.
37. Regenia Gagnier, "The literary standard: working-class lifewriting and gender", *Textual Practice* 3, 1989, p. 41.
38. Myrdal & Klein, *Women's two roles*, p. 84.
39. Audrey Best, Letter to author, July 1994.
40. "Maria Woods" (pseudonym), Oral testimony, 1994.
41. Lella Secor Florence, *Progress report on birth control* (London: Heinemann, 1956), p. 213.
42. Gladys Petty, Oral testimony, 1994.
43. "Maria Woods" (pseudonym), Oral testimony, 1994.
44. Win Kewley, Oral testimony, 1992.
45. *Ibid.*
46. Constance Nembhard, Oral testimony, 1995.
47. "Vi Chambers" (pseudonym), Oral testimony, 1995.
48. Mrs H, Oral testimony, 1995.
49. Constance Nembhard, Oral testimony, 1995.
50. "Mary" (pseudonym), Oral testimony, 1995.
51. Buchi Emecheta, *Second-class citizen* (London: Allison & Busby, 1974), pp. 55–67.
52. Thatcher, "Wake up women".
53. I am grateful to Linda Harrison for the information that the "twilight shift" was called the "granny shift" in Barrow-in-Furness in the 1950s.
54. Norma Steele, "We're in Britain for the money", in *Black women: bringing it all back home*, Margaret Prescod-Roberts & Norma Steele (eds) (Bristol: Falling Wall Press, 1980), p. 10.
55. "Vi Chambers" (pseudonym), Oral testimony, 1995.
56. Cecilia Wade, in *"Sorry no vacancies": life stories of senior citizens from the Caribbean*, Notting Dale Urban Studies Centre (ed.) (London: Notting Dale Urban Studies Centre, 1992), pp. 16–17.

Chapter 7

1. Quoted in Betty Jerman, *The lively-minded women: the first twenty years of the National Housewives Register* (London: Heinemann, 1981), p. 5.
2. Adrian Forty, *Objects of desire: design and society 1750–1980* (London: Thames & Hudson, 1986), p. 167.
3. Mass Observation, *An enquiry into people's homes* (London: John Murray, 1943), p. 50.
4. Bill Schwarz, " 'The only white man in there': the re-racialisation of England, 1956–1968", *Race and Class* 38, 1996, p. 259; Kathleen Paul, " 'British subjects' and 'British stock': Labour's postwar imperialism", *Journal of British Studies* 34, 1995, p. 258.
5. Andrew Nocon, "A reluctant welcome?: Poles in Britain in the 1940s", *Oral History*, Spring 1986, p. 82.
6. Alison Ravetz, "A view from the interior", in *A view from the interior: feminism, women and design*, Judy Attfield & Pat Kirkham (eds) (London: Women's Press, 1989), p. 189.
7. Judy Giles, *Women, identity and private life in Britain, 1900–1950* (Basingstoke: Macmillan 1995), p. 135.
8. This is Margaret Powell's phrase in *Below stairs* (London: Pan Books, 1970), p. 159.
9. Violet Markham, *Return passage* (London: Oxford University Press, 1953), pp. 25, 222.
10. Violet Markham & Florence Hancock, *Report on post-war organisation of private domestic employment*, Cmd. 6650 (London: HMSO, 1945), p. 7.
11. See Nicola Beauman, *A very great profession: the woman's novel 1914–1939* (London: Virago, 1995), pp. 232–3.
12. Christina Hardyment, *From mangle to microwave: the mechanisation of household work* (Cambridge: Polity, 1985), p. 185.
13. Kay Smallshaw, *How to run your home without help* (London: John Lehmann, 1949), p. vi.
14. Jean Rennie, "Every other Sunday", in *Useful toil: autobiographies of working people from the 1820s to the 1920s*, John Burnett (ed.) (Harmondsworth: Penguin, 1977); Powell, *Below stairs*; Winifred Foley, *A child in the forest* (London: BBC Books, 1974).
15. Powell, *Below stairs*, p. 159.
16. Rennie, "Every other Sunday", pp. 244–5.
17. Powell, *Below stairs*, pp. 147–8.
18. Jan Struther, *Mrs Miniver* (London: Virago, 1989, first published 1939).
19. Mary Wylde, *A housewife in Kensington* (London: Longman, 1937).
20. Struther, *Mrs Miniver*, p. 30.
21. Wylde, *A housewife in Kensington*, pp. 195–6, 185–9, 199, 35–6.
22. Markham & Hancock, *Report on post-war organisation of private domestic employment*, p. 7.

23. Markham, *Return passage*, p. 32.
24. Marjorie Bruce-Milne (ed.), *The book for the home* (London: Caxton Publishing, 1956), vol. 1, pp. 344–52.
25. "Elizabeth Arthur" (pseudonym), Oral testimony, 1992.
26. Markham & Hancock, *Report on post-war organisation of private domestic employment*; Christina Butler, *Domestic service: an enquiry by the Women's Industrial Council* (London: G. Bell, 1916).
27. See for example, Lilly Frazer, *First aid to the servantless* (Cambridge: W. Heffer, 1913); Dorothy Peel, *The labour-saving house* (London: John Lane, 1917); "The house without a servant", *Our Homes and Gardens*, December 1919.
28. British Federation of University Women, *The occupational outlook for graduate women: interim report on one-day conference* (London, 1964), pp. 25–6.
29. Sheila Patterson, *Dark strangers: a sociological study of the absorption of a recent West Indian migrant group in Brixton, South London* (London: Tavistock, 1963), p. 101.
30. W. W. Daniel, *Racial discrimination in England, based on the PEP Report* (Harmondsworth: Penguin, 1968), p. 110.
31. "Vi Chambers" (pseudonym), Oral testimony, 1995.
32. *Ibid.*
33. Amanda Murphy, Oral testimony, 1995.
34. Penny Summerfield, "Women in Britain since 1945: companionate marriage and the double burden", in *Understanding post-war British society*, James Obelkevich & Peter Catterall (eds) (London: Routledge, 1994), p. 64.
35. Hannah Gavron, *The captive wife: conflicts of housebound mothers* (Harmondsworth: Penguin, 1968, first published 1966), p. 122.
36. *ibid.*, p. 137.
37. Suzanne Gail, "The housewife", in Ronald Fraser (ed.), *Work: twenty personal accounts* (Harmondsworth: Penguin, 1968), pp. 145, 150.
38. *Ibid.*, pp. 154, 147.
39. Margaret Drabble, *A summer bird-cage* (Harmondsworth: Penguin, 1968, first published 1963), pp. 204–5.
40. Margaret Drabble, *The millstone* (Harmondsworth: Penguin, 1969, first published 1965), pp. 107–9, 71–3.
41. Jerman, *The lively-minded women*, pp. 29, 45.
42. Alison Light, *Forever England: femininity, literature and conservatism between the wars* (London: Routledge, 1991), p. 219.
43. Jerman, *The lively-minded women*, pp. 10, 35.
44. Leonore Davidoff, *Worlds between: historical perspectives on gender and class* (Cambridge: Polity, 1995), p. 12.
45. Ann Oakley, *Taking it like a woman* (London: Flamingo, 1985), p. 67.
46. Giles, *Women, identity and private life in Britain*; Judy Giles, "A home of one's own: women and domesticity in England 1918–1950", *Women's Studies International Forum* 16, 1993; M. J. Daunton, *A*

property owning democracy?: Housing in Britain (London: Faber & Faber, 1987), pp. 17–35.

47. John Burnett, *A social history of housing 1815–1985* (London: Methuen, 1986), pp. 282–3.

48. Central Office of Information, Social Survey Division, *The British household by P. G. Gray based on an inquiry carried out in April, 1947* (London, 1950), pp. 27–9; Central Office of Information, Social Survey Division, *The housing situation in 1960* (London, 1960), p. 49.

49. Quoted in Judy Attfield, "Inside pram town: a case study of Harlow house interiors. 1951–61", in *A view from the interior*, Attfield & Kirkham (eds), p. 221. See also Graham Crow, "The post-war development of the modern domestic ideal", in *Home and family: creating the domestic sphere*, Graham Allan & Graham Crow (eds), (Basingstoke: Macmillan, 1989), p. 22.

50. "Elizabeth Arthur" (pseudonym), Oral testimony, 1992.

51. "Chris" (pseudonym), Oral testimony, 1994.

52. *Ibid.*

53. Michael Young & Peter Willmott, *Family and kinship in East London* (London: Routledge & Kegan Paul, 1957), pp. 62, 18, 23–4.

54. See Mary Stott (ed.), *Women talking: an anthology from the Guardian women's page* (London: Pandora, 1987), pp. 230–1.

55. Rachel Pierce, "Marriage in the fifties", *Sociological Review* 11, 1963, pp. 232–3

56. Carol Smart, *The ties that bind: law, marriage and the reproduction of patriarchal relations* (London: Routledge & Kegan Paul, 1984), pp. 46–8.

57. Markham & Hancock, *Report on post-war organisation of private domestic employment*, p. 7.

58. Bruce-Milne, *The book for the home*, p. 20.

59. Mass Observation, *An enquiry into people's homes*, p. 173.

60. *Ibid.*, pp. xxiii, 46.

61. Gavron, *The captive wife*, p. 58.

62. Mass Observation, *An enquiry into people's homes*, pp. 171–2.

63. *Ibid.*, p. 173.

64. *Ibid.*, p. 48.

65. Attfield, "Inside pram town", p. 219.

66. *Ibid.*, p. 215.

67. Joyce Storey, *Joyce's war* (London: Virago, 1992), p. 163.

68. "Jean Grant" (pseudonym), Oral testimony, 1995.

69. Storey, *Joyce's war*, p. 164.

70. *Ibid.*, p. 162.

71. Joyce Storey, *Joyce's dream* (London: Virago, 1995), p. 8.

72. Storey, *Joyce's war*, p. 141.

73. Storey, *Joyce's dream*, pp. 25, 37, 49.

74. *Ibid.*, p. 89.

75. *Ibid.*, pp. 94–5.

76. *Ibid.*, p. 7.

77. Clifford Hill, *How colour prejudiced is Britain?* (London: Gollancz, 1965), p. 102; Sheila Patterson, *Immigration and race relations in Britain 1960–1967* (London: Oxford University Press, 1969), p. 252.
78. Patterson, *Immigration and race relations in Britain*, p. 209.
79. *Ibid.*, p. 203.
80. W. W. Daniel, *Racial discrimination in England, based on the PEP Report* (Harmondsworth: Penguin, 1968), p. 154.
81. Sidney Jacobs, "Race, empire and the welfare state: council housing and racism", *Critical Social Policy* 13, 1985, p. 19.
82. Patterson, *Immigration and race relations in Britain*, p. 246. Daniel, *Racial discrimination in England*, p. 177.
83. *Ibid.*, p. 210.
84. Daniel, *Racial discrimination in England*, pp. 183–4.
85. Patterson, *Immigration and race relations in Britain*, p. 196.
86. Daniel, *Racial discrimination in England*, p. 152.
87. Central Office of Information, *The housing situation in 1960*, pp. 49–51.
88. Patterson, *Immigration and race relations in Britain*, pp. 194, 204.
89. Terri Colpi, *The Italian factor: the Italian community in Great Britain* (Edinburgh: Mainstream, 1991), p. 199.
90. Daniel, *Racial discrimination in England*, p. 163.
91. Leena Dhingra, "Breaking out of the labels", in *Watchers and seekers*, Rhonda Cobham & Merle Collins (eds) (Cambridge: Cambridge University Press, 1990), pp. 104–5.
92. Buchi Emecheta, *Second-class citizen* (London: Allison & Busby, 1974), p. 55.
93. Mrs B, Oral testimony, 1995.
94. For Polish migrants, see Keith Sword, *The formation of the Polish community in Great Britain 1939–1950* (London: University of London, 1989), p. 377.
95. Una Cooper, "No Irish need apply", in *Across the water: Irish women's lives in Britain*, Mary Lennon, Marie McAdam, Joanne O'Brien (eds) (London: Virago, 1988), p. 142.
96. Constance Nembhard, Oral testimony, 1995.
97. "Urena Phillips" (pseudonym), Oral testimony, 1995.
98. *Ibid.*
99. Elsie George, Oral testimony, 1995.
100. Buchi Emecheta, *Head above water* (London: Fontana, 1986), p. 31; Emecheta, *Second-class citizen*, p. 47.
101. Constance Nembhard, Oral testimony, 1995.
102. "Mrs Wilson" (pseudonym), Oral testimony, 1995.
103. Constance Nembhard, Oral testimony, 1995.
104. Amanda Murphy, Oral testimony, 1995.
105. Emecheta, *Second-class citizen*, p. 73.
106. Sydney Collins, *Coloured minorities in Britain* (London: Lutterworth Press, 1957), p. 55.
107. Mrs Wilson, Oral testimony, 1995; 'Gloria Lewis' (pseudonym), Oral testimony, 1995; 'Vi Chambers' (pseudonym), Oral testimony, 1995.

108. Sword, *The formation of the Polish community*, p. 378.
109. Genowefa Dziewanda, Oral testimony, 1996.
110. Bevereley Bryan, Stella Dadzie, Suzanne Scafé, *The heart of the race: black women's lives in Britain* (London: Virago, 1985), p. 131; Claudette Williams, "We are a natural part of many different struggles: black women organising", in *Inside Babylon: the Caribbean diaspora in Britain*, Winston James & Clive Harris (eds) (London: Verso, 1993), p. 154.
111. Valentina Alexander, " 'A mouse in a jungle': the Black Christian woman's experience in the church and society in Britain", in *Reconstructing womanhood, reconstructing feminism: writings on black women*, Delia Jarrett-Macauley (ed.) (London: Routledge, 1996), p. 90.
112. Bryan, *The heart of the race*, p. 132.
113. Mrs H, Oral testimony, 1995.
114. Quoted in Elyse Dodgson, *Motherland: West Indian women to Britain in the 1950s* (London: Heinemann, 1984), pp. 26–7.
115. "Vi Chambers" (pseudonym), Oral testimony, 1995.
116. Constance Nembhard, Oral testimony, 1995.
117. Cooper, "No Irish need apply", pp. 142–5.
118. *Ibid.*

Epilogue

1. Catherine Hall, The ruinous ghost of empire past, *The Times Higher Educational Supplement*, 8 March 1996.
2. Quoted in Peter Hennessy, *Never again: Britain 1945–51* (London: Jonathan Cape, 1992), p. xiv.
3. Quoted in Humphrey Berkeley, *The odyssey of Enoch: a political memoir* (London: Hamilton, 1977), p. 52.
4. For accounts of Powell's passionate imperialism and subsequent disenchantment see Paul Foot, *The rise of Enoch Powell: an examination of Enoch Powell's attitude to immigration and race* (Harmondsworth: Penguin, 1969); Tom Nairn, *The break-up of Britain: crisis and neo-nationalism* (London: New Left Books, 1977).
5. For the full text of Powell's speech see Enoch Powell, *Freedom and reality* (London: Paperfront, 1969), pp. 281–90.

Bibliography

Life-writing and oral histories

Bousquet, B. & C. Douglas. *West Indian women at war: British racism in world war II* (London: Lawrence & Wishart, 1991).

Broad, R. & S. Fleming (eds). *Nella Last's war: a mother's diary 1939–45* (Bristol: Falling Wall Press, 1981).

Bryan, B., S. Dadzie, S. Scafe *The heart of the race: Black women's lives in Britain* (London: Virago, 1985).

Cant, B. & S. Hemmings (eds). *Radical records: thirty years of lesbian and gay history 1957–1987* (London: Routledge, 1988).

Chapeltown Black Women's Writers Group. *When our ship comes in: black women talk* (Castleford: Yorkshire Art Circus, 1992).

Chew, S. & A. Rutherford (eds). *Unbecoming daughters of the empire* (Sydney: Dangaroo Press, 1993).

Dodgson, E. *Motherland: West Indian women to Britain in the 1950s* (London: Heinemann, 1984).

Emecheta, B. *Head above water* (London: Fontana, 1986).

Ethnic Communities Oral History Project. *The motherland calls: African Caribbean experiences* (London: Ethnic Communities Oral History Project, 1992).

Evans, M. *A good school: life at a girls' grammar school in the 1950s* (London: Women's Press, 1991).

Foley, W. *A child in the forest* (London: BBC Books, 1974).

Forster, M. *Hidden lives: a family memoir* (London: Viking, 1995).

Gail, S. The housewife. In *Work: twenty personal accounts*, R. Fraser (ed.) (Harmondsworth: Penguin, 1968).

Gilroy, B. *Black teacher* (London: Bogle-l'Ouverture Press, 1994).

Grieve, M. *Millions made my story* (London: Gollancz, 1964).

Hall Carpenter Archives/Lesbian Oral History Group (eds). *Inventing ourselves: lesbian life stories* (London: Routledge, 1989).

Hartley, J. (ed.). *Hearts undefeated: women's writings of the second world war* (London: Virago, 1995).

Haythorne, E. *On earth to make the numbers up* (Castleford: Yorkshire Art Circus, 1991).

Heron, L. (ed.). *Truth, dare or promise: girls growing up in the 50s* (London: Virago, 1985).

Hinds, D. *Journey to an illusion: the West Indian in Britain* (London: Heinemann, 1966).

Jewish Women in London Group. *Generations of memories: voices of Jewish women* (London: Women's Press, 1989).

Johnson, B. *"I think of my mother": notes on the life and times of Claudia Jones* (London: Karia Press, 1985).

Lambeth Council & the Voice. *Forty winters on: memories of Britain's post-war Caribbean immigrants* (London: South London Press, 1988).

Lawrence, M. *A telling and a keeping: a writer's autobiography* (London: Women's Press, 1989).

Lennon, M., M. McAdam, J. O'Brien (eds). *Across the water: Irish women's lives in Britain* (London: Virago, 1988).

Lorde, A. *The cancer journals* (London: Sheba, 1985).

McCrinde, J. & S. Rowbotham (eds). *Dutiful daughters* (Harmondsworth: Penguin, 1979).

Markham, V. *Return passage* (London: Oxford University Press, 1953).

Mortimer, P. *About time too: 1940–1978* (London: Weidenfeld & Nicolson, 1993).

Neild, S. & R. Pearson (eds). *Women like us* (London: Women's Press, 1992).

Notting Dale Urban Studies Centre (ed.), *"Sorry, no vacancies": life stories of senior citizens from the Caribbean* (London: Notting Dale Urban Studies Centre, 1992).

Oakley, A. *Taking it like a woman* (London: Flamingo, 1985).

Powell, M. *Below stairs* (London: Pan Books, 1970).

Rennie, J. Every other Sunday. In *Useful toil: autobiographies of working people from the 1820s to the 1920s* J. Burnett (ed.) (Harmondsworth: Penguin, 1977).

Roots Oral History. *Rude awakening: African/Caribbean settlers in Manchester* (Roots Oral History Project, 1992).

Stanley, J. (ed.). *To make ends meet: women over 60 write about their working lives* (London: Older Women's Project, n.d.).

Steedman, C. *Landscape for a good woman: a story of two lives* (London: Virago, 1986).

Storey, J. *Joyce's war* (London: Virago, 1992).

Storey, J. *Joyce's dream* (London: Virago, 1995).

Stott, M. *Forgetting's no excuse* (London: Virago, 1989).

Wilson, A. *Finding a voice: Asian women in Britain* (London: Virago, 1978).

Books, reports, articles and pamphlets published before 1969

Abrams, M. *The population of Great Britain* (London: Allen & Unwin, 1945).

Abrams, M. The home-centred society. *The Listener*, 26 November 1959.

Appleyard, R. T. *British emigration to Australia* (London: Weidenfeld & Nicolson, 1964).

Arreger, C. *Graduate women at work* (Newcastle: Oriel Press, 1966).

Astbury, B. E. Welfare of coloured people. *Social Work* 12, October 1955.

Banton, M. *The coloured quarter* (London: Jonathan Cape, 1955).

Banton, M. *White and coloured: the behaviour of British people towards coloured immigrants* (London: Jonathan Cape, 1959).

Bertram, G. L. C. *West Indian immigration* (London: Eugenics Society, 1958).

Blacker, C. P. *Eugenics: Galton and after* (London: Duckworth, 1952).

Blacker, C. P. (ed.). *Problem families: five inquiries* (London: Eugenics Society, 1952).

Bowlby, J. *Maternal care and mental health: a report pepared on behalf of the World Health Organization* (Geneva, 1952).

Bowlby, J. *Child care and the growth of love* (Harmondsworth: Penguin, 1959, first published 1953).

Brew, J. M. *Girls' interests* (London: National Association of Mixed Clubs and Girls' Clubs, 1956).

British Federation of University Women. *The occupational outlook for graduate women: interim report on one-day conference* (London, 1964).

British Medical Association. *Venereal disease and young people: a report by a committee of the British Medical Association on the problem of venereal disease particularly among young people* (London, 1964).

British National Conference on Social Work. *The family* (London: National Council of Social Service, 1953).

Bruce-Milne, M. (ed.). *The book for the home*. vo. 1 (London: Caxton Publishing, 1956).

Butler, C. *Domestic service: an enquiry by the Women's Industrial Council* (London: G. Bell, 1916).

Campbell, O. *The report of a conference on the feminine point of view* (London: Williams & Norgate, 1952).

Care of Children Committee. *Report* Cmd. 6922 (London: HMSO, 1946).

Central Office of Information. *Children in Britain* (London: HMSO, 1959).

Central Office of Information, Social Survey Division. *The British household by P. G. Gray based on an inquiry carried out in April, 1947* (London, 1950).

Central Office of Information, Social Survey Division. *The housing situation in 1960* (London, 1960).

Chapman, D. *The home and social status* (London: Routledge & Kegan Paul, 1955).

Church of England Moral Welfare Council. *Moral crisis: the Church in action* (London: Church Information Board, 1950).

Church of England Moral Welfare Council. *The family in contemporary society* (London: SPCK, 1959).

Clarke, J. *Disabled citizens* (London: Allen & Unwin, 1951).

Collins, S. The social position of white and "half-caste" women in colored groupings in Britain. *American Sociological Review* **16**, December 1951.

Collins, S. *Coloured minorities in Britain* (London: Lutterworth Press, 1957).

Committee on Homosexual Offences and Prostitution. *Report*, Cmnd. 247 (London: HMSO, 1957).

Constantine, L. *Colour bar* (London: Stanley Paul, 1954).

Cooper, C. *The illegitimate child* (National Council for the Unmarried Mother and her Child, 1955).

Cousins, E. G. *Sapphire* (London, Panther, 1959).

Curran, C. The new estate in Great Britain. *Spectator*, 20 January 1956.

Curran, C. The politics of the new estate. *Spectator*, 17 February 1956.

Curran, C. This new England: the passing of the tribunes. *Encounter*, 6 June 1956.

Daniel, W. W. *Racial discrimination in England, based on the PEP Report* (Harmondsworth: Penguin, 1968).

Davison, R. B. *West Indian migrants: social and economic facts of migration from the West Indies* (London: Oxford University Press, 1962).

Davison, R. B. *Black British: immigrants to England* (London: Oxford University Press, 1966).

Departmental Committee on Human Artificial Insemination. *Report*, Cmnd. 1105 (London: HMSO, 1960).

Douglas, J. W. B. The feminists mop up. *The Economist*, 21 April 1956.

Drabble, M. *A summer bird-cage* (Harmondsworth: Penguin, 1968).

Drabble, M. *The millstone* (Harmondsworth: Penguin, 1965).

Drake, St C. The "colour problem" in Britain: a study of social definition. *Sociological Review* **3**, December 1955.

Elkan, I. Interviews with neglectful parents. *British Journal of Psychiatric Social Work* **3**, 1956.

Ellison, M. *The adopted child* (London: Gollancz, 1958).

Lord Elton. *The unarmed invasion: a survey of Afro-Asian immigration* (London: Geoffrey Bles, 1965).

Fabian Society. *Population and the people* (London: Allen & Unwin, 1945).

Family Welfare Association. *The West Indian comes to London* (London: Routledge & Kegan Paul, 1960).

Ferguson, S. & H. Fitzgerald. *Studies in the social services* (London: HMSO & Longman, 1954).

Fisher, L. *Twenty-one years and after: the National Council for the Unmarried Mother and her Child 1918–1939* (n.d.).

Fletcher, R. *The family and marriage in Britain* (Harmondsworth: Penguin, 1968, first published 1962).

Florence, L. S. *Progress report on birth control* (London: Heinemann, 1956).

Frazer, L. *First aid to the servantless* (Cambridge: W. Heffer, 1913).

French, E. The young mother at work. *Biology and Human Affairs* **17**, January 1952.

Friedan, B. *The feminine mystique* (London: Gollancz, 1963).

Fyvel, T. R. This new England: the stones of Harlow, reflections on subtopia. *Encounter*, 6 June 1956.

Fyvel, T. R. *The insecure offenders: rebellious youth in the welfare state* (London: Chatto & Windus, 1961).

Galton, L. *New facts for the childless* (London: Gollancz, 1954).

Gavron, H. *The captive wife: conflicts of housebound mothers* (Harmondsworth: Penguin, 1968).

Good Housekeeping. *Home encyclopaedia* (London: 1970, first published 1951).

Griffith, E. *Sex and citizenship* (London: Methuen, 1948).

Griffiths, P. *A question of colour?* (London: Frewin, 1966).

E.H., Homeless and fatherless families, *Case Conference* 2, July 1955.

Hadley-Jackson, M. A medical service for the treatment of involuntary sterility. *Eugenics Review* 36, January 1945.

Harrisson, T. *Britain revisited* (London: Gollancz, 1961).

Help for housewives. *The Listener* 35, 11 April 1946.

Henrey, M. The new feminism. *Spectator*, 4 May 1951.

Henriques, B. *The home-menders: the prevention of unhappiness in children* (London: Harrap, 1955).

Henriques, U. The new feminism. *Spectator*, 11 May 1951.

Hill, C. *How colour prejudiced is Britain?* (London: Gollancz, 1965).

Hoggart, R. *The uses of literacy: aspects of working-class life with special reference to publications and entertainments* (Harmondsworth: Penguin, 1969, first published 1957).

Home Office. *Sixth report on the work of the Children's Department, May 1951* (London: HMSO, 1951).

Home Office. *Eighth report on the work of the Children's Department, 1961* (London: HMSO, 1961).

Hopkinson, D. *Family inheritance: a life of Eva Hubback* (London: Staples Press, 1954).

The house without a servant. *Our homes and gardens*, December 1919.

How to welcome a soldier home. *Picture Post*, 21 April 1945.

Hubback, E. *Population facts and policies* (London: Allen & Unwin, 1945).

Hubback, E. *The population of Britain* (Harmondsworth: Penguin, 1947).

Hubback, J. *Wives who went to college* (London: Heinemann, 1957).

Huxley, E. *Race and politics in Kenya: a correspondence between Elspeth Huxley and Margery Perham* (London: Faber & Faber, 1944).

Huxley, E. *White man's country: Lord Delamere and the making of Kenya* (2 vols) (London: Chatto & Windus, 1956, first published 1935).

Huxley, E. *A new earth: an experiment in colonialism* (London: Chatto & Windus, 1960).

Huxley, E. *Back street new worlds: a look at immigrants in Britain* (London: Chatto & Windus, 1964).

Isaacs, S. (ed.). *The Cambridge evacuation survey: a wartime study in social welfare and education* (London: Methuen, 1941).

Jephcott, P. *Rising twenty: notes on some ordinary girls* (London: Faber & Faber, 1948).

Jephcott, P. *A troubled area: notes on Notting Hill, London* (London: Faber & Faber, 1964).

Jephcott, P., with N. Seear & J. H. Smith. *Married women working* (London: Allen & Unwin, 1962).

Klein, V. *Working wives: a survey of facts and opinions concerning the gainful employment of married women in Britain* (London: Institute of Personnel Management, 1960).

Klein, V. *Britain's married women workers* (London: Routledge & Kegan Paul, 1965).

Landau, M. E. *Women of forty* (London: Faber & Faber, 1956).

Lane, Sir W. A. (ed.). *The hygiene of life and safer motherhood* (London: New Age Books, n.d.).

Leybourne, G. & K. White. *Children for Britain* (London: Target Series, Pilot Press, 1945).

MacInnes, C. A short guide for jumbles (to the life of their coloured brethren in England). In *England, half English* (London: MacGibbon & Kee, 1961, first published 1956).

MacInnes, C. *City of spades* (London: Allison & Busby, 1993, first published 1957).

McCleary, G. F. *The menace of British depopulation* (London: Allen & Unwin, 1945).

McCleary, G. F. *Race suicide* (London: Allen & Unwin, 1945).

Marchant, J. (ed.). *Rebuilding family life in the post-war world* (London: Odhams, 1945).

Markham, V. & F. Hancock. *Report on post-war organisation of private domestic employment* Cmd. 6650 (London: HMSO, 1945).

Mass Observation. *An enquiry into people's homes* (London: John Murray, 1943).

Mass Observation. *Britain and her birth-rate* (London: John Murray, 1945).

Myrdal, A. & V. Klein. *Women's two roles: home and work* (London: Routledge & Kegan Paul, 1956).

National Society of Children's Nurseries. *Working wives: what of the children?* (London: 1960).

Newsom, J. *The education of girls* (London: Faber & Faber, 1943).

Newsom, J. & E. *Patterns of infant care in an urban community* (London: Allen & Unwin, 1963).

Orwell, G. England your England. In *Inside the whale and other essays* (Harmondsworth: Penguin, 1971, first published 1941).

Osborne, J. *Look back in anger* (London: Faber & Faber, 1962, first published 1957).

Patterson, S. *Dark strangers: a sociological study of the absorption of a recent West Indian migrant group in Brixton, South London* (London: Tavistock, 1963).

Patterson, S. *Immigrants in industry* (London: Oxford University Press, 1968).

Patterson, S. *Immigration and race relations in Britain 1960–1967* (London: Oxford University Press, 1969).

Pearson, S. *Mothers at work* (London: Epworth Press, 1964).

Peel, D. *The labour-saving house* (London: John Lane, 1917).

Philp A. F. & N. Timms. *The problem of the "problem family": a critical review of the literature concerning the "problem family" and its treatment* (London: Family Service Units, 1957).

Philpott, T. Would you let your daughter marry a negro? *Picture Post*, 30 October 1954.

Pierce, R. Marriage in the fifties. *Sociological Review* 11, 1963.

Pilgrim Trust. *Men without work: a report made to the Pilgrim Trust* (London: Cambridge University Press, 1938).

Priestley, J. B. *English journey* (London: Heinemann, 1934).

Priestley, J. B. *Postscripts* (London: Heinemann, 1940).

Pym, B. *Jane and Prudence* (London: Jonathan Cape, 1979, first published 1953).

Richmond, A. *The colour problem: a study of racial relations* (Harmondsworth: Penguin, 1961, first published 1955).

Robb, J. H. review of Slater & Woodside, *Social Work* 9, April 1952.

Rowe, D. A quick look at the lesbians. *Twentieth Century* 171, 1962–3.

Rowe, J. *Parents, children and adoption* (London: Routledge & Kegan Paul, 1966).

Royal Commission on Marriage and Divorce. *Report*, Cmnd. 9678 (London: HMSO, 1956).

Royal Commission on Population. *Report*, Cmnd. 7695 (London: HMSO, 1949).

Schofield, M. *The sexual behaviour of young people* (London: Longman, 1965).

Shils, E. & M. Young. The meaning of the coronation. *Sociological Review*, December 1953.

Slater, E. & M. Woodside. *Patterns of marriage: a study of marriage relationships in the urban working classes* (London: Cassell, 1951).

Smallshaw, K. *How to run your home without help* (London: John Lehmann, 1949).

Southampton Discussion Group. The neglectful mother. *Social Work* 12, April 1955.

Storr, A *Sexual deviation* (Harmondsworth: Penguin, 1968, first published 1964).

Struther, J. *Mrs Miniver* (London: Virago, 1989, first published 1939).

Tannahill, J. A. *European Volunteer Workers in Britain* (Manchester: Manchester University Press, 1958).

Temple, W. *The hope of a new world* (London: Student Christian Movement, 1940).

Thatcher, M. Wake up women. *Sunday Graphic*, 17 February 1952.

Tippett, L. H. C. *A portrait of the Lancashire textile industry* (Oxford: Oxford University Press, 1969).

Tucker, T. *Children without homes: the problems of their care and protection* (London: Bodley Head, 1952).

Waterhouse, K. Introducing to you the boys from Jamaica. *Daily Mirror*, 8 September 1958.

West Indian Royal Commission. *Report* (London: HMSO, 1945).

Wimperis, V. *The unmarried mother and her child* (London: Allen & Unwin, 1960).

Winnicott, D. W. *The child and the family: first relationships* (London: Tavistock, 1962).

Winnicott, D. W. *The family and individual development* (London: Tavistock, 1965).

Women's Group on Public Welfare. *The education and training of girls* (London: National Council of Social Service, 1962).

Women's Hygiene Committee of the Women's Group on Public Welfare. *Our towns: a close-up* (Oxford: Oxford University Press, 1943).

Wylde, M. *A housewife in Kensington* (London: Longman, 1937).

Young, L. *Out of wedlock* (New York: McGraw Hill, 1954).

Young, M. & P. Willmott. *Family and kinship in East London* (London: Routledge & Kegan Paul, 1957).

Young, W. This new England: return to Wigan pier. *Encounter*, 6 June 1956.

Zweig, F. *Productivity and trade unions* (Oxford: Blackwell, 1951).

Zweig, F. *Women's life and labour* (London: Gollancz, 1952).

Zweig, F. *The worker in an affluent society: family life and industry* (London: Heinemann, 1961).

Books and articles published since 1969

Addison, P. *Now the war is over: a social history of Britain 1945–51* (London: BBC & Jonathan Cape, 1985).

Alexander, S. *Becoming a woman, and other essays in 19th and 20th century feminist history* (London: Virago, 1994).

Alexander, Z. Let it lie upon the table: the status of black women's biography in the UK. *Gender and History* **2**, Spring 1990.

Alvarado, M., G. Robin, T. Wollen. *Learning the media: an introduction to media teaching* (Basingstoke: Macmillan, 1987).

Amos, V. Black women in Britain: a bibliographical essay. *Sage race relations abstracts* **7**, 1982.

Amos V., G. Lewis, A. Mama, P. Parmar (eds). Many voices, one chant. *Feminist Review* **17**, Autumn 1984.

Amos, V. *Women, race and racism: a select bibliography 1970–1983* (Runnymede Trust, 1984).

Anthias, F., N. Yuval-Davis, H. Cain. *Racialised boundaries: race, nation, gender, colour and class and the anti-racist struggle* (London: Routledge, 1992).

Attfield, J. & P. Kirkham (eds). *A view from the interior: feminism, women and design* (London: Women's Press, 1989).

Aziz, R. Feminism and the challenge of racism: deviance or difference? In *Knowing women: feminism and knowledge*, H. Crowley & S. Himmelweit (eds) (Cambridge: Polity, 1992).

Baker, N. *Happily ever after?: Women's fiction in postwar Britain 1945–60* (Basingstoke: Macmillan, 1989).

Beauman, N. *A very great profession: the woman's novel 1914–1939* (London: Virago, 1995).

Berkeley, H. *The odyssey of Enoch: a political memoir* (London: Hamilton, 1977).

Bhachu, P. Identities constructed and reconstructed: representations of Asian women in Britain. In *Migrant women* G. Buijs (ed.) (Oxford: Berg Publishers, 1993).

Bhavnani, K. & R. Bhavnani. Racism and resistance in Britain. In *A socialist anatomy of Britain*, D. Coates, G. Johnston, R. Bush (eds) (Cambridge: Polity, 1985).

Bhavnani, K. & M. Coulson. Transforming socialist feminism: the challenge of racism. *Feminist Review* 23, June 1986.

Birmingham Feminist History Group. Feminism as femininity in the 1950s. *Feminist Review* 3, 1979.

Bourke, J. *Working-class cultures in Britain 1890–1960: gender, class and ethnicity* (London: Routledge, 1994).

Boyce Davies, C. *Black women, writing and identity: migrations of the subject* (London: Routledge, 1994).

Brah, A. Difference, diversity and differentiation. In *"Race", culture and difference*, J. Donald & A. Rattansi (eds) (London: Sage, 1992).

Brah, A. Difference, diversity, differentiation: processes of racialisation and gender. In *Racism and migration in Western Europe*, J. Solomos & J. Wrench (eds) (Oxford: Berg Publishers, 1993).

Brah, A. Women of South Asian origin in Britain: issues and concerns. *Racism and antiracism: inequalities, opportunities and policies*, P. Braham, A. Rattansi, R. Skellington (eds) (London: Sage, 1992).

Brookes, B. *Abortion in England 1900–1967* (London: Croom Helm, 1988).

Brooks, D. *Race and labour in London Transport* (Oxford: Oxford University Press, 1975).

Bryan, B., S. Dadzie, S. Scafe. *The heart of the race: Black women's lives in Britain* (London: Virago, 1985).

Burnett, J. *A social history of housing 1815–1985* (London: Methuen, 1986).

Campbell, B. *The iron ladies: why do women vote Tory?* (London: Virago, 1987).

Carby, H. White woman listen! Black feminism and the boundaries of sisterhood. In *The empire strikes back* Centre for Contemporary Cultural Studies (ed.) (London: Hutchinson, 1982).

Carby, H. *Reconstructing womanhood: the emergence of the Afro-American woman novelist* (Oxford: Oxford University Press, 1987).

Carter, B., C. Harris, S. Joshi. The 1951–55 Conservative government and the racialisation of black immigration. *Immigrants and Minorities* **6**, 1987.

Catterall, P. The state of literature on post-war British history. In *Post-war Britain, 1945–1964: themes and perspectives*, A. Gorst, L. Johnmman, W. S. Lucas (eds) (London: Pinter Publishers, 1989).

Chamberlain, M. Family and identity: Barbadian migrants to Britain. In *Migration and identity: International yearbook of oral history and life stories* R. Benmayor and A. Skotnes (eds), Vol. 3, (Oxford: Oxford University Press, 1994).

Clark, D. (ed.). *Marriage: domestic life and social change* (London: Routledge, 1991).

Cobham, R. & M. Collins (eds). *Watchers and seekers* (Cambridge: Cambridge University Press,1990).

Cohen, R. Frontiers of identity: the British and the others (London: Longman, 1994).

Collins, P. H. *Black feminist thought: knowledge, consciousness and the politics of empowerment* (London: Routledge, 1991).

Colls, R. & P. Dodd (eds). *Englishness: politics and culture, 1880–1920* (London: Croom Helm, 1986).

Colpi, T. *The Italian factor: the Italian community in Britain* (Edinburgh: Mainstream, 1991).

Cosslett, T. *Women writing childbirth: modern discourses of motherhood* (Manchester: Manchester University Press, 1994).

Coward, R. *Our treacherous hearts: why women let men get their way* (London: Faber & Faber, 1993).

Crick, B. The English and the British. In *National identities: the constitution of the United Kingdom* (Oxford: Blackwell, 1991).

Crick, B. (ed.) *National identities: the constitution of the United Kingdom* (Oxford: Blackwell, 1991).

Crow, G. The post-war development of the modern domestic ideal. In G. Allan & G. Crow (eds), *Home and family: creating the domestic sphere* (Basingstoke: Macmillan, 1989).

Crowley, H. Women and the domestic sphere. In *Social and cultural forms of modernity*, R. Bocock & K. Thompson (eds) (Cambridge: Polity, 1992).

Curran, J. & V. Porter (eds). *British cinema history* (London: Weidenfeld & Nicolson, 1983).

Dabydeen, D. & N. W. Tagoe. *A reader's guide to West Indian and Black British literature* (London: Hansib Publishing, 1988).

Dale, J. & P. Foster. *Feminists and state welfare* (London: Routledge & Kegan Paul, 1986).

Daunton, M. J. *A property owning democracy?: Housing in Britain* (London: Faber, 1987).

Davidoff, L. & B. Westover (eds). *Our work, our lives, our words* (Basingstoke: Macmillan, 1986).

Davidoff, L. *Worlds between: historical perspectives on gender and class* (Cambridge: Polity, 1995).

Davidoff, L. & C. Hall, *Family fortunes: men and women of the English middle class 1780–1850* (London: Hutchinson, 1987).

Davies, K., J. Dickey, T. Stratford. *Out of focus: writings on women and the media* (London: Women's Press, 1987).

Davin, A. Imperialism and motherhood. In *Patriotism: the making and unmaking of British national identity*, R. Samuel (ed.), vol. 1 (London: Routledge, 1989).

Doyal, L., G. Hunt, J. Mellor. Your life in their hands: migrant workers in the National Health Service. *Critical Social Policy* 1, 1981.

Dummett, A. & A. Nicol. *Subjects, citizens, aliens and others: nationality and immigration law* (London: Weidenfeld & Nicolson, 1990).

Dunstall, G. The social pattern. In *The Oxford history of new Zealand*, G. Rice (ed.) (Oxford: Oxford University Press, 1995).

Dyer, R. White. *Screen* **29**, Autumn 1988.

Echevarria-Howe, L. Reflections from the participants: the process and product of life history work. *Oral History*, Autumn 1995.

Edgerton, R. *Mau Mau: an African crucible* (London: I. B. Tauris, 1990).

Edwards, R. Connecting method and epistemology: a white woman interviewing back women. *Women's Studies International Forum* **13**, 1990.

Emecheta, B. *Second-class citizen* (London: Allison & Busby, 1974).

Foot, P. *The rise of Enoch Powell: an examination of Enoch Powell's attitude to immigration and race* (Harmondsworth: Penguin, 1969).

Forty, A. *Objects of desire: design and society 1750–1980* (London: Thames & Hudson, 1986).

Friedman, S. Beyond white and other: relationality and narratives of feminist discourse. *Signs: Journal of Women in Culture and Society* **21**, Autumn 1995.

Frost, D. West Africans, Black Scousers and the colour problem in inter-war Liverpool. *North West Labour History* **20**, 1995/6.

Fryer, P. *Staying power: the history of black people in Britain* (London: Pluto, 1984).

Fyrth, J. (ed.). *Labour's promised land?: culture and society in Labour Britain 1945–51* (London: Lawrence & Wishart, 1995).

Gagnier, R. The literary standard: working-class lifewriting and gender. *Textual Practice* **3**, 1989.

Geiger, S. What's so feminist about doing women's oral history? In C. Johnson-Odim & M. Strobel (eds), *Expanding the boundaries of women's history: essays on women in the third world* (Bloomington: Indiana University Press, 1992).

George, R. M. *The politics of home: postcolonial relocations and twentieth-century fiction* (Cambridge: Cambridge University Press, 1996).

Giles, J. A home of one's own: women and domesticity in England 1918–1950. *Women's Studies International Forum* **16**, 1993.

Giles, J. *Women, identity and private life in Britain, 1900–50* (Basingstoke: Macmillan, 1995).

Giles, J. & T. Middleton (eds). *Writing Englishness 1900–1950: an introductory source book on national identity* (London: Routledge, 1995).

Gilroy, B. I write because. In *Caribbean women writers: essays from the first international conference*, S. Cudjoe (ed.) (Wellesley, Mass.: Calaxous Publications, 1990).

Gilroy, P. *"There ain't no black in the Union Jack": the cultural politics of race and nation* (London: Hutchinson, 1987).

Gittins, D. *Fair sex: family size and structure 1900–39* (London: Hutchinson, 1982).

Gluck, S. & D. Patai (eds). *Women's words: the feminist practice of oral history* (London: Routledge, 1991).

Glucksmann, M. In a class of their own?: Women workers in the new industries in inter-war Britain. *Feminist Review* **24**, 1986.

Glucksmann, M. *Women assemble: women workers in the new industries in inter-war Britain* (London: Routledge, 1990).

Gordon, T. *Single women: on the margins?* (Basingstoke: Macmillan, 1994).

Greet, A., S. Harrex, S. Hosking (eds). *Raj nostalgia: some literary and critical implications* (Adelaide: CRNLE, 1992).

Grewal, S., J. Kay, L. Landor, G. Lewis, P. Parmar (eds). *Charting the journey: writings by Black and third world women* (London: Sheba, 1988).

Hall, C. The ruinous ghost of empire past. *The Times Higher Educational Supplement*, 8 March 1996.

Hall, S. Racism and reaction. In *Five views of multi-racial Britain* (Commission for Racial Equality, 1978).

Hardyment, C. *From mangle to microwave: the mechanisation of household work* (Cambridge: Polity, 1985).

Harris, C. Images of blacks in Britain 1930–1960. In *Race and social policy*, S. Allen & M. Macey (eds) (London: ESRC, 1988).

Heilbrun, C. *Writing a woman's life* (London: Women's Press, 1989).

Hennessy, P. *Never again: Britain 1945–51* (London: Jonathan Cape, 1992).

Hill, J. *Sex, class and realism: British cinema 1956–1963* (London: British Film Institute, 1986).

Hinton, J. Militant housewives: the British Housewives League and the Attlee government. *History Workshop* **38**, 1994.

Hobsbawm, E. & T. Ranger (eds). *The invention of tradition* (Cambridge: Cambridge University Press, 1983).

Holdsworth, A. *Out of the doll's house: the story of women in the twentieth century* (London: BBC Books, 1988).

Holmes, C. Historians and immigration. In *Migrants, emigrants and immigrants: a social history*, C. Pooley & I Whyte (eds) (London: Routledge, 1991).

hooks, b. *Feminist theory: from margin to centre* (Boston, Mass.: South End Books, 1984).

hooks, b. *Yearning: race, gender and cultural politics* (London: Turnaround, 1991).

Howes, K. *Broadcasting it: an encylopaedia of homosexuality on film, radio and TV in the UK 1923–1993* (London: Cassell, 1993).

Humphreys, M. *Empty cradles* (London: Doubleday, 1994).

Jack, T. *Countering voices: an approach to Asian and feminist studies in the 1990s.* Women's Studies International Forum **17**, 1994.

Jacobs, S. Race, empire and the welfare state: council housing and racism. *Critical Social Policy* **13**, 1985.

James, W. & C. Harris (eds). *Inside Babylon: the Caribbean diaspora in Britain* (London: Verso, 1993).

Jarret-Macauley, D. (ed.). *Reconstructing womanhood, reconstructing feminism: writings on Black women* (London: Routledge, 1996).

Jeffreys, S. *Anticlimax: a feminist perspective on the sexual revolution* (London: Women's Press, 1990).

Jerman, B. *The lively-minded women: the first twenty years of the National Housewives Register* (London: Heinemann, 1981).

Karah, D. *Adoption and the coloured child* (London: Epworth Press, 1970).

Kay, D. & R. Miles. *Refugees or migrant workers?: European Volunteer Workers in Britain 1946–1951* (London: Routledge, 1992).

Kay, J. *The adoption papers* (Newcastle-upon-Tyne: Bloodaxe Books, 1991).

Keating, P. (ed.). *Into unknown England 1866–1913: selections from the social explorers* (London: Fontana, 1976).

Kessler-Harris, A. Gender ideology in historical reconstruction: a case study from the 1930s. *Gender and History* **1**, Spring 1989.

Knewstub, N. Committed to the young people upstairs. *Guardian*, 15 December 1978.

Kushner, T. *The persistence of prejudice: antisemitism in British society during the second world war* (Manchester: Manchester University Press, 1989).

Kushner, T. *The holocaust and the liberal imagination: a social and cultural history* (Oxford: Blackwell, 1994).

Kushner, T. & K. Lunn. *The politics of marginality: race, the radical right and minorities in twentieth century Britain* (London: Frank Cass, 1990).

Laing, S. *Representations of working-class life 1957–1964* (Basingstoke: Macmillan, 1986).

Lewis, J. (ed.). *Labour and love: women's experiences of home and family, 1850–1940* (Oxford: Blackwell, 1986).

Lewis, J. *Women in Britain since 1945* (Oxford: Blackwell, 1992).

Lewis, J., D.Clark, D. Morgan. *"Whom God hath joined together": the work of marriage guidance* (London: Routledge, 1992).

Light, A. *Forever England: femininity, literature and conservatism between the wars* (London: Routledge, 1991).

Lovell, T. Landscapes and stories in 1960s British realism. *Screen* **31** (4) Winter 1990.

McClintock, A. *Imperial leather: race, gender and sexuality in the colonial contest* (London: Routledge, 1995).

Mackenzie, J. *Propaganda and empire: the manipulation of British public opinion 1880–1960* (Manchester: Manchester University Press, 1984).

Mama, A. Black women and the British state: race, class and gender analysis for the 1990s. In *Racism and antiracism: inequalities, opportunities and policies*, P. Braham, A. Rattansi, R. Skellington (eds) (London: Sage, 1992).

Mama, A. *Beyond the masks: race, gender and subjectivity* (London: Routledge, 1995).

Marcus, L. "Enough about you, let's talk about me": recent autobiographical writing. *New Formations* 1, Spring 1987.

Maughan-Brown, D. *Land, freedom and fiction: history and ideology in Kenya* (London: Zed Books, 1985).

Minns, R. *Bombers and mash: the domestic front 1939–1945* (London: Virago, 1980).

Modood, T. "Black", racial equality and Asian identity. *New Community* 14, 1988.

Mort, F. *Dangerous sexualities: medico-moral politics since 1830* (London: Routledge & Kegan Paul, 1987).

Mugo, M. G. *Visions of Africa* (Nairobi: Kenya Literature Bureau, 1978).

Nairn, T. *The break-up of Britain: crisis and neo-nationalism* (London: New Left Books, 1981).

Ngcobo, L. (ed.). *Let it be told: black women writers in Britain* (London: Virago, 1987).

Nocon, A. A reluctant welcome?: Poles in Britain in the 1940s. *Oral History*, Spring 1986.

Panayi, P. The historiography of immigrants and ethnic minorities: Britain compared with the USA. *Ethnic and Racial Studies* 19, 1996.

Parmar, P. Gender, race and class: Asian women in resistance. In *The empire strikes back* Centre for Contemporary Cultural Studies (ed.) (London: Hutchinson, 1982).

Parmar, P. Black feminism: the politics of articulation. In *Identity, community, culture, difference*, J. Rutherford (ed.) (London: Lawrence & Wishart, 1990.

Patterson, S. The Poles: an exile community in Britain. In *Between two cultures: migrants and minorities in Britain*, J. Watson (ed.) (Oxford: Blackwell, 1977).

Paul, K. The politics of citizenship in post-war Britain. *Contemporary Record* 6, 1992.

Paul, K. "British subjects and "British stock": Labour's postwar imperialism. *Journal of British Studies* 34, 1995.

Personal Narratives Group (ed.). *Interpreting women's lives: feminist theory and personal narratives* (Bloomington, Indiana: Indiana University Press, 1989).

Phillips, A. *Divided loyalties: dilemmas of sex and class* (London: Virago, 1987).

Pieterse, J. N. *White on black: images of Africa and blacks in Western popular culture* (New Haven, Conn.: Yale University Press, 1992).

Pope, R. British demobilisation after the second world war. *Journal of Contemporary History* **30**, 1995.

Porter, R. (ed.). *Myths of the English* (Cambridge: Polity, 1992).

Powell, E. *Freedom and reality* (London: Paperfront, 1969).

Prescod-Roberts, M. & N. Steele (eds). *Black women: bringing it all back home* (Bristol: Falling Wall Press, 1980).

Pugh, M. *Women and the women's movement in Britain 1914–1959* (Basingstoke: Macmillan, 1992).

The question of "home". *New Formations* **17**, Summer 1992.

Ramdin, R. *The making of the black working class in Britain* (Aldershot: Gower Publishing 1987).

Reay, D. Insider perspectives on stealing the words out of women's mouths: interpretation in the research process. *Feminist Review* **53**, 1996.

Rich, P. *Race and empire in British politics* (Cambridge: Cambridge University Press, 1990).

Riley, D. The free mothers: pronatalism and working women in industry at the end of the last war in Britain. *History Workshop* **11**, Spring 1981.

Riley, D. *War in the nursery: theories of the child and the mother* (London: Virago, 1983).

Roberts, E. *A woman's place: an oral history of working-class women 1890–1940* (Oxford: Blackwell, 1984).

Roberts, E. *Women and families: an oral history 1940–1970* (Oxford: Blackwell, 1995).

Robertson, G., M. Mash, L. Tickner, J. Bird, B. Curtis, T. Putnam (eds). *Travellers' tales: narratives of home and displacement* (London: Routledge, 1994).

Samuel, R. (ed.). *Patriotism: the making and unmaking of British national identity* [3 vols] (London: Routledge, 1989).

Scanlon, J. Challenging the imbalances of power in feminist oral history: developing a take-and-give methodology. *Women's Studies International Forum* **16**, 1993.

Schwarz, B. "The only white man in there": the re-racialisation of England, 1956–1968. *Race and Class* **38**, 1996.

Segal, L. Look back in anger: men in the fifties. In *Male order: unwrapping masculinity*, R. Chapman & J. Rutherford (eds) (London: Lawrence & Wishart, 1988).

Segal, L. *Straight sex: the politics of pleasure* (London: Virago, 1994).

Segal, L. A feminist looks at the family. In *Understanding the family*, J. Muncie, M. Wetherell, R. Dallos, A. Cochrane (eds) (London: Sage, 1995).

Sherwood, M. *Many struggles: West Indian workers and service personnel in Britain* (London: Karia Press, 1985).

Sinfield, A. *Literature, politics and culture in postwar Britain* (Oxford: Blackwell, 1989).

Smart, C. Law and the control of women's sexuality: the case of the 1950s. In *Controlling women: the normal and the deviant*, B. Hutter & G. Williams (eds) (London: Croom Helm, 1981).

Smart, C. (ed.). *The ties that bind: law, marriage and the reproduction of patriarchal relations* (London: Routledge & Kegan Paul, 1984).

Smith, H. (ed.). *British feminism in the twentieth century* (Aldershot: Edward Elgar, 1990).

Solomos, J. & L. Back. *Race, politics and social change* (London: Routledge, 1995).

Spencer, I. The open door: labour needs and British immigration policy, 1945–55. *Immigrants and Minorities* **15**, 1996.

Spensky, M. Producers of illegitimacy: homes for unmarried mothers in the 1950s. In *Regulating womanhood: historical essays on marriage, motherhood and sexuality*, C. Smart (ed.) (London: Routledge, 1992).

Stott, M. (ed.). *Women talking: an anthology from the Guardian women's page* (London: Pandora, 1987).

Stuart, M. You're a big girl now: subjectivities, feminism and oral history. *Oral History*, Autumn 1994.

Summerfield, P. *Women workers in the second world war: production and patriarchy in conflict* (London: Croom Helm, 1989).

Summerfield, P. Approaches to women and social change in the second world war. In *What difference did the war make?*, B. Brivati & H. Jones (eds) (Leicester: Leicester University Press, 1993).

Summerfield, P. The patriarchal discourse of human capital: training women for war work 1939–1945. *Journal of Gender Studies* **2**, 1993.

Summerfield, P. Women in Britain since 1945: companionate marriage and the double burden. In *Understanding post-war British society*, J. Obelkevich & P. Catterall (eds) (London: Routledge, 1994).

Summerfield, P. & N. Crockett. You weren't taught that with the welding; lessons in sexuality in the second world war. *Women's History Review* **1**, 1992.

Sword, K. *The formation of the Polish community in Great Britain 1939–1950* (London: University of London, 1989).

Tabili, L. The construction of racial difference in twentieth-century Britain: the Special Restriction (Coloured Alien Seamen) Order, 1925. *Journal of British Studies* **33**, 1994.

Tabili, L. *"We ask for British justice": workers and racial difference in late imperial Britain* (Ithaca, NY: Cornell University Press, 1994).

Temple, B. Constructing Polishness: researching Polish women's lives: feminist auto/biographical accounts. *Women's Studies International Forum* **17**, 1994.

Temple, B. Telling tales: accounts and selves in the journeys of British Poles. *Oral history*, Autumn 1995.

Tizard, B. & A. Phoenix. *Black, white or mixed race?: Race and racism in the lives of young people of mixed parentage* (London: Routledge, 1993).

Turner, B. & T. Rennell. *When daddy came home: how family life changed forever in 1945* (London: Hutchinson, 1995).

Ungerson, C. (ed.). *Women and social policy: a reader* (Basingstoke: Macmillan, 1985).

Ungerson, C. (ed.). *Gender and caring* (Hemel Hempstead: Harvester Wheatsheaf, 1990).

Visram, R. *Ayahs, lascars and princes: Indians in Britain 1700–1947* (London: Pluto Press, 1986).

Walby, S. *Patriarchy at work: patriarchal and capitalist relations in employment* (Cambridge: Polity, 1986).

Walby, S. *Theorising patriarchy* (Oxford: Blackwell, 1990).

Walkerdine, V. & H. Lucey. *Democracy in the kitchen: regulating mothers and daughters* (London: Virago, 1989).

Wandor, M. *Look back in gender: sexuality and the family in post-war British drama* (London: Methuen, 1987).

Ware, V. *Beyond the pale: white women, racism and history* (London: Verso, 1992).

White, D. The Ukes of Halifax. *New Society* **52**, 12 June 1980.

Williams, F. *Social policy: a critical introduction* (Cambridge: Polity, 1989).

Williams, F. The welfare state as part of a racially structured and patriarchal capitalism. In *The state or the market: politics and welfare in contemporary Britain*, M. Loney. R. Bocock, J. Clarke, P. Graham, M. Wilson (eds) (London: Sage, 1993).

Williamson, B. Memories, vision and hope: themes in an historical sociology of Britain since the second world war. *Journal of Historical Sociology* **1**, 1988.

Wilson, E. *Women and the welfare state* (London: Tavistock, 1977).

Wilson, E. *Only halfway to paradise: women in post-war Britain 1945–1968* (London: Tavistock, 1980).

Winship, J. *Inside women's magazines* (London: Pandora, 1987).

Wright, P. On living in an old country: the national past in contemporary Britain (London: Verso, 1985).

Young, L. *Fear of the dark: "race", gender and sexuality in the cinema* (London: Routledge, 1996).

Younger, C. *Anglo-Indians, neglected children of the Raj* (Delhi: BR Publishing, 1987).

Younghusband, E. *Social work in Britain 1950–1975: a follow-up study* (London: Allen & Unwin, 1978).

Yuval-Davis, N. & F.Anthias (eds). *Woman–nation–state* (Basingstoke: Macmillan, 1989).

Index

INDEX